WHAT REALLY SANK
THE TITANIC

WHAT REALLY SANK
THE TITANIC

New Forensic Discoveries

Jennifer Hooper McCarty

and

Tim Foecke

CITADEL PRESS
Kensington Publishing Corp.
www.kensingtonbooks.com

CITADEL PRESS BOOKS are published by

Kensington Publishing Corp.
850 Third Avenue
New York, NY 10022

All Kensington titles, imprints, and distributed lines are available at special quantity
discounts for bulk purchases for sales promotions, premiums, fund-raising, educational,
or institutional use. Special book excerpts or customized printings can also be created
to fit specific needs. For details, write or phone the office of the Kensington special
sales manager: Kensington Publishing Corp., 850 Third Avenue, New York, NY
10022, attn: Special Sales Department; phone 1-800-221-2647.

CITADEL PRESS and the Citadel logo are Reg. U.S. Pat. & TM Off.

First printing: March 2008

10 9 8 7 6 5 4 3 2

Printed in the United States of America

Library of Congress Control Number: 2007937045

ISBN-13: 978-0-8065-2895-3
ISBN-10: 0-8065-2895-8

CONTENTS

PART IV: THE REST OF THE STORY 173

PREFACE

For nearly one hundred years, the public has been enthralled by her story. As the largest man-made moving object of her time, the construction of the RMS *Titanic* was a technological feat, yet her sinking comprised one of the most famous disasters of the twentieth century. A colossal tragedy, the sinking has been shrouded in mystery ever since and has led to unending speculation concerning the details of that fateful evening. Heightened interest has produced a plethora of books, films, and exhibitions in recent years, all probing an answer to the most intriguing question: How and why did the *Titanic*, believed to be man's technological triumph over nature, sink in less than three hours' time?

What follows is the first hands-on forensic investigation into the details of the collision between the ship and the iceberg: how the ship was damaged and how she eventually sank. The authors have nearly ten years' experience working directly with recovered steel and wrought iron from the wreck, including mechanical testing, microscopy, and extensive computer modeling of these and contemporary materials, as well as exhaustive historical research on the ship's construction, best practices, and quality control of the materials that made up the *Titanic*. We propose a scenario whereby substandard materials used in some of the riveted joints of the ill-fated liner caused the first six compartments to flood after the iceberg impact and allowed the largest man-made moving object of the time to sink in a little more than two hours on that night in April 1912.

PART I

THE BACKGROUND

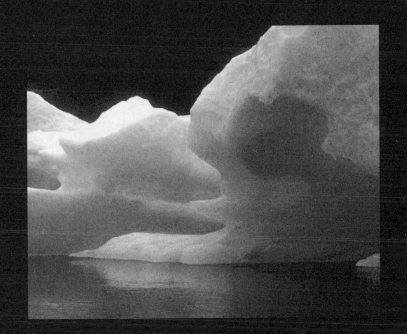

CHAPTER 1

THE YARD

The morning sun rose up from behind the Queen's Road tramcar as it clattered along the track, jostling the dark coats and caps clinging to every last joist on the way toward Queen's Island. As it slowed on the approach toward The Yard, the passengers disembarked into a sea of black, the hustle and bustle of thousands of shipyard workers, undulating back and forth, as crowds merged and streams of men descended from other trams. Here the crowd swelled into a parade of marchers, then narrowed into a long black ribbon, scurrying along the edge of the tracks to beat the 8 a.m. horn.

From another direction, a more distinguished set of men trickled into the main offices, while preparations were underway for a meeting of the managing directors. The board had gone into crisis mode. Faced with the daunting construction of several large vessels at once, the loss of workers to other yards, and a dwindling sense of worker efficiency, Lord W. J. Pirrie, chairman of Harland & Wolff, and his associates were forced to consider a reorganization of laborers that would improve their situation.

The riveters' work at the Yard had been tough during the last few months of 1911 and into the winter of 1912. According to shipbuilding records, the foreman, Mr. Kingan, had resorted to becoming unduly stern with the workers, formally complaining of their idling on the job. Harland & Wolff was one of the most powerful shipbuilders in the world, yet in the early spring of 1912, it certainly didn't need to

3

add laziness to its latest troubles. For the first and last time in history, the White Star sisters *Titanic* and *Olympic* found themselves quartered next to one another at the gantry in Belfast, Ireland, as seen in plate 1.* On March 2, 1912, the older sister, *Olympic* (on the left), was dry-docked after a collision stripped her of a propeller blade, and the *Titanic*, poised to break the record books, instead wallowed months behind schedule, now bereft of a propeller blade.

Each day the workers were forced to move faster, accelerating their speed, pounding away with the precision of a well-oiled machine. Harland & Wolff's board members took to panicking over lost days and diminishing materials, setting in motion a pandemonium of activity to finish the job at any cost, be it financial or human. According to Harland & Wolff's records, before the *Titanic* even left the River Lagan, eight people had died on the job, and a list of those maimed or injured because of work-related accidents "read like a roster of the wounded after battle." A total of 254 work-related accidents occurred during her construction. It's hard to say which employees got the brunt of the criticism; however, it was the riveting squads who were deemed most crucial to the shipbuilder's fame. The faster they worked, the earlier *Titanic*'s structure would take shape and the sooner Harland & Wolff could breathe a sigh of relief.

Even the less-experienced rivet boys, some as young as thirteen, knew that a ramp-up in production meant pressure on the lines. Every iron rivet had to be perfectly heated to just the right color of flaming cherry red. If too hot or too cold, they didn't "rivet up" properly—the shipbuilder's way of saying that the rivet was too loose to create that all-critical watertight seal between the plates.

It was the rivet counter's job to oversee the whole process—a duty that became a source of real animosity among the riveting gangs. In between pointing out weaknesses and reprimanding the lollygaggers, the rivet counter inspected the completed rivets, or at least as many as he could conceivably check during a shift. This manual inspection was more than merely a daunting task—it became an impossibility on a ship built with over three million rivets.

* When we refer to plates, please see the color photo insert.

On the production lines, the rivet boys pumped the stove bellows with their feet until they sweat, getting the coke stoked just right. Fresh in their teens, local boys were plucked for the job from around the Belfast countryside when Harland & Wolff was looking for workers to help on the new passenger steamers. The conditions were gruesome, standing for a nine-hour shift in the bitterly cold weather and unbearable noise. For many, even the hot stove and the steady pumping of their feet weren't enough to warm them from the cold, wet Belfast winter. Despite the hardship, at least it provided the working class with some income.

The magic of the Edwardian Age was that it managed to prolong the Victorian belief in progress and the energy for invention, despite the rampant poverty that pervaded the working class. Belfast had become the industrial powerhouse of Ireland, wooing skilled workers from the surrounding areas to participate on the manufacturing lines. Yet, at the same time, a mass emigration from the surrounding counties supplied Harland & Wolff's inexhaustible needs for unskilled labor. Belfast yards paid more than most to the skilled engineering workers, but only about half that much was offered to unskilled laborers and apprentices, a wage consistently *lower* than in most shipbuilding centers.

At the Yard, Monday morning was the busiest time, because the rivet gangs rushed to drive the first rivets of the workweek. As soon as the horn blew, heater boys clamped their rivets over the coals and watched them heat up until glowing red. The familiar smells of grease, rust, and hot metal wafted through the air, and the men bustled about the gantry, a steel goliath looming over them, while the heater boys picked up *Titanic* rivets in their tongs. The bright red slugs of metal warming their faces signaled a critical moment in the production lines. Once installed, the rivets were the glue that held the ship together, the watertight seals that ensured her flotation. In most cases, ships faced the typical stresses and strains caused by high winds or rough wave patterns at sea. The stakes rose dramatically when a ship's structure was challenged to withstand an iceberg collision.

The evidence to interpret history's most famous marine disaster begins at her beginning—at the shipyard in the hands of common people. Their focus on the job, the attention to detail, and the quality of the materials they used had a direct influence on the success of the ship's maiden voyage, whether good or bad. In 1911, there were 1,728 unskilled workers at the Harland & Wolff shipyard, comprising between 17 percent and 23 percent of the workforce in any one month. They were overworked and under pressure. On October 16, 1911, Lord Pirrie decided against an incentive measure to increase wages for riveters who kept good time on the job. During the next six months, the board discussed idleness on the job, reorganization of the labor force, and sources for additional riveters at every single meeting. Between December 1909 and January 1912, at least four forges were utilized as suppliers of rivet material to make more than fifteen different types of rivets. Just as the great ship, No. 401 *Titanic*, sat poised for completion, a coal strike forced the Harland & Wolff board members to reevaluate the speed of their ships and the distances they could travel. Did any of these factors play a part in the sinking of the unsinkable ship *Titanic*? The human factor cannot be avoided in disaster analysis, and what we know about the lives of the builders of the *Titanic* may help in sifting through the facts.

The shipyard workers and the city of Belfast celebrated with admiration as the ship born from their sweat sprung from the Queen's Island docks into the Belfast Lough on April 2, 1912. The feelings of ownership and the sense of worth that had emerged among a society torn apart by religious animosity and bigotry were overwhelming. The *Titanic* was on view for the entire world to see—a product of the hardworking Irish and a masterpiece formed by the united hands of a city plagued by political strife. The citizens were direct contributors and their men the creators, designers, and builders of the largest manmade moving object on Earth. Spectators crowded together to wave goodbye to the grand manifestation of their hopes and dreams, never suspecting that it would soon become the greatest source of loss and bewilderment that the country had ever experienced.

CHAPTER 2

BUILDING THE GREAT LEVIATHAN

A Guide to *Titanic*'s Details

D espite the workers' plight of the early 1900s, the optimism of early-twentieth-century science and technology could not be squelched. Discoveries and inventions that claimed new feats of mastery over nature were becoming almost commonplace: the discovery of X-rays (1895), the invention of the Zeppelin airship (1897), the first powered flight by the Wright brothers (1903), Einstein's Theory of Relativity (1905), the launching of the first Dreadnought (1906), and Rutherford's model of the atom (1911). The steel industry, the design of huge machinery, and the invention of the internal combustion engine had changed passenger transport forever. The transatlantic Blue Riband race (the world's most glamorous speed record for crossing the Atlantic) began in 1838 and instigated construction of the fastest steamships in the world. People were swept up in a bubble of confidence, marveling with pride at the technological miracles and new discoveries that had carried through the turn of the century. *The New York Times* brilliantly expressed the sentiments of the Golden Age on New Year's Eve 1899, "We step upon the threshold of 1900, which leads to the new century, facing a still bright dawn of civilization."

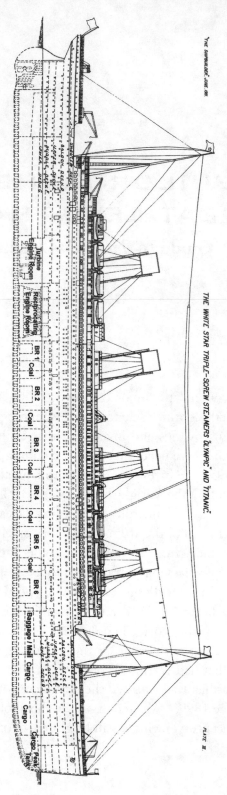

Figure 1.

THE WHITE STAR TRIPLE-SCREW STEAMERS "OLYMPIC" AND "TITANIC."

Turbine Engine Room

Reciprocating Engine Room

BR 1 | Coal
BR 2 | Coal
BR 3 | Coal
BR 4 | Coal
BR 5 | Coal
BR 6 | Coal

Baggage / Mail Cargo

Cargo

Cargo | Peak Tank

Floating Palaces

In the early 1900s, Britain dominated the shipbuilding industry in terms of output, but not without some serious rivalry. For centuries, enormous quantities of available coal and rapid advances in iron and steel production made her impervious to competition from the Germans or the Americans. But by the late 1800s, other players entered the ring. In 1897, British smugness was quickly broken by Germany's offering to the transatlantic passenger trade because the *Kaiser Wilhelm der Grosse* won the coveted Blue Riband trophy. At 627 feet in length and 14,349 tons, this North German Lloyd creation was the first modern luxury liner and received a huge portion of transatlantic business. Soon after, the company followed with three similar ships, and the Hamburg-Amerika line chimed in with the four-funneled *Deutschland*. The Germans had seized the Blue Riband and, with it, Britain's national prestige. The White Star Line had countered with the *Oceanic* in 1899, but this largest and most luxurious liner was not the fastest because her designers favored passenger comfort over speed. In 1902, the American business tycoon J. Pierpont Morgan bought out the White Star Line as part of his conglomerate, the International Mercantile Marine Company, and happily used his capital to extend the sumptuous style and lavish artistry of the company's ships. Morgan deftly formed a partnership with North German Lloyd as well.

Meanwhile, the British government was horrified that the roost it had ruled for centuries was being simultaneously culled by the Germans and gobbled up by the Americans. British businessmen anxiously followed the dwindling passenger lists, sickened by the losses that competing foreign lines had scooped up. A member of the North East Coast Institution of Engineers and Shipbuilders summed it up in a presentation to his colleagues: "There is . . . the larger and more important national view which has to be borne in mind . . . that by far the larger number of the passengers crossing the Atlantic are now carried by the German and the French lines, whilst only a comparatively small number are patronizing the English boats."

The government was certainly not immune to this public embarrassment, and so in support of regaining the transatlantic speed record, it subsidized Cunard to build the world's next great liners: *Lusitania* and *Mauretania*, both Blue Riband winners. Not only did Cunard succeed, the company managed to design the largest, fastest, most luxurious passenger ships to date, using the extravagance typical of English stately homes to create floating palaces. Cunard's creations ushered in the transformation of twentieth-century liners from frugal seagoing transportation to regal accommodation, replete with plush bedrooms, glistening ballrooms, and the very latest in *haute cuisine*. Cunard's feat won incredible support and popularity from the public and quickly stripped the White Star Line of any claims to fame. Under pressure from the success of Cunard's masterpiece and speculation over the lucrative future of German ventures, Lord Pirrie, head of Harland & Wolff, and Bruce Ismay, managing director of the White Star Line, came to the table to devise a counterattack, whose sheer size and magnificence would guarantee headlines.

THE LEVIATHAN OF THE GOLDEN AGE

As the nineteenth century came to a close, the optimism gained from higher productivity and financial success had arrived in more places than just Britain. The United States was growing into one of the most powerful and prosperous nations in the world. Years of civil war were over, western settlements were established, and economic expansion and technology had resulted in a rail network that connected the Northeastern wealth to the rest of the country. Yet, the United States needed manpower to supplement the construction and industry that this new infrastructure demanded. Europeans escaping unsettled lives of rebellions, disasters, and famine looked westward in pursuit of opportunities in the New World. In the late 1800s, it was the combination of massive migration westward and aristocratic American vacationing eastward that brought success to the transatlantic shipping lines. Shipping companies grew and prospered, ships became more accommodating, and passenger liners had tripled in size in just over a decade. To the working class, the new ocean liners represented the tangible means to a better life, while to the elite they were yet another symbol of their well-earned economic triumphs and status.

Titanic was a direct product of the era's growing optimism and its insatiable thirst for expansion and grandiosity. She was, as shipbuilding expert and historian Michael McCaughan called it, "the essence of modernity." *Titanic* symbolized the pinnacle in British shipbuilding technology and gave the nation a welcome boost at a time when the United States had taken control of the lucrative steel industry. She was a source of great pride for all, robustly outfitted and sumptuously decorated. The White Star Line was not shy in emphasizing these sentiments: "The White Star liners *Olympic* and *Titanic*, eloquent testimonies to the progress of mankind, as shown in the conquest of mind over matter—will rank high in the achievements of the twentieth century." Despite a string of accidents starring the White Star Line ships, people were convinced that technology had mastered the seas, and they were encouraged by the press's invincible claims about the world's largest ships.

Although the ship's design was spectacular, luxurious, and grandiose on a scale never experienced, *Titanic*'s construction was not revolutionary in its basic elements. The building of the ship was accomplished in accordance with the highest standards of the day, a characteristic for which her builders Harland & Wolff were well known, yet many of her features had been previously used on earlier ships. Steel plating and watertight bulkhead construction had become commonplace since the late 1800s. The Marconi wireless communication system was outfitted on the *Kaiser Wilhelm der Grosse* twelve years earlier, the first Atlantic liner to have one. Of course, twelve years of development made the system on the *Titanic* innovative in its own right. Even the combination engine, a curiously efficient system, had been tested on the White Star Line's *Megantic* and *Laurentic*. The key was in the whole package, brilliantly proclaimed in White Star's presumptuous marketing campaign. The opulence, the size, and the combination of her mechanical and structural elements provided the "unsinkable" package that society longed to believe in. Even Captain

The Track Record of the White Star Line

In the late 1800s, the White Star Line's safety track record was less than stellar. On April 1, 1873, the *Atlantic, Oceanic*'s sister ship, sank after running aground on Marrs Rock off the coast of Halifax. While fighting off a vicious storm on its way to New York, much of the ship's coal was used up, forcing the captain to divert course for refueling. More than 500 people were killed in the accident, for which the inquiry report ruled that one of the causes was lack of sufficient fuel. Rumors proliferated in the media, concerning the quality of the ship's materials, its design, and Harland & Wolff's craftsmanship. White Star Line appealed to the Board of Trade and won, but the company's luck did not change. In 1893, the world's largest livestock carrier, the *Naronic*, disappeared in the North Atlantic, never to be seen again. In 1899, a blizzard in New York harbor caused the liner *Germanic* to capsize under the weight of the snow and ice. The twentieth century offered no relief from the string of mishaps. In 1907, the *Suevic* lost a sizable chunk from the forward section of its hull after running aground near Cornwall, England. On September 20, 1911, the *Olympic* collided with the HMS *Hawke* off the coast of the Isle of Wight, punching a massive hole in her starboard side. Within weeks of *Titanic*'s maiden voyage, the *Olympic*, fully repaired, lost a propeller after smacking into an obstruction in the North Atlantic. As we well know, history "has an unfortunate habit of repeating itself," and the factors that saved the reputations of both Harland & Wolff and the White Star Line after the loss of the *Atlantic* back in 1873 would again be challenged by an even greater tragedy in the early part of the twentieth century.

E. J. Smith, when discussing his trip across the Atlantic on the *Adriatic*, became a spokesman for the company's achievements, admitting the utmost of faith in modern technology. "I cannot imagine any condition which would cause a ship to flounder. . . . Modern shipping has gone beyond that."

THE SHIPBUILDING BASICS

The RMS *Titanic* was a maritime legend years before she set sail, the largest man-made moving object, constructed with the latest and greatest in shipbuilding features, safety equipment, and opulent extras of mind-boggling proportions. With the culmination of her design on paper, at a meeting between Lord Pirrie and Bruce Ismay, preparations began that would nurture the colossal project all the way from her birth as scribbles on a dinner napkin to the exultant cries of the crowd as she left Southampton more than three years later.

Hull Design

The hull is simply another name for the main body of the ship. Made from many kinds of materials—wood, skin, plastic, or metal—it must be watertight in order to float. The design of the hull determines the shape, size, and carrying capacity of the ship, and it should resist bending and minimize weight.

Titanic's hull was based on a design popularized by Harland & Wolff in the mid-1800s—the "Belfast Bottom." It was a nearly flat bottomed hull with a squared-off bilge, the curve of the ship's bottom that blends into and forms the sides. The brilliance of the design was that it allowed the builders to increase the length of the ship without needing to enlarge the width, thus creating additional room for cargo and passengers.

Titanic's hull was strengthened several times over, using a crisscrossing series of rigid steel "ribs" across the ship and ones that ran along her length. The sections that were created, called frames, started at the double bottom and extended up eight decks to a height of sixty-six feet, spaced at regular intervals of three feet. By incorporating secondary ribs, known as web frames, the basic frame strength was beefed up.

The transverse strength of the ship relied on fifteen 1-inch-thick watertight bulkheads, which were specifically designed and reinforced to withstand high pressures in the event of an accident. The bulkheads were connected by two large angle irons to the decks, the inner bottom plating, and the side shell plating, creating sixteen separate compartments along the length of the hull.

The longitudinal strength in *Titanic* came from the shell (hull) plating, the inner bottom plating, and the deck plating and, most importantly, from a series of uniformly spaced beams, known as longitudinal girders, running from fore (front) to aft (back) along the length of the hull. Massive stanchions, or cylindrical steel columns, supported these girders, a design that was specially planned by Thomas Andrews in order to ensure superior strength of the hull. The backbone or spine of the ship's hull, known as the center keel girder, further stabilized the ship along its length. It was composed of a 1½-inch-thick steel plate (the keel plate), a 3-inch solid steel bar (the keel bar), and a 5-foot-3-inch-thick box section of steel. At the forward end, the framing and plating were further strengthened in order to prevent panting (the in and out vibration of the plates and beams in the bow) and damage when meeting thin harbor ice.

The Ship's "Armor"

By the nineteenth century, warships and ocean liners were based on a shell-built design, whose ultimate strength came from the strength of the shell, or outer skin of the hull. Both the Crimean War and the American Civil War were catalysts for a revolution in naval technology—the ironclad ship. Faced with more threatening and destructive forms of artillery, the major naval powers realized the need to strengthen their ships' wooden hulls against enemy attack. The solution was the ironclad ships of the mid-1800s, constructed by bolting layers of iron plates up to eight inches thick onto the ship's sides. Anxious to mimic the success of such attempts, ocean liners quickly incorporated iron and steel technology as a means to ensure safety and security for their passengers.

The hull material had to be strong and light and also ductile. The nineteenth-century scientist and engineer David Kirkaldy explained the importance of these properties through experiments on wrought iron from the 1859 shipwreck of the iron-hulled *Royal Charter*. Kirkaldy determined that brittle wrought iron was a factor in the ship's sinking. Although the hull was made of very strong wrought iron, its limited ability to stretch caused the hull to shatter into pieces instead of absorbing the stresses of the impact by deforming. Ideally, the hull material should bend and deform with stress, rather than snap or fracture catastrophically.

By the time the *Titanic* was built, open-hearth steel had become the norm for the hull plates. (We'll define this more carefully in the next chapter.) The shell of the *Titanic* was designed to complement her exceptionally sturdy frame and was composed of 1 to 1½-inch-thick steel plates, 30 feet long by 6 feet wide. The plates were attached to the internal frame in vertical sections known as strakes that ran along the length of the ship. The plates were slightly overlapped all the way down the side of the ship, forming ripples on the outer surface known as joggles (see plate 3). These joggles were laid out with just enough overlap for the strakes to be riveted together. In the central region of the hull (amidships) at each of these overlapping joints, known as lap joints, the plates were triple riveted.

Joining the Hull

The hull of a ship should have a strong structure that resists bending, maintains water tightness, and minimizes weight. While at sea a ship must contend with the motion of waves breaking and slamming against it, as well as the vibrations of the propeller and other machinery. So during the nineteenth century numerous scientists and engineers calculated, experimented, and theorized to death about the optimal size, shape, and placement of rivets in order to secure the plates of the hull and provide stability, while still allowing it to give under substantial stresses.

The two types of joints used to construct the *Titanic* are known as

Figure 2. A doubly riveted lap joint creates a joggled surface on both sides.

Figure 3. A doubly riveted butt joint creates a flat surface on the external side and hides the joggled surface on the interior of the structure.

lap joints and butt joints. A lap joint (also, confusingly, called a butt-lap) is created by overlapping two plates and riveting through both of them. This type of joint always results in a joggled surface.

The other type used is the butt joint (also called butt strap or strapping), made by placing two plates end to end and riveting another plate behind them. Since the plates are flush with one another, a butt joint produces a flat surface (on the outside) (see fig. 3). *Titanic*'s design incorporated both wrought iron and steel rivets, which formed joints that were doubly, trebly, quadruply, and sometimes quintuply riveted—that means two, three, four, or sometimes five rivets in a row across a joint. The shell plates, the real armor of the ship, were triple riveted within the middle section of the hull, and double riveted at the bow and stern, to ensure strength in the region of the ship that must withstand the highest stresses as it flexed in the ocean.

THE FIRST INDUSTRY APPROVAL RATINGS:
DID *TITANIC* PASS?

Some people have heard of *Lloyd's Register* in reference to the *Titanic*, but what does that term actually mean? *Lloyd's Register of Shipping* is a publication that still exists today, which describes, classifies, and registers ships based on a series of rules and standards for building vessels. Originally, Lloyd's began as a coffeehouse in London in the late 1600s where merchants and underwriters would convene to discuss and negotiate insurance on vessels and cargo. *Lloyd's Register* has been in continuous publication since 1775 and has been very influential in encouraging critical changes to the shipbuilding industry. Before adding new shipbuilding materials to the *Register*, Lloyd's made prudent choices and carried out lengthy experimentation to ensure that their new rules were safe and accurate. By the 1800s, similar societies existed in France (Bureau Veritas), Germany (Germanischer Lloyd), and the United States (American Lloyd's Register). Although a classification by Lloyd's was not required, it was a highly respected seal of approval and a reputable classification of a vessel's worth.

Yet, unknown to many in 1912 (or even now, for that matter), *Titanic* was not classified by Lloyd's. The classification simply wasn't sought, apparently because it was believed that her specifications far outweighed any requirements of the registration society. After the disaster, the public felt as though they had been misled by this decision:

> We have been solemnly told by men wearing mysterious faces that
> she was not registered!

This shock soon turned to speculation over the care and precision with which she was built:

> But, however excellent the staff of builders, it is arguable that their out-
> look can hardly be so broad as that of such a body as *Lloyd's Register*.

In *The Times* Finance, Commerce, and Shipping section, *Lloyd's Register* decided to make a public statement, exonerating themselves from any responsibility for the sunken liner:

In view of the reports, which have appeared in the Press in connection with the inquiry into the loss of the S.S. *Titanic*, to the effect that
the vessel was built considerably in excess of the requirements of
Lloyd's Register, I am directed to say that these statements are inaccurate. On the contrary, in important parts of her structure the vessel
as built did not come up to the requirements of *Lloyd's Register* for a
vessel of her dimensions.

SAFETY FIRST: *TITANIC*'S "UNSINKABLE" FEATURES

Her Double Bottom

It was the *Olympic*-class ships' well-planned design and impressive
list of safety features that thrilled naval architects and marine engineers of the day, who in turn convinced and assured the public and
press of the ships' near indestructible reputation. The designers had
carefully determined what features would be necessary to ensure passenger safety in the event of an emergency and constructed the ships
accordingly. For instance, the *Titanic* was reinforced by a double-
bottomed hull that provided an extra seal of strength in the event of a
collision. The double bottom was one of the most innovative design
features on the SS *Great Eastern* (see plate 8, top), *Titanic's* ancestor of
1858, which was the first ship to boast a complete wrought iron double hull, the inner and outer layers being separated by nearly three
feet.

Although most warships and merchant ships were incorporating
double bottoms by the early 1900s, the design was typically just that—
a double layer along the bottom portion of the hull. It was considered
a means of protecting the underside of the ship. So, while *Titanic's*
double bottom itself was nothing new, the fact that it extended
through the entire width of an ocean liner was. This was yet another
example of Harland & Wolff's devoted attempts to surpass the norm
by incorporating design features that provided further fortifications to
Titanic's immense frame. The inner and outer hulls along the bottom
of the *Titanic* were separated by enough space for a man to walk
though them. The double bottom was not, however, carried around

and up the side of the hull to the waterline, a detail that would quickly be modified on the other *Olympic*-class ships after *Titanic* sank.

Her Watertight Subdivision

Spared of no expense, the thick bulkheads between *Titanic*'s watertight compartments contained heavy watertight doors that were equipped to close off each compartment securely. The doors were Harland & Wolff's latest design, formed of heavy cast iron, given ribs for strength, and fitted with gears to control the speed of closing to within twenty-five to thirty seconds. Under normal circumstances these doors were open and allowed movement between compartments. However, in an emergency the doors could be closed in three different ways:

1. By the captain using an electromagnetic switch at the bridge.
2. By a lever fitted alongside the door.
3. By an automatic pulley system when water entered the compartment and caused a float to rise. A bell from the bridge gave notice of their closing.

The ship was designed so that if any adjacent two compartments were flooded (the worst scenario the designers could imagine), it would still remain afloat. If three compartments were flooded, the ship could remain afloat with flooding rising to the top of her bulkheads. If four compartments were flooded, water would, not have gotten into any of the other compartments, although it would have risen above some of the bulkheads. Yet according to her designers, she still would remain afloat. It was the official description of the watertight doors in *The Shipbuilder* of 1911 that claimed the ship's immortality on the seas:

[The door] is held in the open position by a suitable friction clutch, which can be instantly released by means of a powerful electric magnet controlled from the captain's bridge, so that in the event of accident, or at any time when it might be considered advisable, the

What Happened to the Third Sister?

Begun in 1911, the third sister, *Britannic*, laid untouched in the slipway of Harland & Wolff for months until the *Titanic* inquiries were completed and her work could commence anew. In the aftermath of the disaster, modifications were incorporated into *Britannic*'s design that were intended to protect her from the demise of her sister. First, the supposed name of Hull 433, *Gigantic*, was replaced in favor of a less boastful moniker. Second, the most significant of the structural changes was the construction of a double hull that stretched around the belly of the ship up to the watertight bulkheads. Moreover, the distance between the inner and outer skin was increased to six feet and was segmented by six huge longitudinal girders or ribs that were supposed to contain flooding in the event of circumstances similar to what occurred to the *Titanic*. Last, five of the watertight bulkheads were extended up to B deck, and the rest came up to E deck. This system, complemented with improved pumping of compartments and better methods for closing the watertight doors, was designed to protect the ship even if six compartments were flooded. Commissioned as a hospital ship at the start of World War I, *Britannic* never served as a passenger ship (see plate 8, bottom). In 1916, she either struck a mine or was torpedoed in the Aegean sea, which blew a hole in her starboard bow and destroyed an extensive area of her forward four watertight compartments, as well as the watertight door leading to the fifth compartment. Unfortunately, at the crucial bulkhead between Boiler Rooms 6 and 5, a damaged watertight door failed to close, allowing water to enter a sixth compartment. Whether the ship's new design would have kept her afloat was never tested, as water quickly filled the ship through portholes left open by the crew, it being hot in the Aegean Sea that time of year. Despite all the new modifications, *Britannic* sank in less than one hour.

captain can, by simply moving an electric switch, instantly close the doors throughout—practically making the vessel unsinkable.

The height of the bulkheads that separated these compartments was calculated in accordance with the Merchant Shipping Acts of 1894, which required that the bulkheads should be high enough to contain the water of a completely flooded compartment after subtracting that volume from the ship's displacement. As the weight of a ship increases it will settle further into the water, increasing the height of the waterline, known as the load-draft line or load line in calculations. As long as the bulkheads are above this new load-draft line, then the compartment is considered watertight, even if it is not sealed off by a watertight deck. Consequently, the fifteen watertight bulkheads on *Titanic* rose to F deck at the bow and stern and E deck through the middle of the ship. This design was yet another admired safety feature that was deemed sufficient, considering that the most feared accident was a broadside collision with a vessel at sea, not scraping against an iceberg. After the *Titanic* disaster, plans were changed on *Britannic* while she was still under construction in the ways. Five of her bulkheads were extended to B deck, partitioning the once generous first class accommodations, while the remaining twelve bulkheads were taken up to E deck.

Marconi Wireless Telegraphy

The turn of the century evolved into the age of the passenger ship, ports crowded with grandiose ocean liners competing for the profits from shuttling hundreds of thousands of businessmen, aristocracy, and immigrants across the seas. As a result, operators along the North Atlantic route began enticing the more lucrative customers with luxurious accommodations, efficient speed, and technological amenities. One such example was the Marconi wireless communication system, which transformed the world of navigation after its installation on the *East Goodwin* lightship (vessel that acts like a lighthouse) in 1899. Considered by some to be the most important safety feature on the

Olympic-class ships, and clearly the most advanced, the Marconi apparatus provided communication between ships and with stations on shore.

Titanic was particularly well equipped with wireless, in that she was the first ship to travel with the new rotary spark discharger developed in 1912. Simply stated, this gave *Titanic* the advantage of a stronger signal than other ships, including her sister ship *Olympic*. *Titanic*'s Marconi room was a central point to which all incoming and outgoing messages were collected, many from the passengers to their loved ones on land. Jack Phillips and his assistant, Harold Bride, were charged with managing that onslaught of communication during the ship's duration at sea, receiving numerous messages concerning ship navigation, especially warnings of ice fields, while at the same time juggling all the passengers' correspondence. Unfortunately, at the time that *Titanic* set sail, there was no required procedure for prioritizing messages, and in fact, Marconi operators, considered Marconi company employees, were contracted primarily to relay personal messages.

From its first use in 1899, the wireless made an important contribution to the rescue of thousands at sea. Ships in danger were no longer alone, as one engineer wrote to the editor of the *Halifax Daily Echo*, September 14, 1899, expounding the advantages of such new technology:

> On [the ship's] way across the ocean she is not cut off from the outer world, for occasionally by night and by day the merry tick of her telegraphic instrument apprises her of the presence of another vessel on the great waters. Signals are exchanged, news imparted and possibly warning given. The latitude and longitude of menacing derelicts of field ice or bergs are given.

That very security was tested in January 1909 when the White Star Line's S.S. *Republic* collided with an Italian steamer, *Florida*, in thick fog southwest of Nantucket Island, Massachusetts. Aboard the sinking *Republic*, over a period of two days in subzero temperatures, Jack Binns, the Marconi radio operator, sent out a total of two hundred messages indicating the stricken vessel's location. Because of his faithful efforts, over 1,700 people were rescued at sea. While the outcome of this latest White Star Line disaster was encouraging, it was a harbinger of much worse things to come.

White Star Line spared no expense in grooming the ultimate in luxury passenger liners. Proudly utilizing workers and supplies from all over the world, the company completed its latest business maneuver with dreams of securing a lasting reputation. And they got it. Staying true to tradition, the *Olympic*-class ships were the "super size" versions of the age, enlarged copies of White Star's previous Big Four—*Celtic, Cedric, Baltic, and Adriatic.* A classic, simple design was given its pizzazz with glitzy decorations and pronounced bulk in every possible way. This family of three giants was considered crucial to gaining and maintaining control of the North Atlantic shipping industry. So, it was with great gusto and a whiff of contagious confidence that White Star, armed with two of the most knowledgeable men in the passenger liner industry, Thomas Andrews and Captain Smith, beamed over *Titanic*'s departure, blissfully unaware that she would become the most famous ocean liner wreck in history.

CHAPTER 3

WHAT THE *TITANIC* WAS MADE OF

The Science of Iron

Scientific investigation and civil and mechanical engineering have become all-absorbing passions, and men fail to acknowledge God as the source of their achievements.

—A. White, *The Titanic Tragedy: God Speaking to the Nations*, 1913

How did nineteenth-century scientific progress lead to the sweeping triumphs of the *Titanic*? The preeminent British iron and steel industry, the technology that created *Titanic*, began with the field of iron metallurgy. It still holds many clues to her design details.

THE BASICS

There are three major types of commercially useful iron: wrought irons, cast irons and steels. All three were hugely important to structural applications in the late nineteenth and early twentieth century, such as the building of bridges and the design of railways, and all were found in abundance on the *Titanic*. Understanding the forensic analysis of later chapters requires a brief introduction to the types of materials that made up the *Titanic*.

Wrought Iron: The Facts

Wrought iron is not only the oldest but (perhaps somewhat surprisingly) the purest form of *smelted* iron, the conversion of iron ore into metallic iron by combining it with the element carbon. Produced for thousands of years before the appearance of either cast iron or steel, wrought iron became the single most important structural material, even after other types of iron came into use. Wrought iron can be simply described as a very pure form of iron, virtually clean from impurities such as carbon, but containing a small amount of something known as slag. Slag is a by-product of the manufacturing process, basically a chemical form of iron, oxygen, and silicon, referred to as an iron silicate. When mixed within the iron, slag gives wrought iron its particular fibrous structure. The interspersed "stringers" of slag within an iron bar give it an appearance similar to wood. The fibers run along the length of the bar like the grain in a plank of wood or a rod of fiberglass. If a nick is cut into the bar and the bar is bent back, the metal tears, exposing the broken ends of the columns of iron and slag, like splinters in wood or the fibers in fiberglass.

It turns out that wrought iron has a slew of properties that make it advantageous to use: it has a high strength along the direction of the fibers, is easy for a blacksmith to hammer weld and has good corrosion resistance. It is also very ductile and, therefore, allows the blacksmith to work it easily into complicated shapes while hot, hence the term *wrought*. Yet because it is so pure, it has a very high melting point. Addition of other elements to iron actually decreases iron's melting point substantially.

By contrast, cast iron is a type of iron with a lot of carbon, from 2.2 percent to 5 percent, along with 1 to 2 percent silicon, which helps it flow easily into moulds. Because up to one tenth of cast iron is made up of elements other than iron, it has a significantly lower melting point than pure iron or steel. This last bit is the important part and helps to define what kind of iron it is. By comparison, wrought iron typically has less than 0.1 percent carbon. The high carbon content of cast iron makes it melt at lower temperatures and helps it flow, but it also produces a very brittle material that cannot be hammered by the smith's tools, forged or wrought, like its low-carbon relative. When broken, the fresh surface of cast iron has many shiny crystalline facets, very unlike the fibrous tearing of wrought iron. As with wrought iron, the term "cast iron" suggests the production method of the metal, which is a direct consequence of its particular chemical properties.

Until the early twentieth century, wrought iron was manufactured in all shapes and forms, but it has since become extinct, replaced by steel as a result of the burgeoning steel industry. It can still be found, though, in many late Victorian/Edwardian structures in the United Kingdom and throughout buildings, ships, and bridges from Colonial to Civil War America. What people today would describe as wrought iron (decorative gates, furniture, and other domestic items) are not wrought iron at all, but rather are made of steel. Over the years, the term "wrought iron" has become synonymous with a particular decorative style and look, but its actual meaning derives from its chemical makeup and its associated easy workability.

Iron Making Ain't Easy: The Plight of the Ironsmith and the Puddler

During the early history of wrought iron manufacturing thousands of years ago, a constant supply of fire was required to convert the iron ore to metallic iron. Several human blowers would often take turns stomping on the bellows to ensure a continuous blast of air to the fire until the transformation of the ore was judged complete. The process was very touchy, was time consuming, and required a significant amount of acquired skill to create a consistent result. One of the world's earliest metallurgical texts describes the art of the ironsmith as such:

> The task of the smith who works in iron is very laborious, indeed far more so than that of the copper smith just described. For he also handles heavy weights continually, and stands constantly erect before the fire of the forge, since the hardness of the iron cannot be soft-

ened except by means of heating and boiling it well. . . . When, finally, I consider what this art is, it seems to me that everything in all
kinds depends only on experience, since these craftsmen are people
without plan, and most of them are crude country people, and if they
know how to do one thing they do not know how to do another.
                    —The *Pirotechnia* of Vannoccio Biringuccio, 1540

The workers knew *what* to do to get a workable product, but they
didn't really know *why*; this self-determined craftsmanship was common in the early years of iron production, and it slowly filtered
through the ages as an apprenticed skill, all the way into the twentieth
century and to the men who made the *Titanic*. The basic workshops of
medieval times produced the critical know-how that gave birth to the
great iron and steel industry more than a millennium later.

During the Industrial Revolution in the eighteenth century,
wrought iron was in high demand, and this long, slow manufacturing
method could produce only limited quantities at one time. With this
laborious process still lagging in the Dark Ages, builders reached a
technological bottleneck.

In 1784, a disenchanted Englishman named Henry Cort came to
the rescue. He created a special furnace that made wrought iron
through the puddling process—a method requiring a worker to constantly agitate or stir a molten "puddle" of iron and slag. Puddling allowed for quicker production of the wrought iron but was very
dependent on the skill of the puddler working the molten charge. It
required constant stirring because the process included the addition of
oxides that needed to be spread throughout the iron and its impurities.
The oxides would react with the carbon, silicon, phosphorus, and
manganese impurities to create a refined metal of nearly pure iron and
slag. With continued stirring, the impurities in the iron were absorbed
into the slag, and the carbon burned off as carbon monoxide and carbon dioxide gas. Rising like blue flames from the bath, these bubbling
fumes were known as puddler's candles.

The constant agitation of the bath was key to producing material
that had consistent properties and quickly became one of the new

skilled labors of the Industrial Revolution. The puddler was faced with an exhausting job: stirring a batch, several hundred pounds in weight, over hot flames and then shaping and turning the lumpy, sticky product of iron and slag as artfully and thoroughly as possible. As was noted by many ironworkers of the late nineteenth century, a hot humid day could be excruciating for a puddler out of his prime. It was not uncommon to "see a puddler drop down dead" from the mere strain of the job. Only a strong, experienced, highly skilled puddler could control the exact proportions necessary for success. Even so, the quality of the wrought iron would vary from batch to batch, and the amount of product was directly limited by the physical strength of the puddler.

The Glory Days of Wrought Iron

By the middle of the century, the production process of wrought iron had been streamlined to its maximum capabilities. In fact, the process used then was the same until the 1960s, when wrought iron became extinct in the United States and Britain. A puddler, and usually an apprentice learning the trade, would work a twelve-hour shift and could typically produce six complete charges, the conversion of a batch of pig iron to wrought iron, during one shift. The process was something like cooking old-fashioned fudge, requiring preparation of the pot, slow addition of ingredients, and constant stirring while the heating took place. During the boiling the iron thickened and had to be stirred constantly by two men who used a long iron hook known as a rabble. When the carbon had been completely removed, the blue flames subsided, and the men struggled to remove the spongy mass from the furnace as quickly as possible.

They would separate the large blob into hundred-pound balls and heave them with huge tongs from the furnace to the hammer (see plate 6, bottom), where they would be beaten to expel as much molten slag as possible. Recall that wrought iron is a mixture of iron and slag and requires working of the product to squeeze out most of the slag and to force the iron to stick together. By using strong hammering and rolling, this step ensured better consistency throughout and would reveal to the puddler how well the wrought iron had been made. If it was a good batch, it would be soft and workable; if it was bad, it would crumble when hit by the hammer. Once it cooled, it became known as puddle bar, or muck bar, the lowest-quality wrought iron. In this form, it was really only useful if it was further processed. At the end of this first step of processing, the slag particles in the wrought iron would be long, thin stringers, all aligned along the direction in which the bar was rolled or squeezed out.

Since it was known that iron's properties would improve with the amount of work done on it, before the muck bar could be sold, it had to be reworked, using a method known as piling. Piling required the stacking of rolled wrought iron product in an alternating pattern. The stack would then be reheated and rolled again to break up remaining long stringers of slag in the mass from the first rolling. This piling operation created more uniform iron (see figs. 4a, 4b, and 4c, pp. 30–32).

In Victorian England (mid-nineteenth to early twentieth century) the piling process was a measure of the quality of the wrought iron, since a larger number of pilings improved the mechanical properties.

Slag Under the Microscope

For the best properties, the slag stringers in wrought iron are not supposed to be big. In fact, the finer their structure, the better. Engineers and scientists of the early twentieth century knew this, yet, unfortunately, as with anything made by a skilled human hand, there will always be variations. In the case of wrought iron from the *Titanic*, there were huge variations. Some slag chunks were so large that cooling following the puddling process took a very long time. As a result, coarse tree-like crystals, known as dendrites, had enough time to form inside of the slag. When large slag chunks are left unrefined like this, they can single-handedly control the wrought iron's mechanical properties.

Figure 4a. A microscope image showing the long, thin fibrous slag stringers that are formed in wrought iron prior to any piling to break them up.

Consequently, a very unimaginative, albeit simple naming system was created, based on the number of times the puddled iron was piled. Number 1 iron, or muck bar, was composed of hammered or squeezed puddled iron that had been rolled without reworking it. This was the first product made by the puddler and the apprentice. Number 1 iron would have had extremely variable properties. Number 2 bar, or "merchant" bar, resulted from a piling, reheating, and rerolling of No. 1. Piling, reheating, and rerolling of No. 2 resulted in (you guessed it) No. 3 bar, or "best" bar. The same process on No. 3 bar produced No. 4 bar, or "best-best" bar, which was typically used for anchors, chains, and rivets. According to the company's Iron and Steel Contract records, Harland & Wolff ordered No. 3 or best bar iron for the rivets of the *Titanic*. In general, the strength and ductility (the amount of stretching before breaking) of the wrought iron was directly related to the number of times this piling process had been performed, hence the

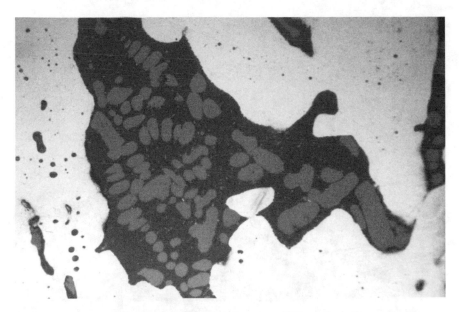

Figure 4b. A close-up of a slag particle in wrought iron that shows the formation of dendrites in the slag. This means that the slag was so large that cooling from the furnace temperature took a very long time, and coarse crystals began to form. Photograph copyright Jennifer Hooper McCarty, Ph.D. diss., The Johns Hopkins University.

difference in quality between a merchant bar and a best-best bar. Nineteenth-century scientists, anxious to study these new metals, soon discovered that piling beyond six times offered no additional strengthening quality and was simply a waste of time. Besides, the names had gotten pretty annoying.

The production of wrought iron by the puddling method proved useful and nearly timeless, used until the material's gradual extinction in the mid-twentieth century. The SS *Great Britain* (1843), the first screw-driven iron ship, wore wrought iron hull plating made by the puddling method. The Eiffel Tower, completed in 1889, was constructed entirely of puddled wrought iron, composed of 15,000 iron components held together by 2.5 million rivets (see plate 9). Although famous for his colossal tower, Gustav Eiffel collaborated on the design of the Statue of Liberty in New York Harbor (1886), designing the wrought iron frame to support the metal skin of the sculpture.

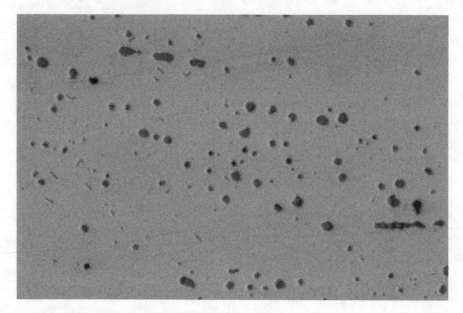

Figure 4c. A microscope image showing nice, round, small slag particles as they appear in properly prepared wrought iron.

The ability to make wrought iron components, and the speed with which they were made, was dependent on a number of factors. Even into the twentieth century, production of wrought iron was limited to batches that were small enough to be puddled by a skilled worker. The quality of each component was controlled by the puddler who stirred the batch and the amount of subsequent piling that it received after it was made. With so many small batches, produced by different puddlers, the results could be highly variable.

Scientific Enlightenment

In the late nineteenth century, in Britain, Sweden, and the United States, wrought iron was manufactured on a large scale for use on bridges, ships' hulls, and as parts of machinery—pretty much any area of high stress and high usage. Despite its high strength, however, accidents did happen. A number of mechanical failures occurred, and the public was especially concerned about reports of the occasional ship-

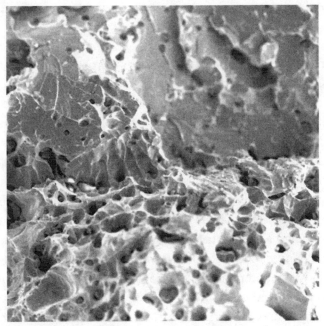

Figure 5. An image from a scanning electron microscope
of the broken end of a wrought iron rivet. Each little hole
contains a broken piece of slag.

wreck. So far it had been the puddler's responsibility to ensure that
good quality wrought iron was prepared. With the stirring of a batch
and the pounding of the smith's hammer, a worker would be able to
tell if his iron was suitable for use. But what actually made the wrought
iron good or bad? Why had some wrought iron failed? What caused
the Versailles railway disaster of 1842? Why did the ship *Royal Charter* sink? How is it possible to explain the collapse of the Basse-Chaîne
suspension bridge that killed 226 people? All these failures had one
thing in common—the catastrophic fracture of wrought iron.

The Tay Bridge Disaster, 1879

The longest river in Scotland, the Tay, runs from the interior, opens into the Firth of Tay and drains into the North Sea. To the delight of the city of Dundee, the two-mile-long Tay Bridge, then the longest span over water in the world, opened in 1878 across the river. The bridge was a daring engineering feat, designed for railroad traffic and was constructed of wrought iron. At the time, necessary inspections and maintenance were severely inadequate, although such regulatory precautions were as yet unheard of in the nineteenth century. Combine this with a lack of understanding about metallurgical properties and inconsistent manufacturing methods, and it was only a matter of time before a defect or damaged region would cause problems. Unfortunately, it took only one year in the case of the Tay Bridge. In 1879, battered by strong vibrations during high winds, a wrought iron girder collapsed while a train was passing over the bridge, killing eighty people. The girders, one of which is on display in the Royal Museum of Scotland, was made of plates of rolled wrought iron, held together by hand-riveted wrought iron rivets.

THE EMERGENCE OF THE STEEL AGE

So What About Steel?

So far the third type of iron has gone completely unmentioned—steel. The definition of steel is particularly complicated, as a huge number of steel alloys, or recipes, have been created over the years, each for a specific use. Basically, steel is an alloy of iron and carbon with a small amount of other elements; it contains less carbon than cast iron but more carbon than wrought iron. It is easiest to subdivide steels into three categories: mild steels (less than 0.25 percent carbon), carbon steels (0.25–1.4 percent carbon), and alloy steels. Alloy steel covers the more modern mixtures containing such additives as nickel and chromium for corrosion resistance, in, for instance, stainless steel kitchenware.

Mild steel is fairly close to wrought iron in chemistry, containing very little carbon, making it soft and ductile, and therefore easy to work. However, it contains no slag stringers. Mild steel has less corrosion resistance than wrought iron but usually has better strength. Mild steel is very commonly used for engineering applications today, and it was the hot new material of shipbuilding in the late nineteenth to the

---

Thank Goodness for Photography

The most extensive study of wrought iron performed in the nineteenth century was by Mr. David Kirkaldy, who completed 1,700 tensile tests over three years (1858–61) using random samples that he selected at Robert Napier & Sons shipyard in Glasgow, Scotland. Kirkaldy found that the quality of the wrought iron and its mechanical properties could be determined by carefully studying its fibrous structure before and after breaking it. The results were extremely useful, both because his studies are carefully detailed in notes and tables and also because he was working independently for the iron manufacturers on the British market. Today we use microscopes to study the structure of the material postfracture, but in the mid-1800s there was no such luxury. Before each experiment Kirkaldy would observe the structure of the fibers and then draw exactly what he saw in his notebooks. When he had successfully broken the sample in his tensile testing machine, he would examine it again and draw a complementary picture. In 1862, Kirkaldy published his findings. He had studied seventy-six kinds of wrought iron, had pulled them in all directions, and had drawn a picture of each and every surface before and after testing. Nowadays, scientists use high-powered microscopes with digital cameras to view the fractured surfaces of metals (see fig. 5, p. 33).

early twentieth century. In 1874, the White Star Line was one of the
first companies to move from building its ships' hulls of wrought iron
to mild steel. *The Shipbuilder* of 1907 boasted the latest in achievements in the construction of Cunard's *Mauretania* and *Lusitania*:

> Mild steel rivets have been used throughout the structure, even for
> connecting the high-tensile steel plates. . . . It was considered prefer-
> able . . . to use mild steel and maintain the necessary strength at the
> butts by increasing the rivet area and using hydraulic riveting ma-
> chines of great power.

By contrast, the White Star Line's *Titanic*, completed in 1912, was
constructed using both wrought iron *and* steel rivets, a choice that will
be scrutinized in the chapters to follow.

The Open-Hearth Alternative to Steel Production

By the 1870s there were two available processes for making steel—
the Bessemer and the open-hearth processes. The open-hearth
method was not too different from a puddling furnace but just a lot
bigger and hotter. These grueling conditions can be seen in plate 6
(top). This allowed steel to be created in liquid form, since temperatures could rise as high as 1,800°C. The Bessemer process, which is
the older of the two, involves blowing hot air through the molten iron,
burning out impurities. The open-hearth process worked slowly and,
therefore, allowed for constant checks on the chemistry of the steel.
The Bessemer process was very fast but was much more limited in
what types of steel it could make. As the turn of the century approached, the steelmaking industry was firmly rooted, signaling the
emergence of good, cheap, mild steel that would slowly replace
wrought iron in rails and ships.

Turn of the Century Developments: What Did *Titanic* Use?

The construction of the White Star Line *Olympic*-class ships was
right in the middle of the transition between wrought iron and steel in

shipbuilding. Both *Olympic* and *Titanic*'s steel plates were made by the open-hearth process, which by 1877 had been accepted as a material for shipbuilding. The steel plates were ordered in accordance with the day's standards. In fact, Mr. Edward Harland of Harland & Wolff had requested a series of tests on Bessemer steel way back in the 1860s, determining that it was too brittle for ships' plating. Lloyd's was soon to follow, banning Bessemer steel completely by the early 1900s. In this sense, Harland & Wolff were forward-thinkers. On the other hand, numerous Harland & Wolff and Board of Trade texts prove that wrought iron was still being used for riveting, showing that very specific riveting guidelines were given during the construction of the *Olympic* and *Titanic*, including the size and placement of wrought iron rivets to secure the hull plates. While Cunard had already moved into using mild steel rivets exclusively, these records reveal that Harland & Wolff chose to use both wrought iron and steel. Part of this investigation will try to determine why the most successful shipbuilder in the world made this choice and whether this is important in light of the disaster.

CHAPTER 4

THE RIVETING PROCESS

*[Riveting] is a difficult trade to learn, a hard and
exhausting one to follow, wearing a man out in his
youth, for no one ever saw an old riveter. . . . Wages
are inevitably high and most of the work is done by
the piece. When the work is to be had, therefore, the
riveter makes a great deal of good money, but at the
expense of his vital energies.*

—*Transactions of the Institute of Naval Architects,* **1899**

The concept of using rivets to secure the *Titanic*'s plates was nothing new. Both the Romans and the Vikings used a blacksmith's long iron nails to fasten the wooden planks of their ships together. Iron bolts were used from the Middle Ages onward for wooden battleships and merchant vessels, and eventually the use of iron rivets became the norm, even after steel became the common shipbuilding material. Eventually, as naval architects and marine engineers were more confident in the advantages of using a new material, they slowly replaced using wrought iron with steel rivets. The *Olympic*-class ships were constructed using wrought iron rivets that were hand driven and mild steel rivets that were hydraulically driven. Since the 3 million rivets on the *Titanic* were the links that held the ship together, their performance was crucial to the overall strength of the ship and definitely merit further consideration in the investigation.

THE BASICS

A Rivet Revealed

A rivet is like a two-headed nail that can hold together plates on ships, skins of airplanes, parts of boilers, bridges, or on any number of other structures. A rivet has two heads, one that is formed before the rivet is placed through the hole in the plate and the other, known as the point, is formed after the rivet is in the hole (see fig. 6). The process of riveting provides a way to clamp several plates together because a hot rivet driven through the holes will shrink when cooled. The result is that the rivet will always feel a strong pulling along its shaft, a tensile stress, that develops because the rivets want to shrink as they cool, but the plates are in the way.

The first iron rivets were made from puddled wrought iron that had been formed into a bar shape. Remember that after the puddler removed the spongy mass of wrought iron from the furnace, it was hammered or rolled into bar stock. Depending on what it was being used for, the bar stock would be piled and rolled again to get the right grade or quality. In the case of rivets, usually a No. 4 iron was needed, which was piled three additional times. Once the blacksmith got the

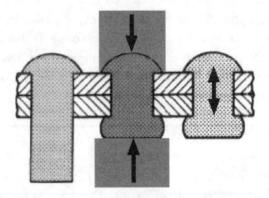

Figure 6. A schematic diagram showing (from left to right): a rivet just after installation; how a rivet's two heads, which are formed while hot (arrows), then cool and shrink, thereby holding the plates together tightly.

An early example of an immense ship-riveting job was the *Great Eastern* (1858), made from 30,000 pieces of iron that were riveted together by hand. It took approximately 3,000,000 wrought iron rivets to complete the job and 200 rivet squads to do it. A rivet squad consisted of two bashers who worked on the outside of the hull, one man inside the hull who held the rivets (the "holder-up"), and three boys who usually assisted the worker on the inside. An accomplished worker could drive home 200 rivets during an eight-hour shift. The 400 bashers who hammered the rivets banged away for over one thousand hours before the *Great Eastern* hull was complete.

At the Harland & Wolff shipyard, the job of a riveter was one of hard work and incessant noise. Once the plates were positioned onto the frame they were ready for the riveters. Often young boys would have the job of heater—in charge of heating the rivet in a portable stove to a red-hot temperature of approximately 800°C (1,400°F) and throwing it up to the holder-up, positioned on the frame. The holder caught the rivet in a funnel and, using a pair of tongs, would place it into position within a prepunched or drilled hole. Immediately, two bashers quickly and accurately struck at the head, taking turns, to form the point. In some cases, both heads would be formed simultaneously, in which case the bashers would stand on either side of the hull hammering until the heads were evenly formed. By the way, the hammers used for the job could weigh anywhere from two to forty pounds.

right quality, the iron was extruded using a machine not unlike a huge Play-Doh Fun Factory to create a long spaghetti-like cylinder about one inch in diameter (see plate 7, top). The correct lengths were then cut to make the rivet shaft or shank. If one head was to be premade before going down to the shipyard, these little cylinders would be heated again, and one head of the rivet was formed using a die.

Rivet Material: Iron vs. Steel and the Red-Hot Rule

Thinking back to chapter 3, recall that wrought iron is nearly pure iron. Because it is so pure, its melting temperature is very high. By contrast, steel is a mixture, or alloy, of iron and a small amount of carbon. As a result of this mixture, steel has a lower melting point than pure iron. Therefore, steel will soften at a lower temperature than wrought iron. There is also another issue to consider. If steel is heated too hot, usually beyond cherry red, it will become brittle and may shatter when hammered (a condition known as hot short), whereas iron, at the same temperature, will still be soft and malleable. As long as a worker was sensitive to which material he was using, then everything was fine. It was when he was not so aware that things could go wrong.

By the late 1800s, as interest in manufacturing and usage increased, steel gradually replaced iron at the shipyard. Despite the growing use of steel plates, shipbuilders avoided using steel rivets until much later. One of the main reasons was that the shipbuilders by nature were cautious. Scientists found that if a steel rivet were heated too hot, it would become brittle and wouldn't rivet up properly. This is signaled by a loss in malleability and the inability to be easily hammered. In this case, a new rivet would have to be driven, wasting time and material. From a worker's standpoint, iron rivets were softer and easier to hammer properly, and they provided more consistent results. Considering that an entire ship could fall apart if a mistake was made, erring on the side of caution is understandable. As the Lloyd's surveyor remarked following a discussion on steel in shipbuilding:

> It would appear to be on the while preferable to adhere for the present, and until further experience has been gained on the subject, to the use for steel ships of rivets of the size that would be required by the Committee for the vessels if built of iron.

Translation: Even the shipbuilding rule makers were not really sure how to accommodate changes when using steel rivets, so in the mean-

During World War I efficient shipbuilding was an essential part of the successful war effort. Beginning in 1918, government programs were organized in the United States that aimed to increase the morale of workers. In particular, shipyard competitions were staged in riveting, which was one of the most important controlling factors in the completion of a vessel. The first record was claimed by a riveting gang in the Baltimore Dry Dock and Shipbuilding Company who drove 658 rivets in eight hours. After it was announced throughout the country, the feat was broken days later when 1,202 rivets were driven in an eight-hour day. The record quickly escalated up to 2,919 rivets, completed in nine hours. Soon, to the satisfaction of government organizers, the news of these fearless record holders made their way to the United Kingdom. Convinced that this was merely "Yankee exaggeration," the British riveting gangs were determined to come out on top. A gang in the yard of Fraser & Fraser, London, succeeded with 4,267 rivets driven in nine hours, upping the ante between the United States and the United Kingdom, as some newspapers began offering cash prizes.

With the efforts of millions of hard workers, the Shipping Board built and delivered over 1,700 vessels during 1918–19. Eventually the government realized that these masterminded competitions were exhausting the riveting gangs, who required extra days of rest after attempting a record. The Shipping Board halted the contests, acknowledging that they had spiraled out of control, but still didn't alienate their production-boosting plans. The "Olympic Games" of riveting were replaced by a universally published ranking system in which each shipyard was scored according to the number of rivets completed each day.

while when they did use steel rivets, they decided to make them exactly like the iron ones.

This all sounds reasonable, but consider the expert view of the nineteenth-century Iron and Steel Institute bigwig, J. S. Jeans. Jeans, a well-respected metallurgist of his day, made a very important point when comparing the overheating of an iron rivet and a steel rivet. Remember that a worker (see plate 7, bottom), often a teenaged lad, would stand next to a bellow-driven stove and warm a preformed rivet until it was red hot. There were no thermometers or digital readouts; he had to know the correct temperature based only on color. When the rivet was cherry red, he would throw it to the worker on the structure, who was supposed to catch it and immediately place it in the hole, so that the bashers could begin straightaway while the rivet was still hot. Similar to the puddling process, riveting was very much controlled by a rivet squad's quickness, experience, and skill. "In hand-riveting it will be observed, that the tightness of the joint and the soundness of the work depends upon the skill and also upon the will of the workman to form the joint and close the rivets."

Back to the rivet being heated in the stove. The steel rivet, as described, if heated too high during the riveting process, will become brittle and "cannot be used at all," whereas the wrought iron rivet is also affected by being too hot, but not so much that it cannot be used. That is, an overheated wrought iron rivet can still be riveted into a structure, despite the fact that it is not really as good as it could be, and it could go undetected by the rivet gang, especially if they are inexperienced.

THE RIVETING PROCESS

The Addition of Machinery to the Assembly Line

Manual riveting was a crucial, very well paid trade. Early on, riveters realized their importance to the shipbuilding trade and organized themselves into a powerful union, the Society of Boilermakers and Iron and Steel Shipbuilders, which insisted on working for piece wages. This meant that for every rivet completed, they would receive a carefully negotiated wage.

In order to replace riveters with cheaper labor, the large shipbuilding companies were determined to bring in new machine riveters that could be manned by less skilled men. During the nineteenth century, engineers and inventors alike tackled the problem by introducing steam-powered hydraulic and pneumatic riveters. The mechanization trend was pervasive in the industry, even for the blacksmiths who formed the rivets. An article published in *Engineering* in 1900 compared hand and machine labor, and concluded that a steam-powered, rivet-forming machine could produce single-head rivets twelve times faster and for a tiny fraction of the cost compared to two blacksmiths working the same job. As early as 1856, engineers were wrestling with machinery as a means to obtain the tightest fit when joining plates:

> The [riveting] machine produces much sounder work, as the time occupied in the hand process allows the rivet to cool, and thus by destroying its ductility, the rivet it is imperfectly closed, and hence follow the defects of leaky rivets and imperfect joints.

By the 1880s more shipbuilding firms had become interested in lowering their labor costs, and so began their dabbling in machinery investment. One of the first mechanized systems can be seen in plate 4 (top). By the turn of the century, hydraulic riveters had been improved upon, and they produced good work "even on the rivets of the highest strain." It was said, "Hydraulic riveting is nearly always of the best possible quality, and for certain important items of structure is almost a necessity so that in every way its extension is much to be desired in ship construction." Eventually, hydraulic riveting was adopted for hulls, and it was used on most of the 4 million rivets on *Mauretania*. In 1908, *Engineering* described the world-class construction project underway at Harland & Wolff, which included a power plant setup and new gantry being built for *Olympic* and *Titanic*. The largest cranes in the world, erected to slide along the entire length of the gantry, were designed to hoist the three-ton hydraulic riveters into place and to move the thousands of tons of material that were necessary for the great ships' construction.

The resistance of the workers' union to losing their high wages continued to keep powered machinery out of riveting. Manual riveting was incredibly exhausting hard work, considered one of the most difficult tasks in shipbuilding, required highly specialized attention, and took many years to perfect. Even then, most men could not continue after middle age because the noisy banging, heavy lifting, and full day of backbreaking hammering would wear them out. Sound familiar?—just like the puddler's plight. Shipyards had an incentive to find a way to lengthen the life of an experienced worker at the yard and to cheapen the rising costs. In 1914, even though machine riveting was in use for most vessels, shipbuilders continued to nitpick about the less-than-satisfactory result of hydraulic shell riveters, yet most agreed that the result was far more consistent than work done by hand.

The Standards of the Industry

By the mid-1800s, government bodies realized that to ensure safety and avoid costly disasters (like what happened to the Tay Bridge), standards had to be established to measure the quality of metals used in buildings, bridges, and ships. Unlike with steel, by the early 1900s it was no longer considered necessary to test "[wrought] iron forgings and bars, unless there [was] reason to believe that the material is not of suitable quality." Lloyd's Rules soon followed suit, indicating that iron need only be tested if the surveyor of the ship required it. Bottom line: as of 1901, if the material was iron, the Board of Trade did not require it to be tested, unless specifically requested to do so.

Meanwhile, the British Standards Institute revised the specifications for structural steel in shipbuilding in 1906, which included steel used for plates and rivets. It required that steel always be produced using the open-hearth process. The steel had to be free from defects on the surface, and then only in the Board of Trade inspector's presence could the samples be tested for tensile strength and ductility.

What About the Rivets?

The Board of Trade settled on standard material tests for rivet bar stock and entrusted the actual rivet testing to the shipyard or some other regulating body. They had decided that beyond the bar stock, it was no longer their problem. Large works, such as David Colville & Sons, who were frequent suppliers to Harland & Wolff (and were partially owned by the shipyard in the early 1900s, then completely bought out by them in 1920), published catalogues to assure buyers of the reputable quality of their goods.

Their procedures included testing both steel rivet bars (before they were cut into rivets) and steel manufactured rivets, but did not include iron. By 1906, more and more shipbuilders were turning to steel rivets exclusively, and while iron rivets were still in use, no new specifications were issued after the beginning of the twentieth century.

For rivets, there were two important properties that needed to be investigated—the tensile strength (the strength to resist being pulled apart) and the ductility (the amount of stretching before breaking). Once in the form of a manufactured rivet, the steel was tested for its ductility again: the shank had to be bent cold so that the tips touched without forming cracks. The rivet heads were tested while hot and were hammered down until they were 2½ times the diameter of the shank. As long as no cracks formed at the edges of the head, they passed. Once a sufficient number of rivets had passed the tests, it was time to use them.

Best Practices: The Secrets of Good Riveting

> *After working about three fourths of the outside plating of the ship, men are set to work at closing up the joints, [reaming] out unfair holes, etc., preparatory to the riveting being commenced. The riveting is generally done by piecework, a set of riveters being composed of two riveters, a holder up, and two boys to heat and carry the rivets. The rivets used in the outside plating are of a conical form under the head, and the heads of all the rivets in the ship are laid up.*
> —Theodore D. Wilson, *An Outline of*
> *Shipbuilding, Theoretical and Practical*, 1873

Although in practice each shipyard had its own guidelines for workers to follow, many engineers wrote practical handbooks that documented important advice for successfully constructing a vessel.

These old handbooks gave a sense of what was expected to ensure watertight work.

Concern Number 1: Does the rivet fill up the rivet hole? Loose clanging and banging inside the hole was bad and signaled a potential leak. When rivet holes were punched into plating, the result was usually a hole with slightly tapered sides near the edge. Filling this extra area with the hot rivet required accurately hitting the rivet head, forcing the region just under it to be squashed around the hole in a conical fashion. Handbooks outlined the proper methods of riveting in order to avoid the catastrophe of loose rivets—the telltale sign of poor workmanship.

> Every loose rivet that may be found cannot of course, be taken as being due to excessive stress: the more frequent cause is indifferent work, evidenced by the fact that neighboring rivets will frequently be found quite sound, though the failure of some will cause a greater stress upon the remainder.

In S. J. P. Thearle's *The Modern Practice of Shipbuilding in Iron and Steel* published in 1891, the author underlines that a rivet should be tight in its hole, and goes on to stress the importance of its temperature when driven (see fig. 7, p. 48). On this point, the handbook warns of problems with overheated rivets, particularly with steel ones, since they were known to become extremely brittle under the blow of the hammer and, therefore, unable to fill the rivet hole tightly. The recommended solution was to give riveters plenty of room to work so that they could properly distinguish those rivets that were loose and needed to be replaced.

Concern Number Two: Is the rivet straight? Crooked rivets were just as bad as loose ones, caused when the holes in the plating were not lined up accurately. According to T. Walton's early-twentieth-century handbook *Steel Ships and Their Construction and Maintenance*, driving a rivet in such a situation was rigorously frowned upon; instead the hole should first be reamed out in order to clear a smooth, well-aligned passage. Unfortunately, riveters who were paid by piecework and re-

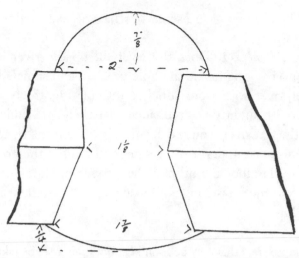

Figure 7. Diagram of a rivet driven into a tapered hole with a flush head, from Francis Carruthers's survey of *Titanic*, 1912.

ceived a standard wage for every one hundred rivets completed were not compensated for this alignment job. At Harland & Wolff, riveters anxious to earn their keep would jump the shipyard wall on weekends to prepare the plating for Monday morning. Following a Sunday afternoon of squaring up plates and securing temporary bolts and washers in place, riveters were guaranteed to be pounding in a rivet by Monday's 8 a.m. horn.

THE INSPECTION PROCESS

As strong as hands can achieve, each rivet of all the millions in a liner (perhaps the most impressive thing one saw) tested separately and certified with its own chalk mark.
        —S. Bullock, *Thomas Andrews: Shipbuilder*, 1912

No standardized method existed for testing the massive number of rivets on the ship, although the testing of iron and steel stock before installation was commonplace by the late 1800s. As the structure took shape and each rivet found its place, a worker known as a rivet counter would count the number completed by each squad and would test them to ensure a tight fit. For this job, the counter made £20 more per week than the hard-toiling riveters, and as a result, one former Harland & Wolff worker explained, "[The rivet counters] had few friends; they were like traffic wardens are today."

The primary concern was to be sure that the rivets were tight against the plates—no rattling, no gaps, and, above all, nowhere for water to seep through. The quickest and most efficient way to test rivets was the tapping method, which was likely the most popular method in the early 1900s. The test consisted of tapping the rivets with a hammer; if the result was a ringing sound, then the rivet had been properly driven; if a dull "thud" was heard, then the rivet was loose and was removed and replaced. This process is referred to in a 1904 handbook: "The tightness of rivets is tested by tapping the side of the rivet head with a small hammer, while two fingers of the other hand rest against the opposite side of the rivet head. An experienced worker can immediately detect a loose rivet. Loose rivets should never be caulked tight [repaired], but renewed and re-riveted." When a rivet passed the test, it was given the seal of approval—a chalk mark. Evidence of these markings can be seen in the lower right-hand corner of a photograph of the *Britannic* (plate 5). These rivets were hydraulically driven as seen in plate 4 (bottom).

Besides the tapping method, smaller areas of the ship were sometimes flooded to check for leaks on the outside. When the outside had been inspected, the water would be released through a small hole drilled in the ship. In other cases, bolts were sometimes used to replace rivets at random in the ship, so that they could be tightened up in order to detect loose rivets nearby.

Late-nineteenth- to early-twentieth-century shipbuilding experienced rapid changes as marine engineers and scientists persuaded the governing bodies, such as the Board of Trade and the British Corporation, to institute the first industrial standards. As the qualified ironworks became more comfortable with high industrial production levels, the testing of wrought iron stock fell by the wayside. As of 1901, the Board of Trade no longer required the testing of iron for use

in shipbuilding. Meanwhile, the shipyard introduced their own inspection procedure for testing the tightness of the rivets. Although
this was considered adequate at the time, a required method for ensur-
ing the strength and ductility of a wrought iron rivet, as undriven
feedstock or once driven, did not exist. *Lloyd's Rules* indicated that iron
was to be tested only if the surveyor of the ship required it.

This laxity in the rules was not trivial to engineers, who had already sought to measure the strength of rivets back in 1869. Their results showed that the quality of the wrought iron mattered:

> The differences in the results [in strength] obtained in the . . . cases
> are no doubt chiefly due to differences in the quality of the rivet-
> iron.

CHAPTER 5

HARLAND & WOLFF'S PROTOCOLS

Terrible as an army with banners
Through the dusk of winter's eve,
Over the bridge
The thousands tramp . . .
Splendid ships they build,
More splendid for
The hearts that dare conceive
Such vastness and such power.
Terrible as an army with banners,
The legions of labour,
The builders of ships,
Tramp thro' the winter's eve.

—Richard Rowley, *The Islandmen*

In May 1911, 14,000 men were employed by Harland & Wolff, three to four thousand of whom were working full time on the fitting out of the *Olympic*. By the end of February 1912, just one month before the *Titanic* left Belfast, the employee count surged to 17,275, with over 10,000 men at work in the yard on Queen's Island, Belfast, racing to finish *Titanic*. The Harland & Wolff shipyard on Queen's Island was the heart of the Belfast economy, having grown from a small facility in

the mid-1800s to a complex of four shipyards that held heavy influence with the Belfast City Council. Messers. Harland & Wolff had become a powerful firm, building ships that traveled the world, and was
well known and respected for the superior quality of its craftsmanship.
The 1911 completion of the largest gantries in the world secured Harland & Wolff's reputation as the world's premiere shipbuilder.

Although a success, the firm was constantly faced with a lack of
skilled labor in Belfast for shipbuilding. To solve this problem, they
successfully recruited and retained highly skilled workers from the
Scotland and England yards during lulls in their competitors' business.
Although wages were not much higher in Belfast, food and lodging
was considerably cheaper, and the booming linen industry meant
guaranteed jobs for female family members. These skilled laborers, often platers, riveters, and caulkers, would act as foremen and squad
leaders and would help in the training of the firm's unskilled recruits.
In just over ten years after Harland & Wolff took control of the
Queen's Island yard, a complete in-house system was in place for
training local unskilled men and boys in the art of shipbuilding. As a
former Harland & Wolff shipyard worker remarked, "Country men
fresh from County Down were transformed into riveters by Harland
& Wolff."

This recruitment and training system worked well and allowed the
shipyard to employ a large number of semiskilled (those who didn't do
a formal apprenticeship) and unskilled workers, as well as apprentices,
all of whom were paid considerably less than the skilled laborers. Before World War I, only about 50 to 60 percent of Harland & Wolff's
employees were skilled workers. With the demands of production at
Queen's Island due to White Star Line contracts and the opening of
the Southampton yard, the number of employees quickly increased
above fifteen thousand. Under extreme pressure to complete *Olympic*
and *Titanic*, the firm forbade visitors to the shipyard and excluded
workers from attending the launching of any vessel. But this was still
not enough to ease the fears of the directors when the *Olympic* was
forced into the Thompson dry dock for repairs in October 1911. In
the Harland & Wolff directors' meeting minutes dated October 28,

Lord Pirrie expressed concern over a shortage of riveters at the yard, suggesting that new squads should be hired from the yards in the Wear shipbuilding district to add to the five new squads hired within the previous three weeks.

In order to finish the *Titanic* even close to her original departure date of March 20, more workers were required. Employment records indicated that the number of Belfast shipyard workers steadily increased over the autumn and winter months, reaching a peak in February 1912. By November 1911, the directors' minutes revealed a reorganization of labor at the Belfast yard in order to complete the fitting out of the *Titanic* as quickly as possible. On February 6, 1912, the directors discussed problems with "idling workers on No. 401 [*Titanic*]" and potential incentives devised to encourage faster production.

By March 11, 1912, after housing the *Olympic* a second time in the Belfast yard while she received one of *Titanic*'s propeller blades, the completion date of the *Titanic* was set at April 1. Due to the lateness of her completion date, the directors decided against a public inspection in Belfast. Within three weeks, the men at the Queen's Island yard had pulled through under fierce pressure to complete the job, exhibiting the efficiency and craftsmanship typical of Harland & Wolff. Number 401, Triple SS *Titanic*, was listed in the record book as delivered only one day later than expected, on April 2, 1912.

Based on Harland & Wolff's reputation, it is no surprise to read the handwritten remarks of Francis Carruthers, Belfast Board of Trade surveyor, as he inspected the *Titanic*, afloat in Belfast, in February 1912:

> The workmanship is of the highest class throughout. The vessel is new and the scantlings and general arrangement are in accordance with the plan, midship section and profile, which were submitted for this vessel and No. 400 [*Olympic*] preceding her.

Such high-quality work was normal and expected of such a world-class firm, and any workers unable to live up to its regulations were punished by deductions from their paychecks. According to Rule No. 16 of those listed for Harland & Wolff employees, which were first published in 1888, "In the event of work being spoiled by the carelessness of workmen, the labor expended thereon will not be paid for, and those in fault will be held responsible for the loss of the material." This rule most certainly extended to riveters. Harland & Wolff was known for its extremely critical standards, and it forbade the occasional caulking chisel used to splay the head of a slightly leaky rivet. Caulking was the final process of creating watertight work, where a chisel would be hammered against the spaces between plates in order to make them lie tightly against one another. By making a slight indentation into the top of two plates, they were pushed more closely together. However important this was as a last finishing process, at Harland & Wolff it was not permitted as a replacement for a sloppily driven rivet. If a rivet was found to be leaking, it was pulled out and a new one was driven in its place.

THE RIVETING PLAN

Of the 3 million rivets used to hold the *Titanic* together, there were the hull (or shell) rivets, bulkhead rivets, porthole rivets, and deck rivets. In addition, there were rivets that held together all the machinery and engines, such as the boiler rivets. The hull rivets were the biggest of all, those in the keel measuring 1¼ inches in diameter, and were long enough to be driven through up to three 1½-inch-thick steel plates, before hammering down the points. They were made of both mild steel and wrought iron. The deck rivets tended to be the smallest and were usually made of wrought iron, except for the plating on the bridge deck. The skeleton of the ship gave the *Titanic* her shape and connected the decks, coal chutes, and watertight bulkheads, the inner guts of the ship, to the shell. All the framing rivets were made of wrought iron, but they had various types of head and point shapes depending on their location. If part of the frame was being riveted to the shell, then the finished points of the rivet were flush with the plating to create the clean lines of a smooth outer surface. In other locations that would go unnoticed by the public, the rivet points were hand hammered into a "snap-point" or semispherical point, which was the most popular type in use and was generally considered to be dependable for most work.

During the building phase the only way to keep track of all these details was to draft specific directions. For each part of the ship's construction (the frame, the shell plating, etc.), a riveting table was drawn up to indicate the diameter, the pitch (separation between rivets), the material, head shape, and point shape for each series of parts that needed connecting. Riveters, holder uppers, and rivet boys would be paid a negotiated price for each type of rivet size, shape, and material. Wages increased with the diameter of the rivet or if the rivets were made of steel rather than wrought iron, since the steel was harder to drive.

By Hand or by Machine: A Measure of Consistency

Machine riveting had become more popular since the late 1890s, and the work produced better and more efficient results. As one of the world's premiere shipbuilders, Harland & Wolff was comfortable with adopting the latest and greatest in shipbuilding technology, and hydraulic riveting was no exception. *Titanic* proudly boasted a sturdy partially machine-riveted hull, despite the general difficulties in using hydraulic riveting for shell work, which arose mainly from the struggle in squeezing the bulky machinery into tight places. A cross-section of the ship published in *Engineering* in honor of *Titanic's* launching is shown in plate 2. Notice that the double bottom was hydraulically riveted, as well as the doubly and trebly riveted breaks along the B and C decks up to the Boat Deck. Detailed specifications for the ship's construction outlined that the shell riveting was to incorporate the machine-driven rivets wherever possible:

> The Shell to be hydraulically riveted from the keel to the upper turn
> of the bilge for the length of the wing tanks, and forward and aft of
> these out to a line tapering into the keel at about the three-fifth

length. . . . The keel plate to be hydraulically riveted as far forward
and aft as possible.

Basically, if the ship is subdivided into five equal sections along its
length, the middle three sections of the hull are riveted by hydraulic
power, while the bow and stern, or the end fifths, are hand riveted.
While engineers agreed that this likely resulted in less consistent work
in the bow and stern, these areas were too cramped to be riveted by
machine.

Titanic's Materials: Tying Harland & Wolff's Specifications to Standards of the Day

Harland & Wolff bought materials from forges, suppliers, and
manufacturers located all over the United Kingdom. As more and
more steel vessels were produced, foundries sprung up throughout
Wales, Scotland, and Northern Ireland, and while the Board of Trade
and Lloyd's were very familiar with the quality of material in the larger
firms, continual efforts were made to certify the new companies' stock.
If Harland & Wolff decided to purchase material from a new foundry,
it had to first be approved by the Board of Trade. A surveyor was required to write a report stipulating the size and type of works, include
a chemical analysis of its open-hearth steel, and had to oversee the cutting and testing of samples before the foundry could manufacture
items for shipbuilding firms. During the late 1800s and early 1900s,
Harland & Wolff utilized its fair share of previously unknown, small
foundries for manufacturing steel boilerplates and rivets.

As the area around Belfast was lacking in active coal mines and
high-quality iron ore, Harland & Wolff also formed partnerships with
a number of iron and steel suppliers in Scotland and England, ordering large amounts at below-market prices. *Titanic*'s steel plates were
made by the Siemens-Martin open-hearth process, the standard shipbuilding steel of the time, and were ordered in batches of 10,000 to
25,000 plates from Harland & Wolff's regular suppliers, D. Colville &
Sons and Dalzell Steel and Iron Works in Motherwell, Scotland. Standard tests of the strength and ductility of the steel plating were re-

quired by the Board of Trade, as it was for all steel used on boilers, bulkheads, and watertight doors.

Harland & Wolff ordered their steel and iron rivets from several companies, always requesting best quality stock that was already tested in accordance with the standards of the day. Rivets and rivet bars of iron and steel were acquired from D. Colville & Sons and James Miller & Co. in batches of 500 to 1,500 tons at a time. According to Harland & Wolff's record book of iron and steel supplier contracts from 1885 to 1911, the cost of steel rivets decreased by 15 shillings per ton, as the cost of iron rivets *increased* by 14 shillings per ton, making the two materials practically equal in price by 1911. This leveling out of prices reflects a general trend toward cheaper steel production and the consequent increase in the use of steel in shipbuilding.

Wrought Iron or Steel: Harland & Wolff's Rationale

Recall from earlier details that the ship's hull was riveted with *both* wrought iron and mild steel rivets. Where exactly was the distinction on the ship? The specifications for riveting on the *Titanic* outlined which rivets to be used in each area, indicating that

1. Iron rivets should be used "for all hand riveting and to be of the best quality. All rivets of and below 1⅛ inches to be iron, except where otherwise specified."
2. By contrast, for all hydraulic riveting, steel rivets should be used. Further pictorial evidence can be gleaned directly from comments on the shell plating diagram of her nearly identical sister ship *Olympic*, which states: "Steel rivets to be used in way of hydraulic riveting. Iron rivets elsewhere." Francis Carruthers' notes during his final inspection of the *Titanic* indicate the use of hydraulic riveting in the three-fifths length of the shell plating.

What is the reasoning behind such a distinction and why would the Edwardian world's most famous shipbuilder choose a material that was rejected in the recent 1906 construction by another yard for the great liner *Mauretania*? It was obvious by the late nineteenth century to naval architects and marine engineers that steel riveting was the way of the future:

> "The tendency to use steel rivets in steel ships is increasing, it being found . . . that more satisfactory results are thereby obtained."

Why Was the *Titanic* Different?

From all the blueprints, drawings, and building instructions it appears that where feasible, Harland & Wolff beefed up the strength of the riveting job, incorporating steel rivets (believed to be stronger) by hydraulic riveting machines (believed to produce better workmanship). These steel rivets were riveted into doubly up to quintuply riveted seams (believed to better resist separation of the plates under stress) all along the three-fifths length, the main body of the ship. This seems reasonable, especially since the highest stresses are felt within the amidships region of a ship's structure. Yet the outer fifths, comprising the bow and the stern, where space on the gantry was definitely more limited, were constructed using wrought iron rivets that were hand riveted. The use of wrought iron for this hand riveting may have been preferable for a number of reasons:

First, riveters were paid more for hammering up steel rivets because it was harder work, so hand riveting iron ones was just easier and likely produced more efficient results. As a nineteenth-century shipbuilding text explains, it was tricky to monitor the temperature and time events of using steel rivets, much more so than iron rivets, requiring that they should be "knocked down and finished off as quickly as possible"—perfect conditions for machine work but not ideal for hand hammering.

Second, and subsequent to easing the workers' struggle, payment for riveting iron would have been cheaper for Harland & Wolff, and last, by the time the *Titanic* was built, although the Board of Trade required that the steel for rivets be suitably tested, it no longer required that the iron be tested. As of 1901, iron bars were not tested by the

Board of Trade surveyors unless under special instructions to do so. Using wrought iron rivets where necessary would have eliminated the prolonged testing period required for the additional steel, as well as any further charges incurred from the Board of Trade.

So here are the facts surrounding *Titanic*'s rivets: (1) Both steel and wrought iron rivets were used. (2) Steel rivets were used on the shell, in trebly riveted seams within the three-fifths length of the ship, and all of them were hydraulically riveted. (3) Wrought iron rivets were found, by contrast, in the outer fifths of the ship's shell, in doubly riveted seams, always riveted by hand. (4) Harland & Wolff probably riveted the ship this way due to time, strength, and financial considerations. These details become useful (and actually interesting) as the events begin to unfold on the night of her sinking.

PART II

THE FACTS

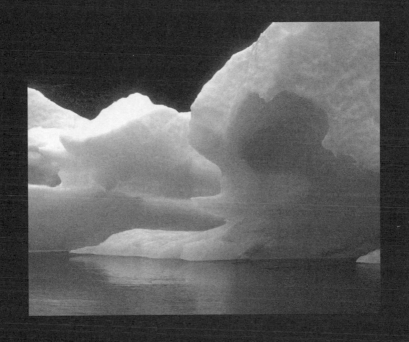

CHAPTER 6

APRIL 14, 1912— WHAT ARE THE FACTS?

SENATOR SMITH: *Was the vessel broken in two in any manner, or intact?*
MR. LIGHTOLLER: *Absolutely intact.*
SENATOR SMITH: *On the decks?*
MR. LIGHTOLLER: *Intact, sir.*

> —Second Officer Charles Lightoller on Day 1, American Inquiry

MR. CROWE: *She broke, and the after part floated back.*
SENATOR BOURNE: *And the bow part, two-thirds of the ship, sank?*
MR. CROWE: *Yes, sir.*

> —Steward George Crowe on Day 7, American Inquiry

Two versions, one fateful night. Only days after the most famous tragedy of the twentieth century, and opposing facts were already running rampant. Add ninety-plus years to the clock, throw in a flurry of sensationalistic media, and notice how the illusions have flourished to mind-boggling proportions.

Descriptions of the night of *Titanic's* sinking have been told a million times over by survivors, historians, marine explorers, naval architects, authors, cinematographers, and a variety of enthusiasts. Yet, despite the variations in their interpretations, these accounts all stem from the same sequence of events. What are they? This chapter offers a straightforward review of the sinking—the pertinent details of an age-old story are synthesized with the data from survivor testimony as well as recent forensic investigations.

What is simply conjecture, and what is hard fact? What type of collision was it, how severe was it, and how long did it last? Here is an examination of the theories and the data that attempt to explain her breakup, and the half-mile separation of her virtually intact bow section from the totally demolished stern on the ocean bottom. What role did the materials play in her sinking? The critical materials, design features, and manufacturing methods will be identified, and the crucial questions surrounding their integrity will finally be scientifically addressed.

A SEA OF SPECULATION: THE CURSE OF EYEWITNESS TESTIMONY

CARPATHIA LETS NO SECRETS OF THE TITANIC'S LOSS ESCAPE
BY WIRELESS
—Headline from the *World*, April 18, 1912

In reality, the accepted story of the most famous shipwreck in history was brewing on the shore only hours after the *Titanic* vanished below the water's surface. Forced to wait in agonizing ignorance, the press, the public, and even President Taft yearned for any news from the ship *Carpathia*, who had picked up the survivors. It would be three full days before they arrived in New York. In the meantime, *Titanic's* rescued wireless operator, Harold Bride, and his *Carpathia* counterpart, Harold Cottam, were only concerned with transmitting lists of the survivors and their personal messages to loved ones. Despite *Carpathia's* unconditional refusal to respond to inquiries or to substantiate claims, the media clamored for answers, cementing fictitious headlines, images, and anecdotes into the public's minds. By definition, nature (and the press) hates a vacuum, and it tends to be filled even if nothing is known. Sociologist Steven Biel described it as the creation of a myth, in which all men became self-sacrificing, courageous heroes, rising to an imminent call of death in order to send their women and children to safety. "By the time that the survivors reached shore, the myth was firmly in place and their testimony could only confirm what the press and the public already knew."

Unfortunately, headline stories that laid the basis of "what the press and public already knew" must have made it more difficult for examiners to extract unprejudiced testimony about the accident. Survivors, feeling shocked and continuously plagued by nightmarish memories, nursing frostbite, suffering from hypothermia, and dealing with an inconsolable sense of loss, were abruptly thrust into the public eye to retell every harrowing detail. While expedient questioning surely provided a more accurate picture of the real events, it could not correct for the pressures of Edwardian society. Certainly, the men wanted to live up to the glorified tales of courage and bravery, just as representatives of the White Star Line and Harland & Wolff wanted to retain the companies' respectable reputations. The officers, stewards, seamen, and directors who had devoted years of their service to the White Star Line and Harland & Wolff did their best to preserve the integrity of their employers, their jobs, and themselves. Of course, survivors' testimonies differed from one another, sometimes producing complete contradictions, as the witnesses struggled to rescue methodically the details already dwindling in their memories.

As a rule, evidence offered by survivors or witnesses must be interpreted very broadly. Today our judicial system strives to evaluate the problems associated with eyewitness accounts, but in the early twentieth century, eyewitnesses were prized for their direct, unfiltered evidence to an event, and personal preferences often guided the judicial decision. Commissions chose whichever version suited their own interests. In the case of *Titanic*'s sinking, most of our notions about the tragedy come from survivors' memories. What can be established from their memories, and what details are necessary to reconstruct the structural disaster?

By nature, survivor testimony of an accident is an extremely difficult thing for investigators to deal with, let alone a jury of normal citizens. Most people believe that eyewitnesses provide the most credible evidence in a court case, but witnesses can be very unreliable, particularly adults, as memories are often tainted by human emotion, concern for reputation, as well as a lack of clear judgment. In one study, nearly 75 percent of the wrongful convictions reviewed had resulted from evidence provided by witnesses. The 1991 book *Witness for the Defense: The Accused, the Eyewitness, and the Expert Who Puts Memory on Trial* describes a 1977 plane crash that was witnessed by sixty people. Two eyewitnesses who had actually seen the airplane just before the impact were called to testify at a hearing for the investigation. One of the eyewitnesses testified that the plane, "was heading right toward the ground—straight down." The witness felt confident enough to offer testimony, but was obviously unaware of a number of photographs that clearly showed the airplane hitting the ground flat and skidding for almost one thousand feet. The National Transportation and Safety Bureau (NTSB) has found that the most reliable witness testimony comes from 8- to 10-year-old children, who seem to function as tape recorders to an event, absorbing facts without significant interpretation. At eight years old, Eva Hart watched the *Titanic* as it sank, recalling that she saw the ship break in two. It was a memory burned into her brain, simply because she remembered hoping that the stern would float away so that her father would be saved.

Over ninety years of discoveries, studies, and analysis have aided in a reconstruction of what the world believes to be the actual sequence of events on April 14, 1912. This analysis attempts to filter out emotion from fact, interpretation from evidence, and inconsequential fluff from crucial clues, in order to provide the background information for the first complete scientific forensic analysis into the loss of the *Titanic*.

AN INTRODUCTION TO THE WITNESSES

Latitude 41° 46′ N, Longitude 50° 14′ W

At 883 feet in length with a gross weight of 46,329 tons, *Titanic* was a floating city in the North Atlantic. Her 3 engines, 29 boilers, and 159 furnaces required flawless synchronization to push her through the water.

As the sun dipped beneath the horizon, temperatures dropped as the ship's crew scurried from deck to deck, passing messages and taking orders so that the *Titanic* could forge her way into the night. Crewmen Frederick Scott and Thomas Ranger monitored the engines, and Fireman Barrett, stationed in Boiler Room No. 6, helped maintain a steady fuel of coal. The workers' jobs were never complete, since full power from the furnaces required shoveling 160 tons of coal every day in around the clock shifts.

By approximately 9:30 p.m., Captain Smith had retired to his cabin. This was his last big run on the Atlantic, having commanded seventeen White Star Liners over a period of twenty-five years and having been appointed commodore of the White Star Fleet. He had ushered *Titanic*'s identical sister, *Olympic*, into service, and despite a string of bad luck that began with the *Republic* in 1889, he was considered a highly skilled mariner. On the way to his cabin, he attended to the ship's business, stopping at the bridge at just about 9 p.m. in order to check on the ship's progress. There he exchanged some words with Second Officer Charles Lightoller, who was in the middle of his watch. As they gazed out over the bridge, Smith showed a concern for the combination of cold air and calm sea, making the telltale clue in spotting icebergs—waves slapping at an iceberg's base—impossible to rely on. Yet, Lightoller recalled that Smith felt the visibility was good enough to spot any impending danger, suggesting that even a blue iceberg (one that recently turned over) would be identified by its reflected white outline. Before he left, he instructed Lightoller to fetch

him if the situation became at all "doubtful," which Lightoller assumed to mean a deterioration in the visibility. Before arriving at his
cabin, Smith stopped briefly at the chart room to log the 19:30 position of the ship calculated by Officer Boxhall.

Meanwhile, according to the testimony, wireless operators Harold
Bride and John "Jack" Phillips (employees of Marconi's Wireless Telegraph Company Limited, not of the White Star Line) were furiously
tapping away in the Marconi room, plagued by a stack of personal
messages that still needed to be sent from the ship's passengers to their
friends and family on the shore. As the number of requests increased,
the operators struggled to keep up against the incoming navigational
messages that were interrupting their flow all day long. By 7:30 p.m.
they had already collected five ice warnings from ships within the area.
As night fell, Phillips continued sending passengers' messages to Cape
Race, Newfoundland, hoping to clear the backlog before he went off
shift. This may have been why he chose not to deliver the *Mesaba*'s
very detailed message to the bridge, instead continuing to relay outgoing messages:

> 9:40 p.m.: "In lat. 42°N to 41° 25′ N, long. 40°W to 50° 30′ W, saw
> much heavy pack ice and a great number of bergs, also field ice.
> Weather good clear."

While the message did contain some navigational notes, it did not
carry the all-important prefix MSG, Master's Service Gram, which required a personal receipt from the captain. Since not one surviving officer recalled seeing or hearing of the *Mesaba* message prior to the
collision, it is possible that Phillips, inundated with work to do, shoved
it out of the way and continued communicating with Cape Race.

At 10:55 p.m., Captain Stanley Lord of the *Californian* instructed
the radio operator Cyril Evans to send a report to the *Titanic*, signaling that they were stopped by very dense field ice. (In fact, Evans made
a similar, if not fatal, mistake to that which Phillips may have committed.) Instead of formally beginning his message with MSG, he simply
began sending with the informal prefix among operators, OM for "old
man." Interrupting Phillips' communication with Cape Race, Evans

nearly deafened him with the strength of the nearby ship's signal. "Shut up, shut up! I am busy! I am working Cape Race!" Phillips replied, understandably angered but completely unaware of the importance of the *Californian's* message. *Titanic* was only twenty-one miles away, but would never receive the *Californian's* warning:

10:55 p.m.: "Say, old man, we are stopped and surrounded by ice. Lat. 42° 00′ W Long. 50° 70′ N."

At 11:00 p.m. Lightoller had already been off his watch for one hour and was preparing for bed. The dropping temperatures had been a concern of his since the beginning of his watch. By 8:45 p.m., with the water temperature approaching 32°F, he had instructed Carpenter John Hutchinson to guard the ship's fresh water supply from freezing. Lightoller recalled a message the captain had shown him earlier in the day from the *Caronia* indicating the position of ice within the Southern track:

9:00 a.m.: "West-bound steamers report bergs, growlers, and field ice in 42° N from 49° to 51° W."

From this information, Lightoller testified that he felt comfortable that they would not approach the region until the end of his evening watch. According to his testimony, ice messages were a regular occurrence on the springtime transatlantic passenger route and did not necessarily result in alarm. It is no surprise then that with an afternoon's activities yet to complete, the Second Officer gave no further thought to the message.

At 6:00 p.m., Lightoller arrived on the bridge to begin his four-hour shift. At some point before dinnertime, Lightoller asked Sixth Officer Moody to calculate when the ship would approach the vicinity of the ice. Moody assuredly answered 11:00 p.m., having used the information on the notice board in the chart room. Slightly surprised, Lightoller recalculated the problem in his head using the *Caronia's* position, concluding that the answer was approximately 9:30 p.m. He decided that the only explanation for Moody's inaccuracy was the presence of some other message. Despite this conclusion, Lightoller never questioned Moody about it. Consequentially, the *Caronia*'s message was the first and only ice warning that Lightoller would ever see.

"If it becomes at all doubtful let me know at once," Lightoller recalled Smith instructing him as he bade the Captain a good night. As the clock ticked into the last half hour of his shift, Lightoller testified that, from the bridge, the surface of the water appeared to be as smooth as a sheet of glass. It was "absolutely flat," without the slightest swell. Despite how clear the sky was and what seemed to be excellent visibility, Lightoller's apprehensions were strong enough to instruct Sixth Officer Moody to warn the lookouts about the approaching ice field. Lookout George Symons remembered receiving a telephone call from the bridge at approximately 9:30 p.m., in which he and fellow lookout Alfred Jewell were instructed "to keep a sharp look out for ice, particularly small ice and growlers."

At 10:00 p.m., First Officer Murdoch relieved Lightoller of his duties, they discussed the weather and the captain's concerns, and Lightoller explained their proximity to the ice region. He then retired to his cabin, admitting that he was clearly aware they were heading straight into an area of icebergs, growlers, and field ice. Lookouts Frederick Fleet and Reginald Lee described taking their positions in the crow's nest, relieving Symons and Jewell, when they were told to watch for "small ice" as per Lightoller's instructions. Fleet and Lee bundled up, settled themselves into position, and concentrated on the view ahead.

Question: What was the ship's speed?

> *You have no right to go at that speed in an ice zone.*
> —Sir Ernest Shackleton, Antarctic Explorer

With or without a grasp of the underlying physics, everyone knows that a car traveling at 60 miles per hour will suffer more damage in a collision than one traveling at 30 miles per hour. To re-create the scene of an accident, investigators must determine the speed of a vehicle at the moment of the collision. The *Titanic* is no different. To assess the damage that occurred during the collision that night requires an accurate estimation of the speed of the ship. Because the logbook was never recovered from the wreck site, the only source of information on the ship's speed at 11:40 p.m. that evening comes from survivor testimony before the American and British Inquiries of 1912. The following analysis incorporates a variety of answers from crew members during both investigations in the hope that a reasonable estimate can be salvaged from their versions of the disaster.

According to Lightoller, *Titanic* was charging ahead at 21½ to 22 knots during his Sunday evening watch. Although he admitted not to knowing the exact speed, he was able to estimate it from the number of revolutions made by the reciprocating engines. He was aware that on Saturday (April 13) an order of 75 revolutions had been given to the engine room, and that is where it stayed, up until Sunday evening—the night of the accident. Third Officer Herbert Pitman corroborated this speed, but added that the ship required a speed of only 20¼ to 21 knots actually to arrive in New York on time—Wednesday, April 17. On top of this, he indicated that attempts at higher speeds were virtually impractical since the ship was low on coal. However, there was no denying that the *Titanic* had slowly picked up speed since Southampton, and although nowhere near her maximum of 24 knots, on Sunday her engines were cycling faster than at any other time on her voyage. Quartermaster Robert Hichens, whose job it was to log the speed, testified that at 10:00 p.m., the ship was moving at 22.5 knots, a notable increase over both of the officers' estimations. Leading Fireman Barrett recalled the lighting of additional boilers on Sunday morning, presumably to increase the ship's speed by Sunday night or early Monday morning. His testimony supports what some authors believe to be a deliberate attempt to race *Titanic* to a surprise finish.

The formal inquiries really helped to solidify the public opinion in 1912 that reckless speeding was one of the factors that contributed to the loss of so many lives. Yet, the U.S. Senate and the Board of Trade Commission never really had any hard evidence as to *why* the ship was not slowed down on the approach to the ice field. The witnesses did not attempt to offer any suggestions. According to the White Star Line's official published time schedule, *Titanic* was scheduled to make the transatlantic passage in six days, arriving in New York Harbor on Wednesday, April 17. While this was by no means a record speed attempt, it required a steady, swift clip.

As far as the officers on the ship were concerned, it seemed perfectly acceptable to continue at the moderate speed of 20¼ to 21 knots, completing the passage in six days. Not only were they lacking in fuel, but it was not even White Star policy to thrust a ship to her full speed during the first journey. There must have been other forces at play. The first clue comes from the testimony of Mr. J. Bruce Ismay, president of International Mercantile Marine Co. and managing director of the White Star Line. During the opening day of the U.S. Senate Inquiry Ismay revealed his own plan to test the new liner's fortitude:

> MR. ISMAY: The full speed of the ship is 78 revolutions. She works up to 80. So far as I am aware, she never exceeded 75 revolutions. . . . It was our intention, if we had fine weather on Monday afternoon or Tuesday, to drive the ship at full speed. That, owing to the unfortunate catastrophe, never eventuated.

As David G. Brown concluded in *The Last Log of the Titanic*, the fact that all the boilers were systematically being put online, combined with Ismay's eagerness to push for 24 knots, suggests that the White Star Line was poised to make a surprise entrance into New York Harbor ahead of schedule. In his final remarks, Senator Smith, commissioner of the American Inquiry, boldly pinpointed what he believed to be the catalyst to maintain high speeds:

I think the presence of Mr. Ismay and Mr. Andrews stimulated the ship to greater speed than it would have made under ordinary conditions, although I cannot fairly ascribe to either of them any instructions to this effect.

From the testimony, it appears that Captain Smith may have been under a great deal of pressure to maintain a high speed at sea, possibly high enough to gain Ismay his publicity, but surely as much as the weather would allow. From the testimony it is reasonable to conclude that the ship had reached a speed of 22 to 22½ knots, about 25 miles per hour, by 11:40 p.m. on the night in question.

Question: What was the size, shape, speed and location of the iceberg?

Consider the car collision analogy again. People understand that a head-on collision between a car and an 18-wheeler will cause more damage than the same collision between two cars. Tens of thousands of icebergs drift throughout the North Atlantic, with the bulkier ones posing a more significant threat than others do. Let's face it—the details of the iceberg make a difference. If the *Titanic* had collided with a 3-foot-high growler, it would not have sunk and this story would not have been written. What is the best way to represent the size and shape of the iceberg that collided with *Titanic?* Was the ice strong enough to puncture steel? Since there is no material evidence from the iceberg itself, only speculative memories and limited comparisons can assist investigators in obtaining clues about the mass of ice that sank the *Titanic*. Using what little that can be gleaned from the testimony, modern scientific research will supplement this information in order to establish a clear model of the massive iceberg.

In the crow's nest, Fleet described "looking all over," scanning the horizon. Lee recalled a "haze right ahead" of them. Within seconds, a "black mass" emerged from the darkness. At that distance, Fleet explained that it was as large as "two tables put together," but both lookouts realized that it was an iceberg. Fleet recalled that he yelled,

"There is ice ahead!" and immediately swung around to the bell, rang three times and telephoned the bridge, as Lee continued to follow the black mass growing larger by the second.

When an iceberg calves from a glacier, it settles about seven eighths of its volume into the water, leaving approximately one eighth out to jut above the water. As the iceberg melts and changes shape, it becomes unstable and will often turn over, exposing the underbelly to the air. When this occurs, the result is an iceberg that appears to be deep blue in color. In the unlucky occurrence of an iceberg overturning at night, the resulting mass may even appear black.

> SENATOR BURTON: *What was the shape at the top?*
> MR. OLLIVER: *The shape was pointed.*
>> —Quartermaster Alfred Olliver on Day 7,
>> American Inquiry

> *There was one of them, particularly, that I noticed, a very large one, which looked something like the Rock of Gibraltar; it was high at one point, and another point came up at the other end, about the same shape as the Rock of Gibraltar. . . . It was not quite as large as the* Titanic, *but it was an enormous, large iceberg.*
>> —Passenger C. E. Henry Stengel on Day 11,
>> American Inquiry

According to the International Ice Patrol's classification system, the iceberg that sank the *Titanic* was most definitely pinnacle shaped, containing "one or more spires." Assuming it was large, any specifics must always rely on survivor accounts that are, at best, questionable. Fleet and Lee testified that it was as high as the forecastle (55 feet), whereas Boxhall guessed that it rose to about the railing on C deck (about 30 feet). Seaman Frank Osman was convinced that he saw the actual iceberg as the sun rose the following morning, and supposed that it was "one hundred feet out of the water." Major Peuchen suggested that the huge icebergs he saw were 100 feet high and 300 to 400 feet long. Despite these discrepancies, what *was* blatantly obvious was that the ship had maneuvered smack-dab into the middle of an obstacle course of icebergs, growlers, and pack ice, just as the *Caronia* had warned.

The limited eyewitness accounts gave a range of heights, from approximately 30 to 55 feet (at the time of collision) to 100 feet (daylight accounts). Using the International Ice Patrol's classification system, the iceberg can be vaguely categorized as medium sized, that is, 51 to 100 feet in height and 201 to 400 feet in width, corresponding to a mass of approximately one hundred thousand tons. Still, this is nothing out of the ordinary for the North Atlantic Ocean.

Just like a collision between two moving vehicles, the speed of each should be considered independently. Icebergs are not stagnant floating bodies; they drift through the water, following currents, waves, and other weather patterns. Their speed is a small fraction of that of a passenger ship, approximately ⅓ mile per hour, but should be put into the equation anyway.

You're Alive Because Ice Is Weird

Water is one of a very few materials that decreases in density when it turns solid. Thus, ice floats. If water behaved like most every other material, the ice that formed on the surface of lakes or on the ocean would sink to the bottom and all of the Earth's water bodies would freeze from the bottom up. Over a short time, this accumulated ice would kill off life cycles and currents in the deep ocean, eventually making the Earth a lifeless ice ball. The fact that ice floats was tragic for the passengers on *Titanic*, but is actually very lucky for the rest of us.

Question: Where on the ship did the collision occur?

To establish details about the collision, the testimony surrounding the ship's maneuvers and the survivors' observations—their feelings and visual clues—of the incident needs to be reviewed and corroborated. Here is where things get dicey. To determine where the collision occurred and how strong the impact was, we must rely on survivor testimony. However, the physical location of each survivor relative to the impact location on the ship must also be considered, since a passenger's perception will be different in the crow's nest than if he or she is in the boiler room. Throughout the chapter, we will use figures to approximate each survivor's location on the ship at the moment of the collision.

The most widely held scenario of events that night represents about ninety years of interpretation of the survivor testimony, a.k.a. "standard scenario." In the standard scenario, it is generally believed that First Officer Murdoch, who was manning the bridge at the time of Fleet's iceberg warning, had decided to swing the bow to the left and then back to the right in the hope of going around the iceberg. He wanted to make a wide right turn around the iceberg. Unfortunately, the iceberg "was too close," and the starboard (right) side scraped against it before he had a chance to order "hard aport." Quartermaster Hichens, who physically carried out Murdoch's orders at the helm, recalled the crunching sound of ice meeting steel, "the grinding noise along the ship's bottom" while the helm was hard astarboard.

In the standard scenario, a left-turning ship (Murdoch's "hard astarboard" order) sustains damage to its starboard (right) side. Based on witness testimony, investigators narrowed down the source of the damage to the front portion of the starboard side. Both Fleet and Lee, who were still stationed in the crow's nest and had a clear view of the iceberg, testified separately that they thought it collided "just before the foremast" on the starboard side. Passenger Major Arthur Peuchen testified that the ship was struck about 40 feet from the front of the bow on the starboard side, based on his perception of the impact from his quarters on C deck. Soon afterward he observed chunks of ice on

A deck that had broken off the iceberg. As did many passengers, he immediately noticed a list to starboard. In fact, many survivors described seeing chunks of ice scattered on the starboard side, forward deck.

Third Officer Herbert Pitman remembered seeing water flowing into the No. 1 hatch (positioned in the forward bow of the ship), "running mostly from the starboard side," corroborating Lee's observation several minutes after the collision. Ismay believed that "the bilge of the ship was ripped out . . . right along the side."

Some researchers have a problem with this theory because it implies that the left-turning ship would have sustained damage to the *front* portion of its starboard (right) side—a scenario that seems to be physically impossible. Think about it. If, in fact, the bow of the ship were turning left, out of harm's way, then the stern would swing to the right, toward the iceberg, suggesting damage toward the *back* end of the ship. This would indicate an apparent gap in our understanding of the ship's maneuvers at that moment.

Recent investigations of the 1912 inquiries have shed new light on Murdoch's instructions that night, relying on the evidence presented by Quartermaster Alfred Olliver, who was delivering messages and had just entered the bridge at the time of the collision, a.k.a. the "Olliver scenario." Olliver insisted that he heard the order "hard aport" given to Hichens, and that it was observed by Sixth Officer Moody. David G. Brown has interpreted this as a right turn just *before* the collision, which sent the starboard bow toward the iceberg, thus bringing the front portion of the ship closer into contact with the iceberg. The only problem is that, according to Olliver, the timing of Murdoch's order to hard aport (right turn) was *after* the collision, evidence which is still in line with Officer Boxhall's testimony.

Here is a situation where all three witnesses, Hichens, Boxhall, and Olliver, are telling portions of the story as they remember them. In the space of several seconds, the crewmen faced a harrowing emergency, steering orders, traumatic messages, ringing bells, and a devastating collision with an iceberg. Difficulty in remembering the order of events, no matter how adept they were, is normal. Although eyewitnesses more consistently verify the hard astarboard version, it does not physically explain the perceived location of the damage.

Accurate knowledge of the ship's maneuvers, combined with details of the ship's geometry, would provide a better picture of what part of the ship was facing in which direction. Even if we regard the Olliver scenario as correct—that Murdoch did order a right turn—and we are therefore able to justify the survivors' observations of the forward starboard collision, there is still next to *nothing* known about the iceberg that would help to pinpoint the specifics of the damage. There is no knowledge of the size beyond a rough estimate, so any calculations about how much energy went into the collision would be based on too many broad assumptions. There is no knowledge of the shape of the part of the iceberg that hit the ship, making detailed calculations about the nature of the localized collision no more than unsubstantiated, hand-waving arguments. Any determinations about these aspects of the disaster need to be inferred indirectly from other observations, such as the passengers' perception of the collision's severity and its location. Because of the inconsistencies within the survivors' stories, there are very few reliable conclusions that can be drawn, and as a result, other investigators of the sinking have proposed various collision scenarios using liberal interpretations. As forensic scientists, we are concerned less with interpretation and more with the most likely conclusion that fits all the data available. What we can learn from the facts will help us to construct a range of possibilities, and, ultimately, the most likely collision scenario.

Question: How severe was the collision?

The survivors gave descriptions of the severity of the impact with the iceberg during testimony before the two inquiries as well as other times after the disaster. When reviewing their comments, it is important to keep in mind that the severity that they felt is going to be affected by their location relative to the impact, so a diagram has been produced that locates each witness's location on the ship (figs. 8a–8k).

At the same time as Murdoch called out his order, he raced to the telegraph on the bridge to alert the engine room. Barrett remembered standing in the depths of Stokehold No. 10, Boiler Room No. 6, conferring with Engineer Hcsketh near the starboard aft corner at the time that their conversation was interrupted by the call for the engines to stop. As the leading fireman, he shouted, "Shut all dampers!" The stokers rushed to close off the draughts to all the fires, forcing the pulleys and slamming the doors shut in a matter of seconds.

Trimmer Thomas Dillon heard the telegraph ring in the Reciprocating Engine Room, where he had been sent to clean up the gear. Two seconds later, he recalled feeling a "slight shock."

Seaman Edward Buley was sitting in the mess room, waiting to relieve the watch on duty, when the slight jar stirred him from his reading. "It seemed as though something was rubbing alongside of her, at the time."

Greaser Thomas Ranger, who was working on the E deck electric store, described the impact as if it threw him from his balance. "There was just a slight jar—just lifted us off our feet."

Seaman Williams Lucas was standing just outside the mess room flailing around in a similarly wobbly scenario, as he nearly lost his footing.

The crunch of the ice against the shell plating sent vibrations through the ship, and in some cases, there was the horrific sound of squealing steel plates and strained joints struggling to resist. "There was a sound that I thought seemed like the ship coming to an anchor—the chain running out over the windlass," insisted Officer Pitman. As the gigantic ship slowly hinged over to starboard, Fleet and Lee guessed that she had squeezed by with just a "narrow shave."

The collision progressed, but based on eyewitness accounts, it

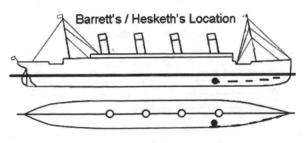

Figure 8a.

lasted for no more than a few seconds. Many described what seemed to be an erratic, eerie rumbling that passed throughout the ship. Quartermaster Olliver remembered it "like she touched something; a long grinding sound" that "did not last many seconds." Passenger Peuchen sensed that the ship was thrown back from the encounter, "I felt as though a heavy wave had struck our ship. She quivered under it somewhat." Able Seaman Ernest Archer didn't feel a shock but described more of a noise, "just a grating sensation." Accounts depended on where the survivors were located, but most were consistent with a shudder beginning in the forward compartments of the starboard side and emanating from there to a weak vibration throughout the ship.

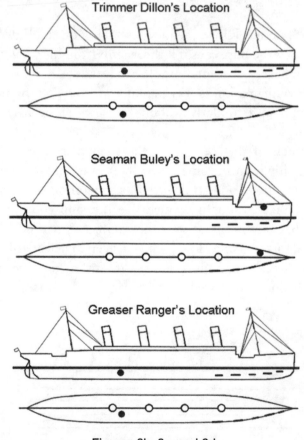

Figures 8b, 8c, and 8d.

The men in the boiler room bore the brunt of the collision's severity. The stokers under Barrett's control were racing to cover the ash
doors over all the furnaces as the ship struck and the starboard side let
loose. The crew manning the boilers didn't hear the crash; they saw it.
A wave of water rushed through the starboard side. "Water came
pouring in two feet above the stokehold plate; the ship's side was torn
from the third stokehold to the forward end," Barrett exclaimed during the Inquiry investigation in London. Trimmer George Cavell was
shoveling coal in the forward starboard bunker of Boiler Room No. 4.
Suddenly he felt a shock and heard the screech of rending metal as the
mountain of coal around him plummeted to the floor, drowning him
in complete blackness.

The shudder that resulted from the collision disguised to many
passengers the destruction that had taken place under the water.
While it was strong enough to awaken some passengers from their
sleep and to jostle others off their feet, most had no idea that an incident of such gravity had occurred. Considering the evidence, it is unlikely that most passengers felt the kind of jolt typical of a head-on

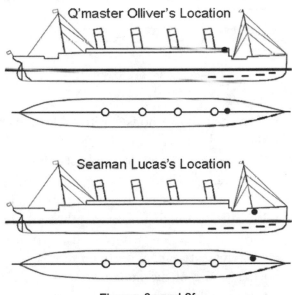

Figures 8e and 8f.

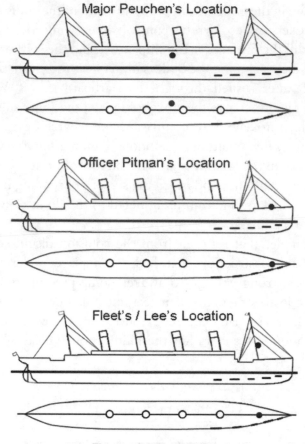

Figures 8g, 8h, and 8i.

collision, but rather, their descriptions confirm a less severe, glancing blow along the starboard side.

Until the 1996 expedition, the world's understanding of *Titanic*'s collision with the iceberg came solely from the survivors' descriptions of the impact—how it felt, what it sounded like, where it came from. During the British Inquiry, Edward Wilding, a naval architect from Harland & Wolff and design partner of Thomas Andrews, listened very carefully to the details in the survivors' testimonies, trying to imagine the views of the damage and the nature of the flooding. At the end of the three months of questioning, Wilding emerged on the stand with a mathematical picture of what he believed the damage looked like. "I cannot believe that the wound was absolutely continuous the whole way. I believe that it was in a series of steps . . ." he began, presenting the commission with the unbelievable conclusion that the *Titanic* had sunk due to several tears amounting to only 12 square feet of damage. "It can only have been a comparatively short length, and the aggregate of the holes must have been somewhere about 12 square feet."

The media quickly latched on to this theory, propagating decades of pictures, stories, and illustrated books showing the doomed liner plagued by a thin scrape extending from the starboard bow. The portrayal stuck as there was no reason to doubt something based on eyewitness accounts. Conventional wisdom is like concrete—it hardens, and there is little you can do about it.

In 1995, a team of naval architects attempted to reevaluate the damage using Wilding's computations and sketches from 1912. Bedford and Hackett applied modern computer modeling tools to seventy-five-year-old evidence and found that Wilding's results were bang on. They concluded the flooding damage to be no more than 12.6 square feet. While this confirmed Wilding's suspicions, it was still relying on eyewitness accounts.

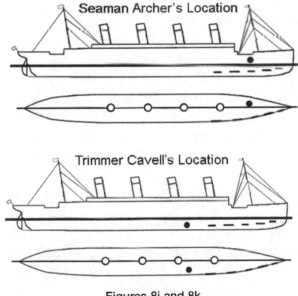

Figures 8j and 8k.

Question: How, when, and at what speed did the ship flood?

> *[I] saw the water rushing in from the starboard side at the
> bottom.*
> —Fireman Charles Hendrickson on Day 5, British Inquiry

Immediately, the electromagnetic relay controlling the watertight
doors in Boiler Room No. 6 kicked in and Murdoch's flick of the switch
took hold. As water spewed into the ship, Barrett and Hesketh dove
under the watertight door as it closed between Boiler Rooms No. 6 and
No. 5. Once in No. 5 Barrett was able to see the remainder of the tear
in the hull's side, the source of water gushing straight into the coal
bunker. While Barrett and Hesketh were making their escape into
No. 5, Fireman Hendrickson recalled that from the deck, glancing
back over the starboard side, he saw an iceberg "just abaft of the engine
room." Minutes later, at the spiral staircase, he testified to seeing water
rushing in from the starboard side into the pipe tunnel, which was located within the lowest part of the ship, connecting the No. 3 compartment to the No. 6 Stokehold. By the time Hendrickson arrived in
Boiler Room No. 6, it was too full of water to enter. Barrett was caught
in the same predicament, ordered to return to a station that was now
eight feet under water. Barrett's testimony pinpoints the location of
damage to the starboard side as far back as Boiler Room No. 5, with
flooding that began instantaneously in Boiler Room No. 6. This is corroborated by Hendrickson's testimony, which reiterates the fast flooding rate between No. 3 compartment and Boiler Room No. 6.

Lightoller testified that based on limited proof he believed that the
forepeak tank (the foremost section of the ship's bow) and compartments No. 1, No. 2, and No. 3 were "pierced." This corresponds to
Boxhall's statement regarding the flooding mailroom, which was located on the starboard side of No. 3. During inspection of the forward
section of the ship soon after the collision, a very brief encounter with
a mail clerk verified his worst nightmare. Boxhall testified that the
clerk told him "the mailroom was filling."

At 12 a.m., Fleet and Lee were relieved of their watch. On climbing their way down from the crow's nest, Lee recalled seeing water coming into the No. 1 (or No. 2) hold. Lee's testimony again confirms damage to the most forward sections of the starboard side.

At approximately midnight, Third Officer Pitman was making his way around the forecastle just before beginning his watch. He recalled hearing that they struck an iceberg and Boxhall's news that "the mailroom was afloat." At the same time, he ran into a gang of stokers telling him that water was coming into their quarters. From these examples, as well as additional survivor testimony, it can be estimated that after approximately twenty to thirty minutes, the first three compartments had filled up to F deck.

Fifteen minutes after the accident, Barrett and Hendrickson testified that Boiler Room No. 6 was under water. In fact, the testimony indicates that the first five compartments had been flooding steadily since the collision. At just about midnight, the *Carpathia's* Marconi operator Harold Cottam received a message from the *Titanic*, requesting assistance:

12:00 a.m.: "Come at once; we have struck a berg. Latitude 41° 46′N, Longitude 50°14′W."

Trimmer Dillon had been ordered to assist in opening the watertight doors manually so that the engineers could get back and forth between the compartments to access valves and pumps. He headed from the stern of the ship to the bow and made it as far forward as Boiler Room No. 4, two compartments back from No. 6. By the time he reached it, although still dry, there was a slow trickle of water leaking in along the floor, inching its way from fore to aft. Dillon's testimony verifies that of Barrett's, who describes seeing the flooding across Boiler Rooms No. 6 and No. 5. The bulkhead aft of No. 6 would not be able to contain the pressure for much longer.

12:15 a.m.: "Come as quickly as possible, old man, the engine room is filling up to the boilers."

Barrett had remained below to assist the engineers in putting out the fires in Boiler Room No. 5 until suddenly a great wall of water rushed through the passageway between boilers. It appears that the bulkhead between Boiler Rooms No. 6 and No. 5 had finally given way. In his testimony, Barrett was asked to describe a fire in the forward coal bunker, starboard side, of Boiler Room No. 5, and what effect this may have had on weakening the bulkhead in question.

Trimmer George Cavell testified to returning to Boiler Room No. 4 to help draw the fires and explained that over the next half hour the water rose in No. 4, gradually reaching knee height. By approximately 1:15 a.m., Boiler Room No. 4, the sixth compartment from the bow, was awash with seawater and no one remained.

From a review of basic facts combined with crew testimony, there is evidence to suggest that the ship hit an iceberg moving at approximately 22½ knots, although very little is known about the iceberg itself. The preponderance of testimony suggests that despite this considerable speed, the collision was barely detectable and hardly catastrophic. In fact, most people never felt it. Workers in the lower decks described water coming from the starboard side of the ship or up through the plates, with Barrett experiencing the most direct observation of water entering through a tear in the starboard side. As will be discussed, modern forensic investigations seem to support his claim. The timeline of the flooding can be constructed based on eyewitness accounts, which clearly showed that water was quickly engulfing the first five compartments. Barrett's testimony of water rushing into Boiler Room No. 5 from the front of the ship suggests the failure of the bulkhead separating Boiler Room No. 6 from No. 5 and implicates the coal fire as having a potential weakening effect.

With knowledge of the facts of this disaster, reinterpretation can begin on the forensic clues that link them together. How was the ship damaged, and how can we pinpoint why it failed?

CHAPTER 7

MATERIALS
INVESTIGATION

The Goal of the Recent Expeditions

The search for forensic evidence to understand the ship's demise began nearly twenty years ago. Just after 1:00 a.m. on September 1, 1985, Dr. Robert Ballard of the Woods Hole Oceanographic Institute was beckoned from his sleep to the control room on the U.S. Naval research vessel *Knorr*. His partner, Jean-Louis Michel and his team from Institut Français de Recherches pour l'Exploitation des Mers (IFREMER) had been painstakingly following the real-time video transmissions of the unmanned submersible *Argo*, now in its eighth day of zigzagging back and forth along the seafloor. At such a late stage in the trip, after countless hours spent scouring the dark sediment, monitoring of the passing images had plunged the crew into a serious case of the doldrums. Suddenly, *Argo* focused onto a large round structure, bulleted with a series of riveted seams. Ballard arrived and hurried to the monitor, instantly sure that it was the characteristic trio arrangement of furnace doors on one of *Titanic*'s boilers. At the end of what appeared to be a fruitless season, with the aid of deep-sea acoustic sonar and video imaging, they had finally found the *Titanic*.

Over four days' time, undersea cameras shot approximately twenty thousand frames of film of the bow section and the debris field, but they were unable to find the stern. As *Argo* grazed along the surface of the wreck, they soon realized that the stern section was missing, apparently torn off because of the massive stresses inflicted during flooding. While they weren't able to determine the position of the missing stern that year, Ballard led another expedition in 1986 and was successful in finding it. With the support of the U.S. Navy, Ballard tested the latest technology in underwater exploration, directing the new manned submersible *Alvin* and a remote-controlled camera known as Jason, Jr., which together produced breathtaking images.

The discovery of the ship in two pieces finally vindicated those passengers who testified that the ship had seemed to split into two at the surface. By all measurements these two expeditions were a triumph. The nation stared in awe as the underwater camera exposed a delicate ceramic doll's head, a forever unopened bottle of champagne, stacks of dishes still intact, and the remnants of a deck bench, now reduced to fragile fragments of metalwork. The site of the most famous shipwreck in history had finally been discovered, but the reasons for her sinking were still as nebulous as ever. The expedition did not succeed in finding the starboard side damage that many had speculated to have taken down the ship, but the wealth of knowledge that the team did uncover provided plenty for researchers to chew on.

With just a small glimpse into the window of an archaeological site over half a mile in length, the world gasped with a mixture of horror and delight, while historians, scientists, and marine specialists pleaded for more information. What did the wreck site look like? What role did design and engineering play in the sinking? Where was the iceberg damage? In what condition was the wreck site? Since 1986, an untold number of expeditions have visited the site (including Ballard himself), many with the express purpose of salvaging artifacts. Thousands of objects have been retrieved from the site, conserved and displayed for inquisitive eyes, and probably an equal number have been pillaged for profit. While legitimate recoveries have formed the basis of some of the most successful traveling exhibits in history, they did little to further our understanding of the accident that night. Of the many visitors to the wreck, far fewer scientific expeditions have been launched with the goal to research those unanswered questions.

After a brief summary of the early studies of the wreck, this chapter concentrates on the 1996, 1998, and 2004 expeditions (three in which the authors have actively taken part) and will describe the twists and turns that have accompanied accumulation of forensic evidence from the wreck site.

1991

Some of the most spectacular images of the wreck site were taken during the production of the IMAX film *Titanica*. Financed in part by CBS Television, National Geographic, and several Canadian firms, the multinational team produced some of the first sharp, brightly lit images of the ship. Using eight 1,200-watt lights specially designed for underwater photography, the two Russian *MIR* submersibles, and the Russian support vessel *Keldysh*, the crew's wide-angle IMAX cameras glided through the eerily peaceful site and provided footage that revealed details and intricacies never before seen within the living, breathing, underwater microcosm that has fossilized the great liner.

With the original discoveries of the 1985 and 1986 expeditions and the renewed interest during filming, theories abounded as to exactly how the failure of the ship occurred. As a first step to understanding the sinking, researchers looked to the hull steel for information. Miraculously, despite expedition rules instructing the team to disturb nothing, a sample of the hull material appeared on land shortly after the IMAX expedition. (During one scene in the movie, the crew members actually argue over whether they should retrieve a suitcase from the seafloor.) The Maritime Museum of the Atlantic, which obtained this sample for its collection, was the first organization to seek further information from *Titanic*'s metallurgy. In 1991, they requested scientists Ken KarisAllen at the Defence Research Establishment Atlantic (DREA) in Halifax, Nova Scotia, and Bob Brigham and Yves LaFrenière at Canada Centre for Mineral and Energy Technology (CANMET) in Ottawa, Canada, to analyze the

Missing Artifacts

As seems to so often be the case with the expeditions to the *Titanic*, this story has an interesting epilogue. A few years ago, Tim Foecke contacted the investigators in Canada to see if he could obtain some of their steel or wrought iron rivet material, or at least some better photographs of the microstructures to do some comparisons with the samples on hand. It appeared that shortly after the publication of the DREA/CANMET findings and an article in *Popular Mechanics*, Ken KarisAllen left DREA for the private sector. James Matthews, another DREA researcher using the study results to promote his work on fractures in bulk freight vessels, insisted that DREA had no *Titanic* materials, implying in an e-mail instead that Ken might have taken them with him. Bob Brigham at CANMET, a scientist loathe to discuss his *Titanic* work after what he felt was a total misinterpretation of the results by the media, confirmed that he had sent all his samples back to DREA. The Maritime Museum of the Atlantic, that had original possession of the artifacts, states quite emphatically in the museum's recently updated website that it had no artifacts recovered from the wreck site, only those found floating in the sea and/or donated or loaned to the museum by collectors. All of this begs the question: What exactly happened to the steel samples recovered during the IMAX expedition? A possible lead was revealed by CNN in March 2007 in a story about Geneva watchmaker Romain Jerome SA, who announced the availability of watches made from *Titanic* steel, which it billed as its "Titanic-DNA" collection. According to the report, the steel came from a piece that was recovered in 1991, that its pedigree was verified (somehow) by Harland & Wolff, and that the seller would remain anonymous. Given all the pirate expeditions to the wreck over the years, there is no certainty this is the same piece of steel, but the IMAX steel is still missing.

steel's mechanical properties. The purpose? To determine the strength of the hull steel and deduce how it may have reacted in the ice-cold water that night.

1996

It took five years to get the data, but interest never died. In 1996, RMS *Titanic*, Inc. (RMSTI), in cooperation with Discovery Channel, invited a panel of specialists to participate in a scientific investigation of the wreck site. The Marine Forensics Panel of the Society of Naval Architects and Marine Engineers (SNAME) is a group of naval architects and marine engineers, materials scientists, marine biologists, underwater technicians, ship historians, and pretty much anybody with interest and experience in marine salvage and investigation. The group had outlined their biggest concerns about the wreck, and in August they set out on the eighth expedition to the *Titanic* to answer as many questions as they could. The result was the first attempt at a marine forensics approach to the study of the *Titanic*'s sinking.

The specialists arrived at sea with a surplus of unexplained mysteries to ponder and, as always, individual research goals to fulfill. The schedule was tight, but it was clear that there were still some very basic problems that needed tackling, namely, the existence of a missing third piece of the hull, the extent of iceberg damage, and the role of the steel's metallurgy, in order to check out the Canadian findings of 1991. While considerable effort was made to solve each of these questions, success was questionable. It is important to state clearly that the 1996 expedition was the only expedition to the *Titanic* conducted by RMSTI that truly gave scientists the access to submersibles and the wreck that was needed to perform legitimate field work, all due largely to the efforts and good will of the late George Tulloch, former president of RMSTI.

Piecing Together the Puzzle

Data from sonar imaging, as well as underwater dives in the submersible *Nautile*, was crucial to mapping a more precise site plan of the wreck and corresponding debris field. A side-scan sonar imaging system was used to determine the size and location of several hundred artifacts and ship debris surrounding the stern section. In addition, sonar imaging located the missing 57-foot middle section of the ship, one third of a mile from the end of the stern section.

Assessing the Damage

With the help of modern technology, sonar imaging was used to scan the hull of the bow section, now buried under nearly 55 feet of sediment on the seafloor, in the hope of finding any evidence of the iceberg damage. Past expeditions were unable to locate any signs of collision damage, since the bow's 35-mile per hour nosedive had embedded it in the muddy seafloor. The new technique, known as sub-bottom profiling, revealed what appeared to be six openings along the starboard bow section of *Titanic*'s hull. Was this the elusive iceberg damage that was hidden from previous expeditions? The location of the openings was consistent with damage described in eyewitness testimony during the Mersey Inquiry in 1912. Of the six openings detected, the most serious of the blows—a 32-foot opening twenty feet below the waterline—ran between Cargo Holds No. 2 and No. 3. The team estimated that the total damage was approximately 11.4 square feet.

Introducing the Big Piece

The 1996 expedition, publicized by RMSTI, was an opportunity to preserve a sizable portion of *Titanic*'s hull, purportedly as a way to keep her memory alive. More importantly, a revitalized chunk of the ship's outer plating offered the perfect addition to its already large collection of precious artifacts, as well as a catalyst to mass media consumption. Enter the Big Piece, a 20-ton section of shell plating that spanned the starboard side across cabins C79 and C81. With the aid of diesel-filled lift bags and search lighting, the crew planned to raise the piece from the seafloor using a series of towlines. The effort was going well until one lift bag disappeared. Then the search lighting from the deck of the *Ocean Voyager* collapsed. Unhindered by the setbacks, the mission continued. With the Big Piece dangling just two hundred feet below the water's surface, Hurricane Edward rolled into the North Atlantic, buffeting strong waves against the towlines, which were of questionable strength anyway, having been bought at the last minute on the dock in Halifax. The swirling currents twisted and pulled them until they began to snap like rubber bands. One by one they gave way, sending the Big Piece back to the seafloor, nearly ten miles from where it was found, and returning RMSTI home emptyhanded on that score.

1998

In August 1998, Discovery Channel organized an expedition to retrieve another section of the ship's hull plating to compare the type of steel used in different plates on the ship. In addition, the expedition completed a successful raising of the by-then famous 20-ton mammoth Big Piece (see plate 11, top). The 1998 season also provided the perfect opportunity to revisit the region around *Titanic*'s starboard damage. After a review of the Harland & Wolff shell plating diagram and a better understanding of the sediment profiles around the bow section, researchers actually hoped this time to visualize with the naked eye the largest opening on the starboard side—the parted seam across Boiler Room No. 6.

During the British Inquiry of 1912, Fireman Barrett testified that water came rushing in through a torn seam extending from Boiler Room No. 6 to No. 5. (British Inquiry, 1868–1893). Using the remotely operated vehicle (ROV) *Magellan 725* and counting plates down the side of the ship, the group was able to zero in on a clear view of the actual parted seam and identify what looked like several empty rivet holes—exactly where Barrett said it was. This is the best evidence thus far that indicates the iceberg damage along the starboard side.

Getting Samples to Study Can Be Hard

As the largest artifact recovered thus far from the debris field, the Big Piece was promptly put on display after the return of the 1998 expedition. Many pledges of samples from the Big Piece were made to scientists involved, as well as to the Discovery Channel, before the 1998 expedition began, all the way up until the piece was set up in the conservation tent. As metallurgists, the authors obviously wanted samples for testing, and the Discovery Channel wanted to film samples being extracted and examined in order to flesh out the story in its show *Titanic: Answers from the Abyss*.

Once the Big Piece had reached Boston, however, all previous pledges were retracted—all bets were off. It was left to Stephane Pennec of LP3 Conservation in France to decide, on site, from where any samples should be removed. Thinking first as a conservator, Pennec pointed to several places where samples could be "shaved off" here and there in the least damaging way possible. Unfortunately, since full-scale mechanical tests were required on the steel and rivets, shavings were not going to cut it. Pennec and Foecke, poised in front of the piece, debated and argued for close to two hours, all the while being "assisted" by the union head of the team sent to do the actual cutting. With the Discovery Channel producer getting more and more anxious over lost shooting time and his thumb poised over the Send button of his cell phone to initiate an irate call to George Tulloch, it was decided to cut off a piece of steel from the extreme corner of the Big Piece, which contained an intact hull rivet. This scene made it into *Answers from the Abyss*, showing a guy on top of a ladder cutting steel with a gas-powered K-12 fireman's saw, sparks showering over everyone, as Pennec cringed in the background (see plate 11, bottom).

Under orders to retrieve all broken rivets (four different types and sizes of rivets can be seen in plate 13, top), they came across several that were brought to the surface for further testing. An additional thirty rivets were obtained for more extensive analysis, resulting in a total of forty-eight rivets recovered from the wreck. Five of those came from the Big Piece.

Additional observation of the middle section's hull plates on the seafloor revealed twisted, mangled chunks of 1½-inch-thick steel, some contorted as much as 180 degrees.

2000

An ill-fated journey to the wreck took place in 2000, with many plans primarily to recover artifacts but also to check up on the corrosion test beds placed in 1998. Unfortunately, technical and financial issues forced RMSTI to give up early and head home without any significant scientific work having been completed. In fact, the management of RMSTI was so infuriated with how the expedition had gone that they fired one of the expedition leaders while still on board the ship.

2001

Following the successful work in his 1997 movie, James Cameron and his team from Earthship Productions spent seven weeks in the late summer of 2001, utilizing the Russian research vessel *Akademik Mstislav Keldysh* and its two deep submersibles, *Mir 1* and *Mir 2*. Their goal was to capture high-definition video of the wreck site and debris field, as well as to test out two mini ROVs, Jake and Elwood, for exploration on the various deck structures. Twenty-four dives were carried out, and many used the ROVs successfully, producing detailed footage of regions within the interior decks that had never been seen before. The resulting nine hundred hours of video were condensed into the forty-five-minute large-format documentary, *Ghosts of the Abyss*, released in 2002. Expedition photos revealed that the decks and their interiors have been steadily collapsing on themselves since Ballard's discovery in 1985.

Keeping Track of Artifacts

During the course of the investigation, we received artifacts for study that were recovered from the wreck site. A few years ago, RMSTI, the salvor-in-possession of the wreck, asked for the artifacts to be returned. This was fine with us, but RMSTI needed to pay for secure shipping. RMSTI's representative asked us to just "mail them in a shoebox to Atlanta." Foecke pointed out the difficulty of this approach, since there was something in excess of 400 pounds of hull, bulkhead, beams, angle iron, rivets, and rusticles in the lab. The representative was flabbergasted and asked where it all came from. The reply was, well, basically, "from all over." Starting with the 1996 expedition, the recovered steel was scattered to the winds among researchers and preservationists, with very little bookkeeping effort to keep track of it. Foecke received pieces from LP3 in France, from Phil Leighly at the University of Missouri–Rolla, from Bethlehem Steel, and from a few other places. When he saw a news article or research paper that mentioned *Titanic* metal, he worked to recover it and store it in the lab. In the end, he had to have made an accession of hundreds of pieces. The accession consisted of photography, labeling, and a best guess of where each piece came from and what had been done to it.

After RMSTI received the bonded and sealed crate, their latest conservator e-mailed to compliment Foecke on the accession, noting that it now formed the *core* of their records on the steel. Foecke decided not to mention the one member of the Marine Forensics Panel of SNAME who claimed that he had a rivet memento on the shelf in his house, since Foecke never actually saw it in person. Very recently, however, it was confirmed that RMSTI retrieved this piece as well.

2004

Since the passage of the late 1990s "*Titanic* Mania," recent work has seen the emphasis shift from salvage to surveillance. In June 2004, in an effort to conserve what little human element actually remained at the site, the U.S. National Oceanic and Atmospheric Administration (NOAA) and National Geographic co-sponsored a scientific expedition, "Return to *Titanic*," with the explicit goal of assessing the condition of the wreck and of determining what, if any, controllable factors are contributing to the ship's rapid deterioration. The overarching motto of this expedition was "look, don't touch."

As part of this two-week trip, Ballard returned to assist in the studies and enlisted the help of technicians from his Institute of Exploration. Using a team of ROVs, scientists were able to capture hundreds of hours of high-definition still and video footage. The results provided an incredibly detailed, up-to-date map of the bow and stern and will serve to build a photo mosaic of the site for comparison with Ballard's images from 1985 and 1986.

During the hours of observation, scientists became acutely aware of the higher levels of deterioration on the decks, where submersibles from previous expeditions had landed. Broken masts, dilapidated decks, and

---

Disrespect and Stupidity

It was reported off the record by one of the scientists on RMSTI's ill-fated 2000 expedition that the debris field of *Titanic* is growing. In that year, one of the officers of RMSTI decided to bring along his son and his son's band to serve as deck hands and gofers. Apparently they thought it would be fun to play "bomb the wreck" with empty beer bottles. The presence of modern bottles on the wreck site was reported in a *New York Times* article by Bill Broad in 2003 and the presence of empty bottles from this particular brand of beer was unofficially confirmed during the NOAA/National Geographic expedition in 2004.

crumbled railings all tell the basic story of corrosion, but at the price of human interference. Lt. j.g. Jeremy Weirich, who was NOAA's chief archaeologist on the mission, revealed that the debris field spanning the area between the bow and stern had changed drastically because visitors to the site pillaged the most heartfelt remains.

Apart from the imaging of the wreck, metal test strips, placed there in 1998 as a means to study corrosive activity, were retrieved and replaced. In addition, further research was carried out to study the effects of rusticle behavior on the overall deterioration of the ship.

While an official report on the scientific findings has yet to be released, NOAA continues to play a key role in the establishment of an international agreement that will provide enforcement authority over the site. Just days after the expedition concluded, the U.S. ambassador to London signed a new agreement that will designate the *Titanic* as an international maritime memorial, legally maintained and protected by the United States, Canada, France, and the United Kingdom.

Stewardship

With RMSTI wrapped up in a protracted legal battle in the Admiralty Court in Norfolk, VA, to both try to gain title to the artifacts while giving up salvage duties on the wreck, NOAA has become the environmental steward of the wreck site. NOAA has had a prominent role in the protection of the *Titanic* wreck site, beginning in 1985 after her discovery. More recently, in accordance with the *Titanic Maritime Memorial Act*, NOAA published *Guidelines for Research, Exploration and Salvage of RMS Titanic*, hoping that through an understanding of international standards, they could promote a list of guidelines that would preserve the integrity of the wreck. Since her discovery over 6,000 of *Titanic*'s artifacts have been salvaged, both legally and illegally. We are active collaborators with NOAA in its conservation and modeling efforts.

CHAPTER 8

DISTILLING THE FACTS
What Are the Possible Scenarios?

After a review of the facts on the night in question, gleaned from survivor testimony, and a summary of the salient facts that resulted from twenty years of expedition research, the next step is to distill the information collected thus far and begin to analyze all possible scenarios to explain how the iceberg damaged the hull.

Fact #1: The iceberg passed along the starboard side and impacted the ship.

Evidence: There are numerous accounts that describe the location of the iceberg with respect to the ship, as well as the feeling of the collision that it was likely along the starboard side. From the evidence that is available, this is the easiest fact to support.

Lookouts Fleet and Lee saw the iceberg emerge from the darkness directly in front of them, and we can assume that apart from Fleet's momentary pause to contact the bridge, the two of them continued to watch it until it physically passed from their sight. This was their job. Whether the ship began to turn to port before or after they identified it, they testified to seeing the iceberg pass to the starboard side and make contact with the ship at approximately "just before the foremast."

99

This was corroborated by the observations of both Third Officer Herbert Pitman and Fireman Frederick Barrett who described water entering the ship from the starboard side. Passengers and crew noted a list to starboard, which was immediately noticed by the captain, as Quartermaster Hitchens testified during the Mersey Inquiry. Even without feeling the collision or seeing the flooding, many survivors noted chunks of ice scattered on the starboard side, forward deck.

Fact #2: It was not a severe collision.

Evidence: Survivor testimony can be used as a guide to understand the severity of the collision. Based on this evidence, it is clear that the ship did not hit the iceberg head-on. The sensations described by passengers imply a collision that was surprisingly light: quivering, shuddering, grating, trembling—anything but a severe blow. Considering the evidence, it is unlikely that most passengers felt the kind of jolt typical of a head-on collision, but rather, their descriptions confirm a

During Day 19 of the Mersey Inquiry, Edward Wilding outlined a rather surprising conclusion about the "what ifs" surrounding that night—had *Titanic* faced the iceberg head-on, rather than trying to veer around it, she would likely have made it to port with very little loss of life. The commissioner was interested enough in this conclusion to press Wilding for a further explanation, in which the witness carefully outlined a scenario that would have saved all the passengers, but would have resulted in enough momentum to crumple up *Titanic*'s bow, approximately 100 feet, killing all the firemen below. His support for such a claim was the fate of the ocean liner *Arizona*, a steamship that broke the transatlantic speed record in July 1879. Four months later the steamship, going full speed, collided head-on with an iceberg in the North Atlantic and managed to float safely into St. John's, Newfoundland, for repairs.

less severe, glancing blow, in which the ship bumped up against the iceberg:

> The sound was like she touched something. It seemed as though something was rubbing alongside of her, at the time.

> I was awakened by the crunching and jarring, as if it was hitting up against something.

> No shock and no jar; just a grating sensation.

> I did not feel the impact at all. It did not wake me up.

> It gave just a little vibration.

> Just like thunder, the roar of thunder. There was just a small motion, but nothing to speak of.

> What awakened me was a grinding sound on her bottom . . . but I would not get up as I thought there was nothing the matter.

> There was a slight jar followed by the grinding—a slight bumping.

After reviewing the survivor testimony, Harland & Wolff's naval architect, Edward Wilding, came to the same conclusion: "This contact seems to have been a particularly light one . . . because we have heard the evidence that lots of people scarcely felt it."

Fact #3: Not only was the collision not severe, but the damage described is not consistent with a catastrophic impact, that is, there was no huge hole reported in *Titanic's* side.

Evidence: In fact, our best source for evidence to describe what the damage looked like is Barrett who was down in No. 10 Stokehold, located in Boiler Room No. 6. "Water came pouring in two feet above the stokehold plate; the ship's side was torn from the third stokehold to the forward end," Barrett recounted during the Inquiry investigation in London. Yet, Barrett not only described water flowing from the damage into Boiler Room No. 6 but also into the coal bunker of Boiler Room No. 5, ostensibly from the same tear. Barrett recalled the water rising in No. 6 up to eight feet in a matter of minutes, but he notes that in No. 5 "the hole was not so big in that section as it was in No. 6 section." In fact, Barrett was able to stay in No. 5 without ever seeing water rise above the floor plates. It was only when the bulkhead separating the two boiler rooms had collapsed that a wall of water rushed into the compartment.

Barrett's description is the key to understanding the size, width, and location of the damage. He was the only person who actually lived to tell the world about it. The fact that he *did* live implies that the tear from Boiler Room No. 6 to No. 5 was not wide enough to emit a head of water large enough to drown someone instantly. It was quickly filling the compartment, but it was manageable.

Fact #4: The damage resulting from the collision extended along some length of the starboard side.

Evidence: Numerous accounts record the rapid, steady flooding rate of the starboard compartments of the ship. From the *Wreck Commissioner's Report Description of the Damage to the Ship*, we know the following about the flooding within the first ten minutes:

According to Able Bodied Seaman Poingdestre, No. 1 cargo hold contained seven feet of water. Hendrickson testified that in the No. 2 cargo hold, five minutes after the collision, he saw water rushing in at the bottom of the firemen's passage on the starboard side. This led to the conclusion that damage on the side of the ship was deep enough to pierce three and a half feet into the starboard side, thus flooding both the hold and the passage.

Many survivors, including Stewardess Annie Robinson, Officer Boxhall, First Class Passenger Norman Chambers, Night Watchman James Johnson, and Second Steward Joseph Wheat provided evidence about the flooding rates in the No. 3 cargo hold. The mailroom, located in No. 3 on the Orlop deck, starboard side, was filled soon after the collision.

According to Barrett, at the time of the collision in Boiler Room No. 6, water poured in to approximately two feet above the stokehold plates, on the starboard side, at the aft end of the boiler room. Some of the firemen immediately went through the watertight door opening to Boiler Room No. 5 because the water was coming in quickly. Witnesses explained that approximately ten minutes later, the water had risen to eight feet above the double bottom in Boiler Room No. 6.

On his escape to Boiler Room No. 5, Barrett described the damage to the ship's side in the starboard forward bunker at approximately two feet above the stokehold plates and two feet back from the watertight bulkhead between Boiler Room Nos. 5 and 6.

All in all, the flooding rates within the first six compartments of the ship seem to be approximately equal. There was no testimony describing the starboard side as being stove in, or severely punctured, despite the commission's attempts to get more detailed information from Barrett.

> MR. ROCHE: You cannot say how much water was coming through at all?
> BARRETT: No.
> THE COMMISSIONER: I do not understand this. Was a teacupful of water coming through?
> BARRETT: No.
> THE COMMISSIONER: What was it?
> BARRETT: A continual pour of water.
> THE COMMISSIONER: Now, describe the pour of water. It was not like Niagara Falls, I suppose, but try and tell me what it was like.
> BARRETT: Just the very same as an ordinary fire hose would come in.

Although aft of the perceived damage location, in Boiler Room No. 4, Trimmer Dillon testified that the water was seeping in through the floor, that it was "damp," and that only "small quantities" came in, rather than the gushes that would be expected with serious damage. This is not the type of description that implies a catastrophic barrage of water, but rather a steady filling of the ship, which was controllable through pumping for at least a period of time during the ship's flooding.

Fact #5: The sinking was the result of a very small amount of initial damage.

Evidence: The survivor testimony of 1912 gave naval architects enough information to begin calculating the approximate size of the damage and the flooding rates that brought down the ship. Wilding utilized these details to generate his own model of the flooding sequence. His conclusion? That the *Titanic* sank due to 12 square feet of damage. "My estimate for the size of the hole required (and making some allowance for the obstruction due to the presence of decks and other things) is that the total area through which water was entering the ship, was somewhere about 12 square feet. . . . A hole three quarters of an inch wide and two-hundred feet long does not seem to describe to me the probable damage, but it must have averaged about that amount."

Wilding's findings were confirmed using modern computational techniques by Harland & Wolff's naval architects John Bedford and Chris Hackett. Using many of Wilding's sketches and calculations but reevaluating some of his assumptions, they concluded that the flooding damage was no more than 12.6 square feet.

From the facts assembled using the eyewitness testimony and the available evidence, the bottom line result is the following: there was a long, thin array of damage to the starboard bow over several hundred feet in length, comprising a total area of 12 square feet. This damage flooded six compartments simultaneously. After nearly three months of testimony, the *1912 Wreck Commissioner's Inquiry Report of the Loss of the "Titanic"* summarized the extent of the damage with the following: "The collision with the iceberg, which took place at 11:40 p.m., caused damage to the bottom of the starboard side of the vessel at about ten feet above the level of the keel, but there was no damage above this height. There was damage in the forepeak, No. 1 hold, No. 2 hold, No. 3 hold, No. 6 boiler room, No. 5 boiler room. The damage extended over a length of about 300 ft." From 1912 until 1996, the world concurred with this conclusion.

The discovery of the *Titanic* on the ocean floor offered new opportunities to investigate the damage and support or disprove the testimony. With what has been learned in the years since, many new theories have emerged to explain how and why the *Titanic* sank. The next five chapters will examine each one individually, using the testimony, historical facts, and scientific evidence to analyze all the possible scenarios.

PART III

THE ANALYSIS

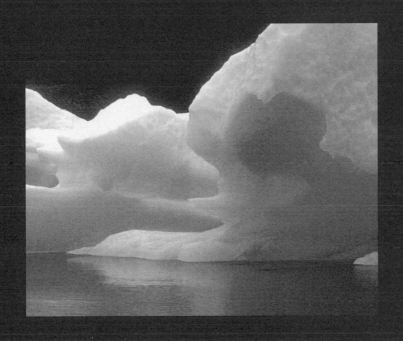

CHAPTER 9

THE 300-FOOT GASH

*My theory would be that she was going along and
touched one of those large spurs from an iceberg . . .
that she struck one of those on her bilge, and that
she ran along that, and that opened up her plates,
the lining of her plates, and the water came in; and
so much water got in that I think her bulkheads
could not stand the strain . . . and she must have
struck along on her bilge and opened herself
outright along as far as the engine room, sir.*

—James Moore, Master of the SS *Temple*, Day 9,
American Inquiry

F ollowing both the American and British Inquiries in 1912, the public was presented with the conclusion that the *Titanic* had sunk due
to a 300-foot gash that ran along the starboard bilge (the curved
portion between the double bottom and the side of the ship). The *Illustrated Times of London* produced a sketch of the collision as seen in
plate 16, depicting the iceberg slicing like a saw blade straight through
the steel hull plates. Could ice really slice through steel? This chapter
will examine additional evidence to support or dispute the 300-foot
gash, including excerpts from neglected parts of the 1912 testimony,
the physical properties of ice, and the last ten years of expedition observations.

ICE VS. STEEL: WHAT DOES SCIENCE TELL US?

Two large moving bodies collide in the ocean—a North Atlantic iceberg and the largest man-made moving object in 1912. The ultimate goal in the investigation is to quantify what ice can actually do to steel. First, let's consider the average hardness and strength of a North Atlantic iceberg. The hardness of ice varies with its crystal structure, which depends on the conditions under which it formed—the temperature and pressure within the glacier. While it may get as cold as −15°C within the core, the surface of a North Atlantic iceberg is at an overall temperature of about 0°C, both above and below the waterline. This means that among all the bits of the iceberg involved in the collision with the *Titanic*, the chunks that fell onto the decks or the rugged underwater spur that collided with the hull, there was very little variation in hardness and strength properties. Even at the inner core, where the ice is hardest, it is still no more than 2 percent of the hardness of the steel used to make *Titanic*'s hull.

An iceberg's breaking strength will vary with the temperature of the ice, as well as the speed of the collision, from as little as 500 pounds per square inch (psi) to as much as 3,000 psi—the faster the collision, the stronger the ice. These values correspond to a maximum of only one twentieth the strength of *Titanic*'s steel plates. How, then, do iceberg collisions result in so much damage? What physically happened when the ice met *Titanic*'s steel plates?

Using some of the general observations described in the survivor testimonies, we have estimated the iceberg as a typical North Atlantic, medium-sized, pinnacle-shaped iceberg, corresponding to a mass of approximately 100,000 tons and moving at about ⅓ mile per hour. *Titanic* was 882 feet long and had a displacement (the weight of the ship and its contents) of 52,310 tons. From the testimony, her speed was estimated at 22½ knots, which is about 25 miles per hour.

Science tells us that the strength of ice is a mere fraction of that of steel, even at fast collision rates. Yet, throughout history many ships have collided with icebergs, have suffered irreparable damage, and have sunk as a result. Even today a ship's collision with an iceberg has the potential to end in disaster. In March 2000, the shrimp trawler *BCM Atlantic* struck an iceberg in the North Atlantic and sank within five minutes. What controls the amount of damage? Why is it that steel can be crumpled, fractured, or torn by ice, a material that is significantly weaker? It is the enormous *momentum* involved in the collision of two huge bodies. The collision of the *Titanic* and the iceberg, no matter how big it was, resulted in the transfer of momentum, generating some amount of force on the hull that may or may not penetrate the steel. Momentum relates to how hard it is to stop an object from moving and, therefore, depends on only the mass and the velocity of the object, *not* the object's strength or hardness.

Passengers on the ship feel this change in momentum as an *impulse*. They may shift sideways, fall to the ground, or feel a gentle jerk one way or another. Depending on how easily the two bodies can move, the passengers will feel more or less of an impulse. Ramming a ship into a dock at port will cause more of an impulse than a collision with the same dock floating in the water because the momentum is transferred much more quickly. In addition, *Titanic*'s mass was so large relative to her passengers that it disguised the huge transfer of momentum taking place.

Ice has the ability to damage the steel hull of a ship severely, but the question with the *Titanic* is to determine how this damage may have looked. Without specific details about the angle of contact between the two bodies and the area over which this contact occurred, no one will ever really be able to estimate accurately the forces that were generated. However, inferences can be made from the survivor testimony and the expedition observations of the damage. In addition, by establishing scenarios that match what physically makes sense provides a more accurate picture of what really happened. For instance, is it more likely that the steel was cut open, or did the riveted seams let go?

WILDING'S CONTRIBUTION:
HOW FAST WOULD THE SHIP SINK?

During his testimony Edward Wilding was asked to describe what he believed to be the extent of the damage, the volume of the water that had entered the ship, and the length of time it took to fill the damaged compartments. While the committee took away an image of a long, continuous gash, Wilding had actually suggested otherwise. "I cannot believe that the wound was absolutely continuous the whole way. I believe that it was in a series of steps, and that from what we heard Barrett say in his evidence, it was the end of one of the series of wounds which flooded the different spaces." Later he went on to describe his calculations in more detail, "It can only have been a comparatively short length, and the aggregate of the holes must have been somewhere about 12 square feet."

On this second point, when he was asked to speculate on the size of the damage, Wilding explained that about 16,000 tons of water would have been necessary to enter the ship in order for it to flood over the approximate 40 minutes described. Assuming that No. 1, No. 2, and No. 3 holds, as well as No. 6 and No. 5 boiler rooms were flooding at the same time due to a continuous gash, the distance covered from fore to aft is about 500 feet along the starboard side. Using the testimony to determine the flooding rates, Wilding felt that the width of the gash could have been no more than ¼ inch and no more than 200 feet long in total. Any wider and the ship would have flooded much more quickly than what is consistent with the story told by survivors and witnesses.

Instead, Wilding suggested that the ship might have banged against numerous spurs along the iceberg's side, producing a series of holes over the six compartments:

> MR. ROWLATT: I suppose it is possible that a piece of ice made a hole and then got itself broken off?
> WILDING: Yes, quite probable.
> MR. ROWLATT: And then another piece of ice made another hole, and so on?
> WILDING: Yes, that is what I believe happened.

THE UNDERWATER EVIDENCE BUILDS

Despite Wilding's documented claims, for the next eight decades it was generally accepted that a long, piercing gash had brought down the ship. Since there was never any proof to settle the difference definitively one way or the other, Wilding's statements were disregarded. During the 1996 expedition, modern technology provided the first evidence to support Wilding's claims. Sonar imaging revealed the "aggregate of holes" on *Titanic*'s starboard side—six openings along the bow section of *Titanic*'s hull. Since the location overlapped perfectly with the damage described during the 1912 inquiries, it appeared that after eighty-four years, there was finally some physical proof to reinforce Wilding's claims. The long, continuous gash was nowhere to be found. But were these the long, lost facts that would fill in the blanks about the *Titanic*'s sinking? Not just yet.

The sonar imaging of openings along the starboard side might have been conclusive—the final proof of *Titanic*'s iceberg damage—except for that fact that similar damage was found on the port side. This often-neglected piece of information (in fact, completely omitted from the SNAME report, as well as subsequent media versions on the discovery) calls into question whether what was seen by sonar was actually iceberg damage. It is interesting, however, that the calculated area of the damage is nearly identical: 11.4 square feet versus Wilding's 12 square feet. If split seams are clearly visible on both sides, then it is virtually impossible to distinguish between the damage caused by the iceberg and damage resulting from impact with the seafloor. While it may be plausible that the iceberg collision was an intermittent sideswipe along the starboard side, the work carried out in 1996 did little to prove it.

Over time, it has become increasingly difficult to confirm the sonar imaging results, as even Paul Matthias of Polaris Imaging has refused to defend what Garzke and others declared in the SNAME paper. This was a classic case of overstated findings, disagreement among investigators, and deceitful scholarly practice. Ultimately, it resulted in a division among the panel, some of whom did not grant permission for use of their names, and was one of the prime motivating factors in ending the authors' ties with the ongoing panel's investigations.

In the end, what the sonar images *did* indicate was that considerable damage had occurred regularly near or across riveted seams, whether iceberg related or not. Still riding on a wave of optimism, the 1998 Discovery Channel–funded expedition returned to the wreck using ROVs to zoom in on these purported areas of damage. Recently unearthed from the seafloor, the large tear described by Fireman Barrett was actually visible with the naked eye and revealed to the team undeniable proof of a parted seam plus what looked like several empty rivet holes. Not only did these two seasons provide the best evidence thus far to indicate iceberg damage along the starboard side, but the results also formally dispelled the 300-foot continuous gash theory finally.

The 1998 expedition offered additional clues to fuel the fire, producing more salvaged material to investigate. Results from the two trips had further concentrated the iceberg damage to a series of very thin openings, many of which were near (based on sonar) or included (based on ROV observation) riveted seams. Coupling the damage observations with documented views at the wreck site of twisted steel plates that were missing rivets, as well as rivets that were missing heads, the focus would be turned away from serious design issues and toward the wreck's metallurgical clues in hopes of reconstructing the damage. The investigation required a detailed study of *Titanic*'s materials. Now, to the most highly publicized explanation surrounding the *Titanic*'s sinking—the "brittle steel theory."

CHAPTER 10

HULL STEEL = BRITTLE STEEL?

D id shortcomings in the quality control of *Titanic*'s hull steel lead to her tragic sinking? Ask most people today and the likely response will be something about "bad steel," "brittle steel," or "poorly made steel." A few might even recall: "Wasn't it full of sulfur or something?" Thanks to extensive media promotion and Discovery Channel reruns, the public has been barraged with heavily massaged technical half-truths. What is the scientific evidence to support those claims? Was the steel really of inferior quality? Studies of the hull steel salvaged in 1991 led several scientists to conclude that *Titanic*'s steel was "brittle as glass, shattering on collision with the iceberg"—known by many as the brittle steel theory. Yet, the authors' scientific findings indicate the contrary—that *Titanic* steel had sufficient toughness in the ice water temperatures. This chapter provides a careful presentation of the data and supporting evidence for both camps of thought, using testimonials, photographs of damage to the *Olympic* in 1911, and metallurgical analysis.

Titanic's steel plates were made using the open-hearth process, which was the same type used on all ships in the early twentieth century. The plates were 1 to 1½ inches thick, 30 feet long by 6 feet wide, and weighed several tons apiece. The steel was rolled and cut to size at the steel mill, and then rivet holes were cold punched at the Harland & Wolff works using a steam-driven punching machine. As mentioned earlier, the plates were ordered in batches of 10,000 to 25,000 from Harland & Wolff's regular suppliers, D. Colville & Sons and Dalzell Steel & Iron Works in Motherwell, Scotland. Standard tests of the strength and ductility of the steel plating were required by the Board of Trade, as it was for all steel used on *Titanic*'s boilers, bulkheads, and watertight doors.

ROUND ONE

Titanic Science Hits the Big Time

As mentioned earlier, the first tests on *Titanic* steel recovered from the wreck site occurred in 1991, performed by a team of scientists at DREA in Halifax, Nova Scotia, and CANMET in Ottawa, Canada. Ken KarisAllen and Jim Matthews of DREA performed some mechanical tests on hull plate, and they found that the steel fractured in a completely brittle manner at ice water temperatures. Details of what they found were published in an internal CANMET publication and later in an article in *Popular Mechanics*, and the story was picked up and republished by media worldwide. This caused many people to believe that the brittle character of the hull steel in ice water might have been a major factor, or even the only factor, in the sinking of the ship. It was considered probable that the impact of the hull with the iceberg, though minor, would have been strong enough to shatter the brittle hull plates in the bow, allowing the rapid flooding of the ship. This was an impressive conclusion, meriting a very close examination of their investigation to understand what these investigators did and why. First, we begin with a better definition of the type of mechanical testing that they used—the Charpy impact test—and the information that it provides.

The Charpy impact test is an experiment designed to test a material's toughness. Toughness is a measurement of the amount of energy that a material can absorb before it cracks—the higher the amount of energy absorbed, the tougher the material. During the Charpy impact test, a small rectangular bar with a V-shaped notch on the side is broken by a heavy pendulum hammer, which swings from a fixed height and breaks (or bends) the sample when it reaches the bottom. After the specimen is broken, the amount of energy absorbed can be calculated from the height that the pendulum swings up to after the impact—the lower the swing, the more energy that the sample absorbed from the hammer and the tougher the material.

The toughness of a material can be measured in cold or hot conditions using the Charpy impact test at a range of temperatures. The results are plotted on a graph that shows how the amount of absorbed energy changes with temperature. Some metals change from ductile to brittle as the temperature decreases. This is more intuitive than it might seem—it is easy to imagine cold steel cracking and hot metal bending. The temperature at which this change happens is characteristic of each metal and this change is known as the ductile-to-brittle transition temperature. In the case of the DREA/CANMET study, two data points were used to create a trend line showing that the ductile-to-brittle transition temperature of *Titanic* steel was well above 32°F. Translation: *Titanic* steel is brittle in ice water. Despite the fact that the measurement of the change from brittle-to-ductile behavior is a very subjective and fuzzy procedure to quantify, the published DREA/CANMET results stated emphatically that the *Titanic* steel acted in a brittle manner during the collision.

Besides the test data, the DREA/CANMET study cited the collision of the sister ship *Olympic* with the HMS *Hawke* near the Isle of Wight in September 1911. The result of this crash was a 40-foot hole in *Olympic's* starboard side, as partially seen in a photo taken by Harland & Wolff (plate 10, top). The DREA/CANMET scientists used this photo as support for their conclusions, noting that the straight edges of the punched-in hull piece in the upper portion of this picture suggest brittle fracture, as if the steel cracked on contact with the *Hawke*.

But that wasn't all. They included in their study a chemical analysis that revealed high amounts of sulfur and phosphorus present in the steel—high in comparison to modern-day requirements—suggesting that sulfur or phosphorus embrittlement could have caused *Titanic* hull steel's less-than-ideal mechanical behavior.

The media coverage of the results was sensational, claiming that the mystery had finally been solved, that *Titanic* steel was of inferior quality, too brittle for the application, fracturing on contact with the

You can see for yourself how a material breaks differently depending on temperature, like the hull plates of the RMS *Olympic*. Pick up a chocolate bar. Break off one end, and you see how the thickness of the bar is the same all the way out to the broken end. Now, heat up the rest of the bar until it is slightly soft. Tear another piece off, and you see how the bar thins gradually as you get closer to the break. This is an example of an important clue that a forensic metallurgist uses to determine whether something broke in a brittle or ductile manner—the thickness profile near the fracture surface.

iceberg. It was a neat, clean package: too much sulfur, bad steel, cracks, sinking. The media couldn't have asked for a more oversimplified, easy-to-digest story. It was picked up everywhere, and over the years, it has become something of an assumed "fact"—it was the steel, wasn't it? Time has come to subject conventional wisdom to some in-depth analysis.

Researchers were eager to learn more, ready for further studies, when in August 1996 Discovery Channel formed a team that was charged with a scientific investigation into the causes of the sinking of the *Titanic*. RMSTI, headed then by the late George Tulloch and salvor-in-possession of the wreck, provided access to the wreck and facilitated the investigation. Of particular importance to metallurgists was a large section of the *Titanic's* hull steel, along with several hull and bulkhead rivets, recovered and turned over to the team for analysis. It was at this point that we got involved.

ROUND TWO

Confirming the Data

Metallurgical testing on the 1996 hull steel was directed by Professor H. P. Leighly at the University of Missouri–Rolla, who was later assisted by Tim Foecke in his laboratory at the National Institute of Standards and Technology (NIST). Chemical analyses were performed by Leighly and also by Dr. Harold Reemsnyder of the Homer Laboratories of Bethlehem Steel in Bethlehem, Pennsylvania.

The group at the University of Missouri–Rolla performed a series of Charpy impact tests over a range of temperatures from –55° to 179°C (–67° to 354°F), at last providing a complete curve to compare to DREA/ CANMET's two data points. Three different plates were tested—two from the *Titanic* and one made from modern ASTM A36 steel (see fig. 9). The results indicated a low-impact energy (brittleness) in the *Titanic* specimens at low temperatures. The ductile–brittle transition happened at about 30°C (86°F)—a nice sunny day in Florida and well above

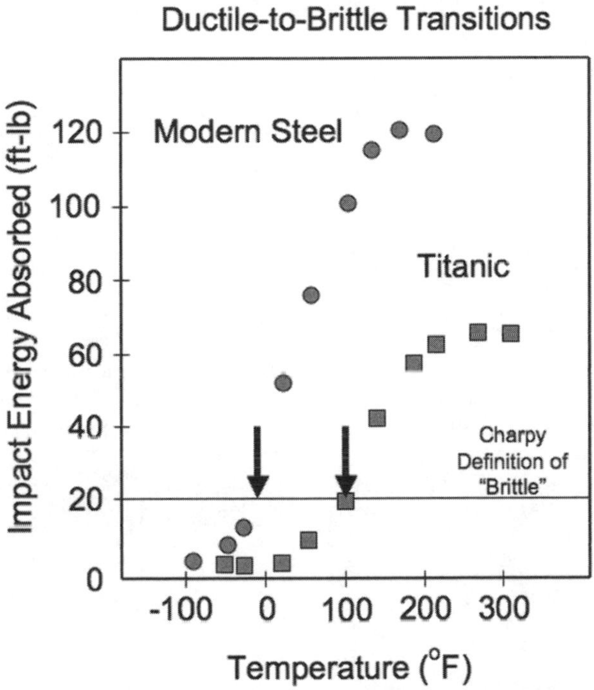

Ductile-to-Brittle Transitions

Figure 9. This graph shows the results of a series of Charpy impact tests that were completed on *Titanic* steel and modern (A36) steel. Notice that the *Titanic* data intercept the ductile-to-brittle transition line well above 32°F, showing that the steel is brittle at ice water temperatures.

ice water temperatures. Okay, no smoking gun, but the results did add credence to the DREA/CANMET conclusions—brittle behavior.

A Microstructural History

Metallurgical forensics links us to the history of a piece of material. By studying a sample in detail, scientists are able to deduce how it was made, how it was used, and how it may have failed. This requires measurements of the metal's strength, fracture behavior, chemistry, and microstructure. It's the combination of all these data that forms the chain of clues used to reconstruct any possible role of the material in an accident.

To examine the microstructure of the *Titanic*, samples were cut from each plate recovered from the wreck, polished to create an extremely flat surface, and then etched in nitric acid to reveal the fine

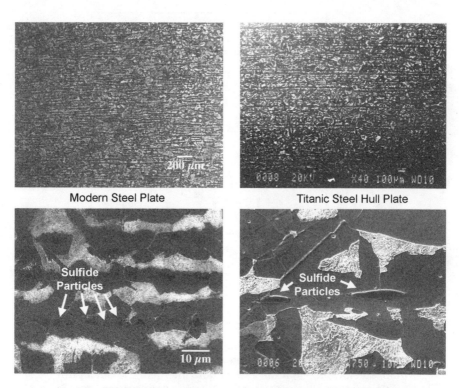

Figure 10. Four scanning electron micrographs showing the difference in microstructure of modern (AISI 1018) steel on the left and *Titanic* hull plate (on the right).

Titanic and *Olympic* sit next to one another in the double gantry. This is the last photo of the two together, just weeks before *Olympic* set sail.

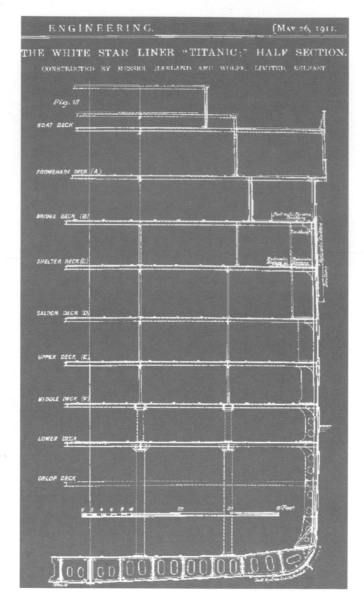

A blueprint of the *Titanic*'s hull showing all nine decks in cross section.

This photo taken during *Titanic*'s construction shows the joggled surface that was created by *Titanic*'s overlapping steel plates. (Harland and Wolff Photographic Collection, © National Museums Northern Ireland, Ulster Folk Transport Museum)

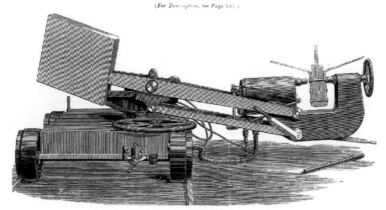

HYDRAULIC KEEL RIVETTER; (TWEDDELL'S SYSTEM).

CONSTRUCTED BY MESSRS. FIELDING AND PLATT, ENGINEERS, GLOUCESTER.

(For Description, see Page 541.)

A sketch of Tweddell's Riveter as seen in the technical journal *Engineering*, December 10, 1880. Tweddell's Riveter was one of the first mechanized riveting systems to be used for shipbuilding.

A riveting crew uses a hydraulic riveter to complete the keel section of *Titanic*'s sister ship *Britannic*. (Harland and Wolff Photographic Collection, © National Museums Northern Ireland, Ulster Folk Transport Museum)

A shipyard worker uses a hydraulic riveter on *Titanic*'s sister ship *Britannic*. Notice the white markings in the lower right-hand corner. These indicate that the rivet counter had inspected them for adequacy. (Harland and Wolff Photographic Collection, © National Museums Northern Ireland, Ulster Folk Transport Museum)

Grueling conditions at the furnaces where workmen had to protect themselves from the intense heat and noxious gases as they worked the molten charge.

Huge tongs were used to remove a batch of molten slag from the furnace after the stirring of the puddling process.

The wrought iron charge is run through an extruder to shape it into a bar, which is subsequently cut and formed into rivets.

A boy heating rivets down at the shipyard slip. (Photo reference 1811/252/17 from the Tyne & Wear Archives)

Brunel's *Great Eastern*, the largest ship in the world when she was launched, off the coast of Newfoundland in 1866.

White Star Line's *Britannic* outfitted as a hospital ship during World War I.

The Eiffel Tower under construction in 1878. The structure is built completely of wrought iron and held together by 2.5 million rivets. (Photographic Collection of the Bibliothèque Nationale de France)

A photograph taken by Harland & Wolff following the *Olympic*'s crash with the HMS *Hawke* shows the extensive damage to her starboard side—and the mangled steel and open rivet holes that resulted. (Harland and Wolff Photographic Collection, © National Museums Northern Ireland, Ulster Folk Transport Museum)

Another Harland & Wolff photograph cataloguing the damage that resulted from the *Olympic–Hawke* collision in 1911. The plate thinning and angle of fracture seen in the *Olympic* hull steel indicates a lot of plastic stretching during cracking. (Harland and Wolff Photographic Collection, © National Museums Northern Ireland, Ulster Folk Transport Museum)

The infamous Big Piece, a chunk of *Titanic*'s hull that spans across the length of two cabins, shown on display in Boston in November 1998.

An ironworker using a gas-powered K-12 saw "removes a sample" from the Big Piece for forensic examination, much to the pain of the conservationists.

Patch from the 2004 NOAA /
National Geographic expedition.

Tim Foecke's jacket from the
1998 expedition.

Tim Foecke *(near left)* is at the University of Rhode Island with other
scientists, linked by satellite (monitors on wall) to the NOAA ship
Ron Brown, which was exploring the wreck with an ROV in 2004.
(Kimberly Foecke)

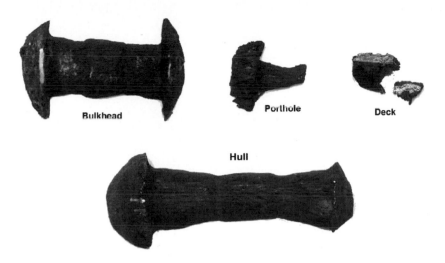

Examples of the 4 different types and sizes of rivets recovered from the wreck of *Titanic*.

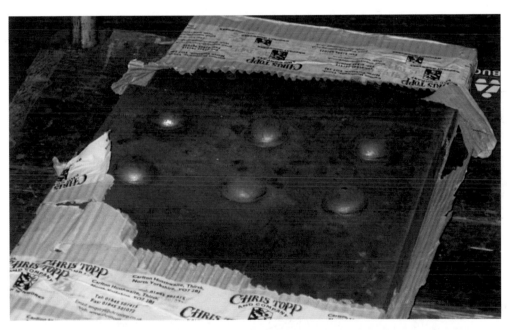

The reproduction hull pieces have arrived from the blacksmith in Yorkshire. Can you believe they used FedEx?

Edge-on view of the reproduction *Titanic* hull seam just before testing.

The reproduction joint after failure. It failed at only 60 percent of the load that a good quality joint should have held.

A closeup of the broken rivet after testing the reproduction joint. A small "button" from inside the head has remained attached to the end of the shaft—typical also of the recovered broken *Titanic* rivets.

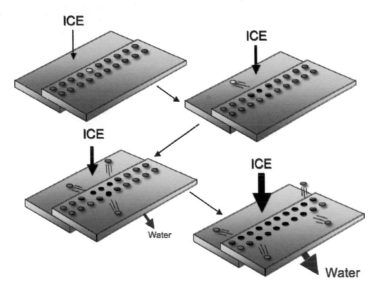

Diagram showing how a bad-quality rivet (yellow) can start a seam unzipping by dumping its load onto neighboring (red) rivets, overloading and snapping them too, and opening the seam and letting in seawater.

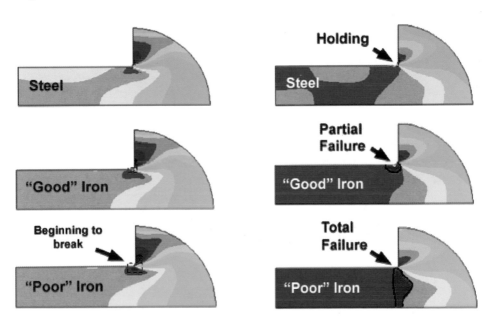

Stresses that develop when the rivets are cooled from 400°C. Keep in mind that the stresses are about the same but the steel is stronger, so it is not as close to breaking as the iron. Note that the poor wrought iron has already begun to break, as shown in the boxed region. (Copyright Jennifer Hooper McCarty, Ph.D. dissertation, The Johns Hopkins University)

Stresses that build up when the rivet is stretched by 5 mm (less than a 1/4 inch) in the computer model. The regions outlined in black have exceeded their ultimate strength and have failed. (Copyright Jennifer Hooper McCarty, Ph.D. dissertation, The Johns Hopkins University)

A drawing from the *Illustrated Times of London* in the days after the sinking. Everyone assumed that the damage to the hull from the iceberg must have been enormous for the great *Titanic* to go down so fast.

microstructural details. Examination with an optical microscope and a scanning electron microscope yields the first set of clues as seen in figure 10. To a metallurgist, the first obvious thing is a microstructure containing large ferrite grains (the dark regions of the background) and large, coarse pearlite colonies (light regions that contain iron carbide) that are varying in thickness. Second, the *Titanic* microstructure shows a large amount of banding in the rolling direction. That is, the microstructure is not randomly distributed but it shows layers of one type of grain and then the other. Third, manganese sulfide (MnS) and oxide particles (the darkest regions that almost protrude from the surface) are seen throughout the material and are also quite large. The MnS particles have been flattened into lens shapes like flying saucers, instead of being melted into long lines of droplets.

So much for the metallurgist-speak. What do these clues tell us? The large grain size and coarse pearlite are significant. Given lots of time at high temperatures, the larger grains tend to grow by absorbing iron from the smaller grains, so the presence of these large grains tells us the plate was hot for a long time. It is also apparent that the steel was allowed to cool slowly, probably by sitting in the open air after it came off the rolling mill.

The large, lens-shaped MnS sulfide particles support the case for slow cooling and provide evidence for a fair amount of sulfur present. (This could be a bad thing.) Their flattened shapes tells us at about what temperature the steel was rolled. MnS is a chemical compound, and it has a melting temperature of 1,100°–1,600°C, depending on purity. When the steel billet is cast from the molten steel, MnS particles form as droplets and are roughly spherical. When the steel is rolled, they are deformed. The shape of the particles in the *Titanic* hull steel shows that the MnS was soft, but not melted, when the plate was rolled. Thus, the rolling temperature was less than 2,939°F. This is lower than typical rolling temperatures used today, where it is more usual to see the MnS squeezed out into a little line of particles, showing that it was a liquid when the steel plate was rolled. Since the *Titanic* steel was not as hot during rolling, it was probably rolled several times to get it to its final thickness, and so it had to be hot for a long time—another indicator as to why the grains are big.

Every one of these observations is consistent with what we know about early-twentieth-century steel-making processes, where a vat of dirtier steel (compared to today) was cast into an ingot, rolled at a moderate temperature (at a lower temperature than today), and air cooled. This was the norm in turn-of-the-century British steel making, indicating that there is nothing out of the ordinary about the *Titanic* steel for its time period.

A comparable modern steel grade is AISI 1018, which has a similar chemistry. Micrographs of a modern 1018 steel show a finer grain size, much finer pearlite, and smaller and less numerous MnS particles. This microstrcture is typical of that produced in a modern high-speed mill, followed by a series of heating and cooling treatments.

The University of Missouri–Rolla analysis suggested that the coarse grain structure was one of the factors that contributed to *Titanic*'s brittle behavior, since large-grained steels are known to be more brittle than fine-grained steels, all other things being equal. This is not to say that the *Titanic* steel was inferior. In fact, its mechanical properties fall within the design requirements for 1911 of "15–20 tonnes per inch squared" as specified by Harland & Wolff (see table 1). Bear in mind, though, that the 1911 tests used to verify the quality of the steel only supplied information about the strength and ductility, not the toughness. The Missouri researchers' conclusions found that *Titanic* steel had low fracture toughness at ice-brine temperatures, something that *Titanic*'s designers knew little, if anything, about and did not specify or test.

TABLE 1: TENSILE TEST RESULTS ON *TITANIC* HULL PLATE.

Plates recovered in:	1991	1996
Yield stress	38 ksi (262 MPa)	41 ksi (280 MPa)
Ultimate Tensile Strength (UTS)	62.5 ksi (430 MPa)	62.6 ksi (432 MPa)
% elongation (50mm gage length)	29	30.9

Harland & Wolff design specifications in 1911 were 40 ksi yield stress and 30% elongation.

Chemical Fingerprints

Just as important as the microstructure, chemical composition is the fingerprint of the material; it can tell us what type of process was used to make the steel, what contaminants it contains, and where it was made. Two chemical analyses were made on the hull steel recovered in the 1996 expedition and one of the 1991 material. These are summarized in table 2. From these results, a metallurgist would conclude that the hull is made up of a steel that is chemically roughly the same as a modern AISI 1018 mild steel, with somewhat elevated levels of sulfur and somewhat lower manganese. The low nitrogen levels seem to show that the steel was produced in an open-hearth furnace and not by a Bessemer process. This is another batch of technojargon, but again, these are all observations that fall in line with what we know about steel making in 1911. No surprises.

The brittle steel theory was reinforced by the observation of a low ratio of the amount of manganese to the amount of sulfur (Mn:S) and a high phosphorus content. Higher than desired levels of sulfur and phosphorus set off metallurgical alarm bells because these "tramp" el-

---

There is something that you might have around your house that undergoes embrittlement too, though it does it because of passing time and not contamination—cheddar cheese. Try this. Cut a rectangular bar of mild (unaged) cheddar cheese, and bend it till it breaks. See how the broken curds have the same sort of lines on them as the images of the broken Charpy bars? (See fig. 11, p. 126.) These curds represent the crystal grains in the steel. Now do the same with very sharp (aged) cheddar cheese. Aging has strengthened the curds, so now the points where the curds stick together are the weakest. See how the boundaries of the curds are now showing on the broken end? This is intergranular fracture.

ements tend to wind up on the grain boundaries between the crystals in the steel, causing the bonds in them to weaken and increasing the chance of a crack at those sites. The reason that the Mn:S ratio is important is simple: manganese loves to bond with sulfur. If sulfur is tied up as particles with the manganese, it will eliminate the threat posed by a bunch of rogue sulfur atoms just waiting to nestle into a grain boundary and crack it open. A comparison of the Mn:S ratio in the *Titanic* steel with the modern 1018 steel reveals a discouraging trend— it is much lower than permissible amounts in modern steel—a scenario for embrittlement disaster.

TABLE 2: CHEMICAL CONSTITUENTS OF *TITANIC* STEEL.

Element	1991 (CANMET)	1996 (U.Mo–Rolla)	1996 (Beth. Steel)	AISI 1018 (ASM)
Carbon	0.20%	0.21%	0.21%	0.18–23%
Sulfur	0.065%	0.069%	0.061%	0.05% max
Manganese	0.52%	0.47%	–	0.60–1.0%
Phosphorus	0.01%	0.045%	–	0.04% max
Nitrogen	0.004%	0.0035%	–	0.0025%
Oxygen	–	0.013%	–	–
Mn/S	8.0:1	6.8:1	–	12:1–20:1
Mn/C	2.5:1	2:1	–	3:1–7:1

The bottom line after the 1996 investigation: Although the steel was of superior quality for its time, it was not appropriate as a structural material in cold conditions. The high sulfur and phosphorus impurities implied grain boundary embrittlement and a catastrophic loss of toughness in the hull steel. Maybe it was the steel.

At the conclusion of the 1996 expedition and publication of the results, it was once again media mayhem. In 1997, Discovery Channel produced *Titanic: Anatomy of a Disaster*, highlighting the dramatic moment of the scientific investigation when a *Titanic* steel sample fractured catastrophically during a Charpy impact test. Millions of people watched as the (considerably audioenhanced) cracking noise of splitting steel echoed through the laboratory, forever solidifying in their memories that inferior materials had doomed the *Titanic*. Conventional wisdom was once again reinforced.

Have we yet again simplified the storyline? Was the greatest marine disaster of the twentieth century literally summed up by bad steel? A large portion of the ship is still intact on the seafloor, much of it deformed, bent, or twisted, even doubled over on itself—far from the cracked or shattered plates that such conclusions would seem to imply. Without examining the actual plates damaged in the collision, the effects of MnS particles and grain size were difficult to conclude firmly; yet there are certainly more accurate techniques to study and many more questions to ask. A forensic investigation examines every possibility in an effort to determine the mechanism of failure. Here is where our story begins.

ROUND THREE

Fractography of Charpy Results

Fractography is the detailed study of the broken end of a failed part and provides another critical technique in metallurgical forensics. The patterns created on fracture surfaces provide a means to qualify, and sometimes quantify, the type of failure. Fracture surfaces cut from the Charpy test specimens from the 1996 plate were examined in the scanning electron microscope in late 1997. In the case of *Titanic* hull steel, fracture was entirely transgranular (through the grains) (fig. 11, bottom left—see p. 126) with no indication that the grain boundaries had broken. This means that fracture did not occur in a manner consistent with problematic sulfur and phosphorus. One more time: Regardless of the suggestions that too much sulfur was causing the steel to be brittle, the images of fracture surfaces do not show any proof to

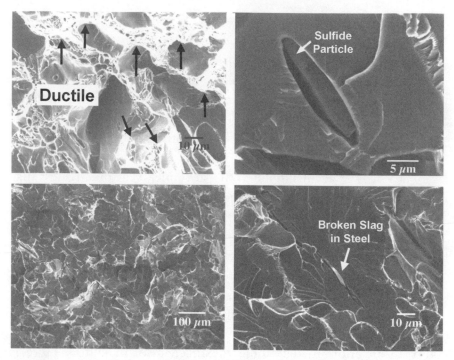

Figure 11. Scanning electron micrographs of the fractured surfaces of the *Titanic* hull steel showing that the fractures occurred across the grains, suggesting that high sulfur did not cause the steel to become brittle.

support this suggestion. This observation is very significant. If the cause of the brittleness of the steel had actually been due to sulfur, we would expect to see sulfur sitting on the grain boundaries and some evidence of fracture in between the grains. Some cleaved grains were found, and some were seen to start at broken MnS particles. This was determined by tracing the crack lines on the broken grains back to where they converge (fig. 11, bottom right). This indicates that in some cases the MnS particles broke and started cracks, which is another way that sulfur can cause brittleness, but the number of these nucleated patches amounted to less than 10 percent of the surface area of the Charpy bar. So while the MnS particles were guilty of causing some cracking (as it often does when mild steels fail), it was not nearly as much as previously thought and was not a major factor.

At ice-brine temperatures, the fracture of the 1996 samples was *nearly* entirely brittle—the broken surfaces were composed of mostly clean faces and sharp lines, indicating a metal that "split" apart, rather than "stretched." The DREA/CANMET study described the behavior of its sample as 100 percent brittle even at room temperature, but here in the 1996 sample, even at 32°F, proof of a small amount of toughness was seen on the fracture surface, around 5 percent of the area (fig. 11, upper left). The bubbly, rounded holes on the ridges in this photograph are known as microvoids and are evidence of the stretching that occurs during the ductile failure of metals. This offers the proof that at ice-brine temperatures the steel's fracture behavior is not entirely within the brittle region—there is an unmistakable region of ductility even when the steel is at ice water temperature.

Where Is the Sulfur Hiding?

We can speculate about whether all the sulfur and the manganese are tied together, but truly to know for sure requires techniques beyond just ordinary chemical analysis. Fortunately, techniques to find out where exactly the manganese, sulfur, and phosphorus reside within the metal are available. Using very sophisticated analysis such as secondary ion mass spectroscopy (SIMS) and parallel electron energy-loss spectroscopy (PEELS) in the transmission electron microscope (TEM), imaging of the chemical distribution within the steel showed that the sulfur was almost entirely tied up in MnS particles and was not located within the iron grains or on the grain boundaries. The data show that sulfur and manganese are consistently found as particles throughout the *Titanic* steel. There was plenty of Mn to get the job done, and it appears that the slow cooling kept the steel hot long enough for the manganese and sulfur to find each other.

Scientific investigation shows that impurities are in the steel, but is this really a problem? Exhaustive studies on the subject have been performed in the decades since 1912, particularly in the 1950s and 1960s on steels used on naval vessels, and results have shown that several types of impurities can increase or decrease the toughness of steel.

The sulfur level measured in the *Titanic* hull steel is higher than that acceptable in modern steels, as is the phosphorus concentration. Both of these elements can decrease how tough a steel is at room temperatures, but they do not affect the temperature at which the steel *changes* from ductile to brittle. Leighly and his co-workers did not consider all the work that had been done in this area, and the effect they tried to pin on the particles was too simplistic.

Some believe that the sulfur content of the hull steel was significantly higher than the standard of the time because the engineers of the ship had chosen material that was substandard. However, it is important to look at the sulfur content standard over time and to understand why it was set at any given level. Always you must put yourself into the mind of the engineers—what should they have known?

Today the sulfur content standard for structural mild steel is 0.05 percent maximum. In 1906, the standard, which would have been in place at the time of the ship's construction, was placed at 0.04 percent. This would indicate that the steel from the hull was even more substandard in 1911 than it would be today. However, a further investigation of the literature reveals that the standard had been revised to 0.055 percent and 0.05 percent at various times between 1906 and the present day. There is no evidence that the concentration level was set in reaction to particular data linking sulfur concentrations to a problem with the mechanical properties of steel. Steelmakers had a feeling that sulfur was a problem in steel, so they guessed at a level that would be "safe." Bottom line: there was no "standard," from a scientific point of view, so how could they fail to meet it?

Metallurgists of the turn-of-the-century era had an empirical knowledge (seat-of-the-pants feeling) that elevated levels of certain tramp elements, most notably sulfur and phosphorus, increased the likelihood of cracking in steel under certain service conditions. The effect had been known in general terms for nearly a century, but an actual quantitative analysis was not performed until the analysis of Liberty Ship failures during and after World War II. So any allegation that the engineers constructing the *Titanic* should have been able to link a chemical analysis showing high sulfur in a plate to an obvious risk of brittle fracture is unfounded. They simply didn't have the knowledge yet.

Microstructural Analysis

The large grain structure and large MnS particles have been blamed for partially causing the hull steel's brittle behavior. This problem could have been fixed with a finer microstructure, where the grains are smaller, which would produce a significantly tougher material. This could have been obtained by rolling the steel at a higher speed and temperature and then subjecting the plate to a series of heat treatments—to result in a microstructure more similar to the modern 1018 steel shown in figure 11.

This is very easy to say, but doing so makes us guilty of placing twenty-first-century scientific explanations onto early twentieth-century understanding. The quality of steel used in British shipbuilding was state of the art in 1911. But that does not mean that metallurgists were capable of identifying critical issues before they were discovered to be important. The concept of notch sensitivity of steels (that is, the tendency to fracture in the presence of a surface defect, such as a notch, crack, or scratch) was little understood, and the first quantitative ways to begin to evaluate the toughness of a material, among them the Charpy V-notch test, were only devised in the five or so years before the construction of the ship. It was suggested in a rather offhand manner in the Mersey Inquiry of 1912 that Charpy-like testing should have been performed on the steel of the hull. However, in 1911, the only materials being routinely tested for fracture toughness were ordinance steels used in cannons, where failures by fracture were thought to be much more likely than in a structural steel under normal use. Therefore, it would not have been intuitive for the designers and builders of the *Titanic* to test the hull steel for notch sensitivity. Even if they had, they had no information about what makes steel notch sensitive in the first place or any idea of how to fix it. Specifications of the time for steels called for only a range of tensile strengths and tensile ductility, which we now know are poor indicators of fracture toughness.

The Effect of Shipbuilding Techniques

Besides microstructural and chemical considerations, several practices that were common in turn-of-the-century British shipbuilding may have contributed to making brittle-behaving steel a factor in the sinking, and we should look at them closely. Although we mention them as potentially important contributors, there is no evidence to suggest that the engineers and builders of the time knew, or should have known, about their effects. Of course, these are only possibilities, as the exact effect each may or may not have had on the sinking will never be known for certain, since we have not been able to examine the damaged plates directly.

1. *Stress concentrations:* Something that is loaded will experience a much higher stress in small areas near sharp edges and corners. These areas are known as stress concentrations. Because of a lack of understanding of how stress concentrations affect steels, there was no attempt to remove them from the architecture of the ship. These are commonly found at hatch corners, strake junctions, and the like, and were a major cause of failures, for example, as sources of brittle cracks in Liberty Ships during and after World War II.

2. *Cracks at rivet holes:* A crack may be thought of as both an extreme type of stress concentration and an ideal location for failure to start. The rivet holes in the hull plates of the *Titanic* and of all its contemporaries were cold punched using a hydraulic ram. Upon close examination, these rivet holes were sometimes found to contain small cracks around the edge. In general, the shipbuilders did not worry about them because they were so small. They thought that a well-driven rivet would clamp them shut, and this would eliminate any risk. In reality, the residual stresses in the plate from the punching process would have been quite large, and the stress was oriented so that it would tend to make these cracks grow. In fact, the only stress that could have resisted crack growth would have been the friction of the rivet head rubbing on the hull plate, and this would have been very

---

Liberty Ship Failures

During World War II, a ship was designed that could be easily mass produced and carry 10,000 tons of cargo from the United States to England without refueling. The result was the Liberty Ship, with a pair of steam-driven engines that could propel her at 11 knots. Most Liberty Ships utilized welded construction rather than riveting in order to speed up production.

During (and after) the war, a small number of Liberty Ships and T2 tankers (the tanker equivalent of a Liberty Ship) broke in half, some while underway in the cold North Atlantic and even one at a dockside in the Caribbean. A combined U.S./UK commission was assembled to study the problem. After considering and rejecting bad welding, poor quality steel, and riveted joints that might have stopped the cracks, they pinned the blame on notch sensitivity of steel. Sharp corners at hatches, strake junctions, and other structural locations magnified the stresses in the ship and started high-speed cracks that parted the ship in two. Once they modified these sharp corners, the problem mostly vanished, although it happens a few times a year even today in freighters.

Constance Tipper, a metallurgist from Cambridge, UK, noted in her book *The Brittle Fracture Story* that despite historical evidence for steel being notch sensitive, it was not among the first things considered by the commission and was found to be a surprising result by the members. She termed it "the most *re*-discovered phenomenon in science."

---

small. The common belief at the time was almost exactly the opposite of reality. Upon impact of the plate at low temperatures, these cracks could have grown and linked up, resulting in failure of the plate.

3. *Plate variability:* The plate fragments recovered from the wreck and analyzed to date have exhibited significant differences in mi-

crostructure and fracture properties. The microstructure appears to show that they were rolled at different temperatures. This effect of plate variability in the hull was also seen in the detailed analysis of Liberty Ship failures. They found that the plates in which the cracks began were the most brittle, the plates through which the cracks grew were a little tougher, and the plates within which the cracks stopped were the toughest. This variability is not unexpected because the *Titanic* and her two sister ships were twice as large as any previously built, and iron feedstock was being assembled from all over the United Kingdom. Also, the plates were being produced in 40-ton batches versus the 500-ton batches typical for today, and the properties varied from batch to batch.

Can We Re-create the Collision with the Iceberg?

The goal in a metallurgical forensic analysis is to reenact how the material behaved during the disaster. We can talk ourselves blue in the face about Charpy test results, but if the test does not represent the conditions during the type of collision experienced, it is pretty much useless. The reason is this: steels are well known to exhibit strain-rate sensitive fracture behavior. All this means is that the faster the crack is loaded, the more brittle the fracture character. To put it another way, a change in how fast a piece of steel is loaded can change the behavior from brittle to ductile without changing the temperature. A perfect (although nonmetallic) example is Silly Putty: pulled apart slowly, it will stretch and deform into a long strand; pulled apart quickly, it will snap into two. In the case of steel, it is absolutely conceivable that at 0°C, a catastrophic, high-rate impact, such as a Charpy test, can cause brittle fracture, while slow, gradual loading may produce ductile-type bending and tearing.

There is both direct and indirect evidence that the steel used in the hull of the *Titanic* and her sister ships exhibited this behavior. Participants in the 1996 and 1998 expeditions noted that the images of the hull of *Titanic* by *Nautile* showed considerable buckling, resulting from the impact with the seafloor. Computer simulations of the sinking completed by the Marine Forensics Panel showed that this impact was

gradual and that these plates deformed at low strain rates. Yet, for almost ninety-five years, the public has assumed that the impact of the
ship with the iceberg at 22.5 knots occurred at high rates, more in line
with a Charpy impact test. At this rate, the steel would exhibit more
brittle behavior.

Additional evidence comes from the 1911 photographs of the
damage to the *Olympic*'s starboard side. As mentioned on page 117, the
DREA/CANMET study focused on the upper portion of this picture,
plate 10 (top), noting that the straight, cracked edges were consistent
with brittle fracture, and supported the idea that *Titanic*'s steel plates
acted in the same manner. However, ductile cracks can grow straight
in this manner too, and this conclusion seems unlikely if we examine
other regions of the damage. A close inspection of this photo, as well
as additional close-ups, that we have viewed, provides an exceptional
opportunity to perform macrofractography analysis ninety-five years
after the fact. It's amazing what evidence can emerge if you look hard
enough.

First, in the bottom of the photo there is considerable bending of
the plates around the hole—very uncharacteristic of brittle-type fracture and an observation ignored by the DREA/CANMET study. Note
that a large number of rivet holes are empty, implying that the rivets
may have failed before the steel. Reports of the physical damage from
the incident include a mention of a triangular piece of hull that fractured into the ship. This would be consistent with a high strain-rate
impact-causing fracture and then progressively slower deformation as
the two ships pressed together, causing bending instead of cracking.

Plate 10 (bottom) is another 1911 photograph taken during inspection by Harland & Wolff. It reveals a cross-sectional view along
the edge of the plate that was broken during the *Olympic–Hawke* collision. Next to it is the plane view of the same plate. In both there is
evidence of 45° angles of fracture around the rivet holes and a lot of
plate thinning near the region of failure—all characteristic of ductile-
type fractures. These cracks may have been straight, but they were not
brittle.

With evidence such as this, the case for 100 percent brittle fractures becomes highly questionable. The argument is too tempting given the following facts:

- Presence of small amounts of ductility is found on fracture surfaces even at ice water temperatures.
- Images show transgranular, not intergranular fractures, thus eliminating sulfur embrittlement as a factor.
- Data show that sulfur is tied up as MnS particles, which are positioned within the grains and, therefore, not causing problems at the grain boundaries.
- Underwater footage and photographic evidence show that the *Titanic* steel's fracture behavior is rate sensitive.
- A large variation in microstructure and fracture behavior is evident among the hull plates.

Considering all these observations, Foecke, in his initial report from the 1996 investigation, suggested that the steel might have behaved in a brittle nature in the ice-cold temperatures, more likely contributing to the splitting of the ship at the surface than during the initial collision.

At the time, this evidence stirred enough reasonable doubt to suggest further investigation, because the exact loading rate on *Titanic*'s steel during the collision with the iceberg was not really known. Time to rewind, consider the basic facts that have been extracted about the collision and look for more insights:

- The collision was not felt by most passengers.
- Those who did feel it described it using the "glancing blow" portrayal: "A slight shock," "It seemed as though something was rubbing alongside of her, at the time," "No shock and no jar; just a grating sensation," "there was a kind of shaking of the ship and a little impact," "I did not feel the impact at all," "It did not wake me up. It gave just a little vibration," "There was just a small motion, but nothing to speak of."
- The ship was moving at a speed of 22–22½ knots.

- It's possible that the iceberg was a barely moving mass of approximately 100,000 tons, but there are no real data about the geometry of the collision or the shape of the part of the iceberg involved in actual contact with the ship.
- In fact, despite nearly a century of research, researchers are not even sure where on the ship the iceberg hit.

With the facts presented, does it appear that the Charpy impact test used in previous studies is the best representation of the conditions of the collision? Recall, the test involves hitting a notched rectangular bar with a big hammer. The hammer swings on an arm that is about three feet long and reaches a speed of about 20 miles per hour at the bottom where it hits the sample. The stress concentration of the

Now, in all fairness, having ourselves been through media interviews with reporters of various integrity, we cannot ascribe all the statements in the *Popular Mechanics* article directly to the researchers. In fact, one scientist at CANMET absolutely refuses to discuss his work because it has been so misconstrued in the media. On the other hand, defenders of the DREA/CANMET "brittle steel" theory have used the results of their study to justify additional work at DREA on the toughness of modern ship steels, ultimately putting the scientists' objectivity into question. Many, many theories have been put forth regarding *Titanic*'s exact sinking scenario, most of them drudging up circumstantial evidence, combined with detailed reinterpretations of 1912 testimony. While most researchers, historians, and *Titanic* aficionados will do no more than simply gaze at her remnants, we have spent ten years characterizing the structure, strength, and chemistry of the materials that made up the ship. This is the additional evidence that will not let us dismiss the sinking as simply a case of brittle steel.

notch is aimed in the direction of the hammer swing, so the amplifi-
cation of the stress is at a maximum and all the energy of the swinging
hammer is dumped directly into the tip of the crack. The Federal Railroad Administration has stated that they consider Charpy a good test
for steels being loaded in a railroad-switching yard, where cars nor-
mally come to a dead stop in a collision from 15 to 20 miles per hour.
Certainly not "a little vibration."

From this perspective, the Charpy test seems to be a rather poor
representation of a steel ship/iceberg collision that most people barely
felt. If anything, cracks or stress concentrations that might be on the
face of the hull wouldn't be loaded so directly by an iceberg's glancing
blow, but they would experience a slow loading as the side of the ship
flexed inward under the pressure of the iceberg. Looking at it in this
way makes the Charpy test appear too severe to represent the events
of that night and suggests that knowing something about the rate-
dependent cracking behavior of these steels could be very important in
deciphering this data.

Fortunately tests are available that measure a material's fracture
toughness at slow loading rates, possibly more akin to those experienced that night, which are much more controlled and standardized.
An example is a slow three-point bend test, in which a sharp notch is
made in the sample and it is loaded to failure by bending it between
three pins. Measurements are made of applied load, the loading rate,
the temperature, and the size of the crack as it grows. Combining all
these results provides a measurement for the fracture toughness of the
material at different temperatures.

To test the "low fracture toughness" hypothesis, Foecke performed a slow three-point bend test on six samples of *Titanic* hull steel,
three at room temperature (25°C) and three at 0°C. The data demon-
strated that the hull steel was by no means a brittle material. In fact,
the results show indisputably that *Titanic* hull steel is a very tough material under slow loading rates, with fracture toughness values ranging
from 49 to 55 MPa-m$^{1/2}$ at 0°C. To put these numbers into context: a
typical glass has a fracture toughness of about 0.1 MPa-m$^{1/2}$, while
metal alloys can range from ten to hundreds of MPa-m$^{1/2}$.

These results seem to prove that the steel was not of inferior quality—it had sufficient fracture toughness, well within typical *modern* fracture toughness values, even at ice-brine temperatures. This is tangible confirmation that the fracture behavior of *Titanic* steel was rate sensitive, possessing ductile qualities at slower loading rates and brittle qualities at fast loading rates.

It appears that both the DREA/CANMET and University of Missouri studies fell into the same trap: that Charpy impact results were the critical measure of the steel's behavior. In addition, DREA/CANMET made the additional error of running two tests on a single sample and extrapolating this to the whole ship. The piece they worked on, as shown in the photo from the KarisAllen *Popular Mechanics'* article, had fractured surfaces all around its edges. This means that it was cracked out of the center of one hull plate and found lying in the debris field. Scientists studying a failure would call this a "self-selected" sample. That is, if you hit a structure hard enough, a piece of the worst-quality material will be the most likely to fall off. It is highly probable that this sample came from a hull plate at one extreme end of the steel quality "distribution curve" and was not at all representative of the ship, only of how bad things could be.

Assume for the moment that the loading rate was too slow to fracture the shell plating, that it was slow enough to be more similar to its description among passengers—a bumping scrape along the starboard side. If the iceberg was too soft to cut the steel open and the steel did not shatter because it was cold, then what else? How did the damage to the hull occur?

Consider the hull damage found using sonar imaging during the 1996 expedition. Whether the six intermittent tears in the hull were the result of the collision or impact of the hull with the ocean bottom as has been theorized, the damage appears to line up with riveted seams. During the 1998 expedition, investigators were able to see with the naked eye the largest opening on the starboard side, an opening that corresponded exactly to the location of survivor Fireman Barrett's torn seam in Boiler Room No. 5. The researchers gazing via the ROV *Magellan* attested to seeing what appeared to be empty rivet holes, just like those in the *Olympic/Hawke* collision in plate 10.

A clue to the answers may lie in how rivets are designed to work and how they were loaded during the collision with the iceberg. Rivets on skins, whether on the *Titanic*, an airliner, or a canoe, are meant to hold two large flat plates together against a uniform pressure being applied to the surface. The pressure can be water, air, or vacuum, but the important point is that the pressure is uniform. When the pressure is uniform, the rivet is loaded in shear (perpendicular to the rivet shaft), since flexing the plates in or out forces them to slide against one another, pulling the rivet heads in opposite directions. On the other hand, if a riveted skin is loaded at one single point, the corresponding rivets are loaded along the shaft in tension. Then, the ends begin to stretch apart as one side of the joint is pressed in, and the other side is not.

Rivets generally perform much less efficiently in tension than in shear, so point loads, like an iceberg hitting a hull, would put the rivets into situations for which they are *not* best suited. As a result, the quality of the rivet materials and how well they were installed become much more important to how they perform. In the investigations that followed the Versailles railway accident of 1842, the collapse of the Basse-Chaîne suspension bridge in 1850, the sinking of the *Royal Charter* in 1859, and the 1878 Tay Bridge disaster, the quality of the wrought iron came under scrutiny.

Here's an experiment to illustrate the different loads on a rivet. Hold your hands out in front of you, such that the fingers of your right hand are on top of the fingers of your left hand, palms down, like a hull lap joint that you are looking at edge-on. Put a pencil between your fingers through your lap joint. Now imagine the iceberg pushing down on your left hand only and, thus, on one side of your joint. How is the pencil being pulled? In tension. Now imagine water pressure on both of the backs of your hands, pushing them down the same (do not let your elbows move—they are sitting on beams). How is the pencil loaded? It tips sideways, showing that it is in shear.

Is it possible that the rivets, not the steel plates, were the weak link in the ship's structure, failing under the collision load and causing the opening of the ship's plates? Of course, rivets will fail in any structure that is loaded past its design limits. So is there something particular to the rivets in the *Titanic* that contributed to the sinking? Historic photographs, images of the wreck site, Barrett's testimony, and discrepancies in the brittle steel theory amount to a definite, undeniable "maybe." The investigation now leads to a close examination of the rivets that held the *Titanic* together.

CHAPTER 11

DOES THE ANSWER LIE WITH THE RIVETS?

*It may not be out of place to remind ourselves that
a steamer is designed for the purpose of carrying
human lives and merchandise across the ocean, and,
what is more, of carrying them safely, so that surely
her first qualification should be that of being able
to easily withstand the severe and continuous stresses
to which we know she will be subjected.*

—*Transactions of the North-east Coast Institution
of Engineers and Shipbuilders*, 1903

I t is the our belief that the evidence presented shows conclusively that the steel used for the hull plates on the *Titanic* were state of the art and had enough strength and toughness to resist cracking during the impact with the iceberg. If the steel possessed sufficient toughness and met the design parameters of 1912, could what was holding the plates *together*—the rivets—be to blame? This chapter details the thought process and the data behind the newest scientific theory to explain what may have happened on the night of April 14, 1912.

Recap of the Facts

Let's collect the facts established thus far that point to rivet failure as the cause of the hull openings.

How the Ship Was Built

Recall that the *Titanic* was assembled using some 3 million rivets, both hand and hydraulically driven. They were made of both wrought iron and steel. The single quality-control test used to determine if the rivets were acceptably installed was a tap with a hammer—if the rivet gave off a clean "ring" it passed, if the sound was a dull "thud," the rivet was drilled out and another driven in. Harland & Wolff's building specifications required that the three-fifths length (the central 60 percent) of the hull be completed with steel rivets, while the outer fifths should be built with wrought iron rivets.

Harland & Wolff designed the riveting of the ship this way due to time, strength, and financial considerations. Wrought iron rivets were easier to drive into the plates, making them cheaper to install, and the material did not need to be tested prior to usage to satisfy regulations. In cramped locations, such as the bow and stern, where the hydraulic riveter could not be used to install steel rivets, bashers could squeeze in and get the job done by hand with iron.

Titanic's shell was triple riveted (and sometimes up to quintuple riveted) over the three-fifths length, where hydraulically driven steel rivets were used. Doubly riveted seams, formed from the wrought iron rivets, were utilized in the bow and the stern. Doubly riveted seams had been used since the mid-1800s throughout the entire ship until 1885, when Lloyd's required triply riveted seams over a considerable amount of the hull, where the ship must resist the highest stresses. From the testimony and the flooding scenario, it appears that the impact with the iceberg occurred in a region of the ship constructed from doubly riveted seams, formed from hand-installed, wrought iron rivets.

Historical Evidence

On September 20, 1911, the RMS *Olympic* collided with the HMS *Hawke* off the coast of the Isle of Wight. The photographs of the damage reveal a 40-foot hole in her side toward the stern. Magnification of these photos reveals dozens of empty rivet holes, suggesting that the rivets failed during or because of the collision, maybe even prior to some of the hull plating.

Clues from the Collision

Fireman Barrett testified at the Mersey Inquiry that "water came pouring in two feet above the stokehold plate; the ship's side was torn from the third stokehold to the forward end. . . . About two feet from where I was standing." He was standing two feet from the side of the ship, and he survived to tell the world about it. Barrett's testimony confirms that the damage could have been no more than a thin gash or he wouldn't have withstood the force of the water. Sonar imaging from the 1996 expedition confined the damage to regions along parted seams, the largest of which is consistent with the location specified by Barrett's eyewitness testimony. Further examination of the openings during the 1998 expedition revealed what appeared to be empty rivet holes surrounding Barrett's tear. This is consistent with damage that is a thin gash, but not through the plates. Instead, it suggests that the damage may have occurred when seams opened. These pieces of evidence naturally lead to an examination of the quality and performance of the rivets that held *Titanic* together—were they up to the task?

What We Know About the Material

Remember that in the late nineteenth and early twentieth century, wrought iron was produced using the *puddling* process, a method requiring a skilled worker to agitate a molten pool of iron and slag constantly in order to produce a mix with consistent properties. Puddling required constant stirring but allowed for quick refining of the wrought iron. This method, however, was difficult work and made the result very dependent on the skill of the puddler working the molten charge. Quality, therefore, varied from batch to batch and puddler to puddler, with each individual order formed and rolled separately, meaning that large structures like the *Titanic* contained thousands of pieces of wrought iron that were all slightly different.

Revelation

In 1997, after completing his tests on the hull plate steel, Foecke decided to take a cursory look at two rivets from *Titanic*, salvaged during the 1996 Discovery Channel expedition. The hull steel debate was still raging at that point, but his slow three-point bend test results had definitively shown that the steel was by no means brittle under slow loading conditions. The other remaining culprit was the rivets, as yet untouched. Metallographic analysis required their careful preparation—cutting them in half using a diamond-blade saw; mounting them in a hard, transparent material known as epoxy; and then polishing them to a flawless mirror finish.

The results were no less than astounding. Using an optical micro-

---

Carrying a *Titanic* Rivet Around

In the course of giving talks about the *Titanic* to schools around the Washington, DC, area, Foecke found himself quite often with a bulkhead rivet in his pocket. The *Titanic* was a great topic to use to get kids thinking about science, with the movie having just been released and most kids familiar with the basic details of the tragedy. Bringing along a piece for the kids to see and touch was always the highlight of the visit. The investigation had centered on the "brittle steel theory" for so long that no one had even considered rivets yet. Little did Foecke realize that the piece of metal rattling around in his pocket for eight months would prove so crucial a piece of evidence.

scope, sections of the rivets were imaged and the wrought iron microstructure was examined. The first rivet contained large, long stringers of slag that comprised over 9 percent of the total material. This is more than three times the normal, expected amount of slag in wrought iron or at least the expectation since people began measuring it. In fact, the second rivet had a slag stringer so large that it could be seen with the naked eye. But the most telling feature by far was the stringers that ran along the length of the rivet shaft, like a jumble of cables, which abruptly turned 90 degrees at the base of what appeared to be a missing head. Here was an example of a wrought iron rivet that contained too much slag, which was in the form of extraordinarily large pieces and whose head appeared to have popped off. Was there a connection?

In Victorian times, wrought iron was classified by the number of times it was refined; that is, extra processing meant better mechanical strength and ductility. The first study confirming this was published in 1857. By the mid-1800s, following a number of catastrophic structural disasters, scientists and engineers began to realize that wrought iron was very anisotropic (its properties vary with direction in the metal). They had rightly concluded that along the direction of the slag stringers the material properties were enhanced, making wrought iron tougher and more ductile, but that this didn't hold in the direction across the stringers.

Parallel to the direction of the slag stringers, the tensile strength is about that of a strong mild steel, while at right angles to this, the measured strength is significantly less. More strikingly, the ductility, which is one of two parameters generally specified in 1911 for the quality of wrought iron, is ten times lower across the slag stringers than along them. What this means is that wrought iron can stretch much further in the direction of the slag stringers than it can across them. The slag helps to strengthen the iron in one direction, while it can cause cracking, and eventually fracture, in the perpendicular direction.

The images of this bulkhead rivet sparked the beginnings of the "weak rivet theory." Figure 12a shows magnified regions within the rivet where the distribution of slag stringers follows the method of processing. Slag in the center is aligned parallel to the shaft of the rivet, following the extrusion direction during formation of the rivet bar. Near the top, the slag branches out evenly where the head would have been formed out of a section of the bar while still hot. At the bottom near the inner head, or point, the stringers turn a sharp right angle, the result of hammering the head into place in the bulkhead as the rivet cools. With this microstructure, the wrought iron would have been strong along the rivet shaft, but weak where the inner (hammered) head meets the shaft.

Figure 12a. A series of microscope images that show how the slag is reoriented when the final head is formed as it is being installed on the ship. Note the missing head at the bottom, and the direction of the slag fibers.

Figure 12b. A bulkhead rivet that has rusted,
and the internal stress has caused a piece of
the head to peel away.

A properly driven rivet contains a considerable amount of residual tensile stress, as described in chapter 4. This develops as the rivet cools and shrinks, clamping the two plates together. Residual stress decreases the amount of additional stress needed to "pop" a rivet during a collision. Once a rivet already contains a certain amount of stress, only a small amount of plate deflection (bending) is needed for a rivet to fail during an impact. Shipbuilders knew about these concerns by 1911; they just didn't know how to test for them. The presence of high stresses in the *Titanic* rivets can be seen in the badly corroded bulkhead rivet in figure 12b. The head of the rivet has peeled apart and the slag stringers have spread, driven by the residual stresses in the head, as the iron rusts away.

Nineteen *Titanic* rivets of the forty-eight studied are missing a head. Many of those were found on the ocean floor, separate from their steel plating, and therefore may very well represent the weaker rivets of the collection. On the other hand, five hull rivets were retrieved from the Big Piece and four more came from a riveted bulkhead section, fully intact and still doing their job. The million-dollar question is whether we can differentiate between those that failed and those that didn't by examining their structure under the microscope.

An important point to mention is that not all rivets need exhibit these undesirable characteristics for the rivets to have played a role in the sinking. If a load from the iceberg impact were borne by the rivets of a joint at the edge of a plate, failure of a small fraction of the rivets (for whatever reason) would transfer this load onto the remaining in-tact rivets like a domino effect. This load transfer would occur mainly onto the rivets immediately next to the failed ones. This could bring the stress level in these neighboring rivets to the failure level and propagate the failure of the joint, even if the neighboring rivets are of standard quality.

After Foecke's initial findings, McCarty, along with Professor Timothy Weihs, at Johns Hopkins University, joined in the efforts, and for her doctoral research, they began the forensic analysis to char-acterize the remaining *Titanic* rivets—looking at what they were made from, what the quality was like, and how strong they really were. This also meant comparing the rivets with their steel counterparts, as well as with other wrought iron samples made during roughly the same time period.

PROBING FOR CLUES

The Search for Slag

The first order of business was to find out how much slag was ac-tually in the recovered wrought iron rivets and to determine what that slag looked like (for example, to see if there were enormously long stringers or small, spherical blobs). Using optical microscopy, the mi-crostructure within the rivets was examined. Thousands of digital im-ages were taken over each rivet and pieced together in order to create a mosaic. Digital image analysis provided information about the size and shape of each slag particle in the rivets. In total, over forty-six thousand digital images were taken and analyzed.

The results for thirty-one rivets revealed a big variation in the amount of slag present. Data from tens of thousands of images showed that a *Titanic* wrought iron rivet contained an average of as little as 1.1 percent and as much as 12.8 percent slag, depending on which rivet was studied. With an average value of over four times the normal slag content, the results were significant. Rivets were full of poorly mixed, abnormally large slag stringers, which created small regions in the heads and shaft that contained as much as 20 to 40 percent slag. With uneven mixtures in a material like this, there will always be localized differences in properties, making weak regions more likely to fail when highly stressed.

Comparing the *Titanic* wrought iron quality to other metals of the day is difficult, as most of it has rusted away. Thankfully, small amounts in various places around the world still remain, and they have proved useful for the rivet studies. A comparison with nineteenth- to twentieth-century wrought iron from England, Northern Ireland, Scotland, Germany, and the United States indicated that the poorer quality *Titanic* rivets contained two to four times as much slag as their international counterparts, with up to 85 percent of it in particles that were longer than 1 millimeter. This evidence suggests that the *Titanic* wrought iron stock was not worked for a sufficient puddling time (not enough time to mix it well) and at too low of a temperature (not enough heat to squeeze out the excess slag easily) to refine the slag stringers into more consistently spherical-shaped, smaller particles. Also, the unusually large amount of total slag would suggest that the puddler was not careful about the amount of slag he left in the mix.

Steel rivets were found in the portholes, some bulkheads, and the hull. Of the six hull rivets that have been salvaged (identified by their size or location), five are steel and one is wrought iron. The five steel rivets are those retrieved intact from the Big Piece, while the wrought iron hull rivet is, in fact, only a head, breaking along the shaft before its recovery from the wreck site. The wrought iron hull rivet contained a whopping 9 percent slag.

Figure 13 compares the microstructures of typical *Titanic* wrought iron and *Titanic* rivet steel. The images reveal two distinctly different materials. The wrought iron on the right shows large stringers of slag that indicate some kind of rolling or extrusion during processing and a definite strong direction in its properties. The majority of slag particles in the wrought iron were larger than 1 millimeter in length; that's about the size of a grain of sand—large enough to be seen by the naked eye. By contrast, the steel contains small, spherical impurities of manganese sulfide and iron oxide, less than 15μm in size, dispersed evenly like tiny speckles in granite, and its properties are much more isotropic (similar in all directions).

 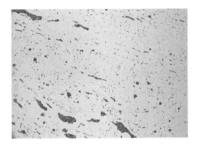

Figure 13. Direct comparison of a typical *Titanic* mild steel rivet (left) to a typical *Titanic* wrought iron rivet (right). Photo copyright Jennifer Hooper McCarty, Ph.D. diss., The Johns Hopkins University.

The construction blueprints for the *Titanic* required hydraulically driven steel rivets in the amidships section, the portion of the ship that feels the highest stresses when riding large waves. Even by the late nineteenth century, engineers and naval architects knew that steel offered a distinct advantage over wrought iron as a building material, mostly because of its higher strength. At the same time, some engineers were beginning to realize that slag inclusions (whether in iron or steel) were a double-edged sword—their presence increased the strength of the wrought iron but also acted as sites for catastrophic cracking and failure. In 1909, three years before *Titanic's* completion, an article by the International Association for the Testing of Materials was published in the magazine *Engineering*, calling for "further attention . . . to the microscopic appearance of some typical forms of slag enclosures taken from objects which had failed in service as results of an excessive quantity of these enclosures."

Every single *Titanic* rivet studied, both wrought iron and steel, exhibited particles that were reoriented when the inner head was formed during installation on the ship. Apparently, however, they were not at all the same in the way they performed. In total, seventeen of the eighteen wrought iron rivets examined were missing their heads, while all but two (both small porthole rivets) of the seventeen steel rivets retained both heads within their structure. What can this tell us about the strength of each type of rivet during the collision?

Mechanical Testing

The only way to determine the variation in strength and ductility of the *Titanic* rivets was to test them using a tensile testing machine. Very small dog-bone-shaped samples were cut from both the *Titanic* and the non-*Titanic* comparison material and polished until smooth. Before testing, each sample was examined using the optical microscope in order to study its microstructure. Specimens were loaded (pulled at both ends simultaneously) along the direction of slag stringers or perpendicular to them until they broke in half, and their ultimate tensile strength and ductility were calculated. A total of forty-three wrought iron and fifteen steel specimens were tested.

The tensile testing results revealed what was suspected: when wrought iron is loaded perpendicular to the slag stringers, it is an average of 20 percent weaker and nearly four times *less* ductile than along the slag stringers. What this means is that wrought iron pulled across the large slag stringers will always be weaker and will fracture earlier than when it is pulled along the slag stringers.

Examination of the broken pieces after failure of the sample confirmed that the higher slag content, and especially the presence of large slag chunks, was responsible for low ductility and lower tensile strength. Combine this result with observations that show large slag stringers lying at the junction of the rivet heads and the shaft, and we begin to see a problem. If during installation of the millions of wrought iron rivets, large slag pieces happened to wind up at the junction between the shaft and the head, the strength of the rivet would be compromised. This analysis provides a clear indication that hammering the heads during installation produced weaknesses in a significant portion of the *Titanic* wrought iron rivets near the junction of the head and shaft, not because of how they hammered them, but because of the quality of the wrought iron feedstock that came from the shop.

Contrast the wrought iron results with those of the *Titanic* rivet steel. According to McCarty's tensile test results on the rivet steel, it is 40 percent stronger and *three* times more ductile than wrought iron's weakest orientation. The steel has a tensile strength of over

1,400 psi higher than even that of the longitudinal wrought iron—the stronger orientation. By 1911, shipbuilders not only knew of the benefits to using steel rivets as opposed to wrought iron but were actually putting it into practice. Overall, the rivet steel boasts a significant advantage in strength and ductility, and of particular importance when compared to wrought iron, the properties of which do not vary with direction. The small MnS particles, common in steels even today, are nearly spherical in shape, so reorientation due to the riveting process has no effect. From this we can conclude that *Titanic* steel rivets would *not* be susceptible to the same weakening in the head during installation.

The rivet steel is stronger, tougher, and more ductile. Its properties aren't affected by a change in orientation, so the hammering process during installation would have no measurable effect on the strength of the rivet at the junction of the head and shaft. However, wrought iron has a strength close to that of steel in the longitudinal direction, and its ductility far outweighs that of steel. This is why historically made wrought iron was advantageous for use in chains, suspension cables, or anything feeling a tensile load in one direction. But (and this is a big but) its lower strength and extremely low ductility in the transverse direction means that only a very small amount of "stretching" can take place in that direction before it fractures.

So far, the results show a better understanding of how the two different rivet materials behave, but what happens when these materials are crafted into rivets and then faced with the additional stress of an iceberg collision? Can we reproduce the observed failures for each rivet? To take the analysis one step further, computer models of several types of rivets were created to determine just how rivets made from each material would react under the stress of a collision.

Taking the Computer to Task

To study the mechanical response of an entire hull rivet, we used a computer modeling technique known as finite element analysis (FEA) to complete McCarty's research. FEA works by mathematically slicing an object into many small pieces (called elements) throughout its volume. In this case, each rivet was split into 6,033 elements that needed to be "filled" with wrought iron or steel and then given their respective mechanical properties. Ultimately, the model was used to compare the critical conditions for the failure of a *Titanic* wrought iron rivet and a *Titanic* steel rivet under the loading they would experience during the iceberg collision. The computer-generated wrought iron rivet was a model that represented the microstructure and mechanical properties of the *Titanic* rivets studied: it was high in slag, had large stringers, and had a distinct variation in properties at the junction of the head and shaft. By contrast, the computer-generated steel rivet was composed of elements containing the properties of the rivet steel: it had small particles, was very well mixed throughout, and had properties that were the same in all directions from the head through the shaft.

The Rivet Geometry

Using a combination of geometries and measurements from the Board of Trade inspection notes, the 1911 *Encyclopedia of Shipbuilding*, and *The Shipbuilder* from 1911, the sizes and shapes of *Titanic* hull rivets were estimated. Although many geometries were examined, the least severe loading case was chosen for this comparison. If we simulate the least severe condition (sometimes referred to as the most conservative case) and we still see a significant difference between iron and steel, then more accurate conditions would surely produce an even greater effect. Since manual riveting caused the highest stresses in the head, both the wrought iron rivet and the steel rivet were instead modeled with a hydraulically driven "snap" point, which basically resulted in a semispherical-shaped head. The rivets were surrounded by steel hull plating with properties based on the mechanical testing completed on the hull steel in 1996.

Cooling Down a Red-Hot Rivet

The first step in the model was to mimic the cooling of the rivets during their installation at the shipyard, from the red-hot riveting temperature of the rivet boy's stove to the air temperature of the rivet once it was formed, installed within the ship's plates, and cooled. This will give an idea of the stress inside the installed rivet and will give a measure of how much more stress is needed to break it. Late-nineteenth- and early-twentieth-century sources describe the process of warming preformed rivets until red hot, prior to driving them into a structure. Iron glows at a very predictable color at each temperature and the somewhat vague red-hot wrought iron can translate to a range of temperatures, depending on its intensity. Cherry red is approximately 850°C, while blood red is considered to be about 550°C. Assuming that the rivet was at 800°–900°C when leaving the warming stove, by the time it was caught and driven into the steel plates, heat loss may have reduced its temperature to 600°C or even 400°C.

Plate 15 (bottom left) shows the stress that forms within a wrought iron rivet and a steel rivet after cooling from 400°C. Recall that as the

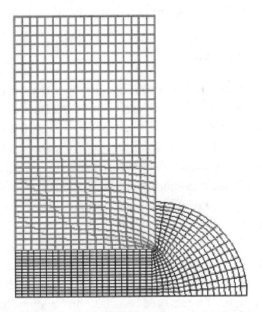

Figure 14. Diagram of the rivet (bottom) and hull plate (top) in the computer model used to simulate load on the rivet during the collision. Copyright Jennifer Hooper McCarty, Ph.D. diss., The Johns Hopkins University.

rivet cools, it shrinks and pulls the plates together, making a tight joint. Once the rivet is constrained by two 1½-inch-thick steel plates, it cannot contract, and what results is a residual stress. The same photo also shows that the high-stress regions build up within the heads because of this cooling. Yielding (permanent stretching) is already occurring in the entire head of the wrought iron rivet, and one region has even reached its ultimate tensile strength (UTS), meaning that it has theoretically broken there. However, the highest stress in the steel rivet, found in one very small area where the head meets the shaft, is still only 75 percent of the steel's UTS. Before the additional stress of the collision is applied, the "bad" wrought iron rivet has already begun to deform permanently, drastically reducing any additional load that it is able to bear before failure. Because of the low strength produced by the reorientation of slag within the head, the high stresses at the corners exceed the material's ultimate tensile strength. The mock collision has not even occurred yet, and it appears that this rivet is already having a hard time.

Creating the Collision

The second step in the model re-creates the strain on the rivet during the iceberg collision. Riveted joints are used on things that undergo a uniform pressure over their surface: aircraft wings, ship hulls, pressure boilers, and so forth. When used this way, as the pressure increases, the joint deforms sideways, putting the rivets into a sideways or shear stress. A unique feature of the iceberg collision with the *Titanic* is the *nonuniform* way in which it impacted the outside of the hull plates, but not the inside. This kind of "point load" would produce a tensile stress, pulling on the heads instead of shearing the shaft.

The computer model re-creates this tensile stress by pushing on the underside of the rivet head with the hull steel, imitating the load on the rivet. The goal was to see how far the head could be pushed before the stresses would exceed the rivet's UTS, the point that signals failure. The speed of the collision was slow, more akin to the observations of the passengers and crew, and amounted to only a few millimeters per second. Not surprisingly, the "bad" wrought iron rivet was the first to fail, unable to withstand even a 5-mm deflection of the hull plate as can be seen in plate 15 (bottom right). The cause? Poor ductility within the head. Five millimeters corresponds to an increase of only 7 percent in the rivet's length. But just like the tensile testing samples, the bad rivet head could stretch only millimeters before it began to fail as stresses mounted well above the UTS. On a ship that is 883 feet long and 92.5 feet wide, flexing as it pounds through the North Atlantic (never mind hitting an iceberg), having 5 mm (less than a ¼ inch) is not much stretch-to-failure as a safety factor.

Amazingly, McCarty's dissertation concluded that the steel rivet required five times higher load than the bad wrought iron rivet in order to fail. The steel's higher yield strength, tensile strength, and ductility allowed it to withstand not only large residual stresses on cooling but made it more suitable to bearing higher loads and to stretching farther before failure.

Building the Case

The high percentages and large pieces of slag within the *Titanic* wrought iron rivets are a significant forensic finding. The data from microscopy and mechanical testing show that this type of slag determines the weak points within the rivets. They are the points of low strength and ductility and, ultimately, failure if oriented in the wrong direction.

Images of poorly mixed wrought iron show that the feedstock was not heavily worked or extensively refined. Yet, as early as 1722, scientists recognized that it was the arrangement and size of the slag in wrought iron that determined its properties. Despite nineteenth-century knowledge that better properties resulted from longer times spent puddling or the number of times it was piled, tens of thousands of images reveal that the *Titanic* was made with wrought iron rivets full of ruinous chunks of brittle slag. At the same time, Harland & Wolff's choice to rivet the center three fifths of the ship's hull with steel rivets clearly suggests that they understood the advantage of using the new material over wrought iron in at least some situations. With many scientific studies identifying the critical differences between the two materials, it is safe to say that steel's superior properties were common knowledge in the early twentieth-century shipbuilding world.

Harland & Wolff ordered their wrought iron rivet bars in batches of 500 to 1,500 tons at a time, yet wrought iron manufacturers were limited by the amount that one puddler could mix. A weak puddler, then, was like a critical bottleneck in the assembly line on which the largest shipbuilders in the world depended. During the first decade of the twentieth century, D. Colville & Sons, one of Harland & Wolff's biggest suppliers, was forced to increase output and efficiency to meet the needs of the shipbuilding industry in a highly competitive market. As one scholar noted in the 1925 *Journal of the Iron and Steel Institute*, "There is no question that productivity would have been greatly enhanced had the Scottish works not had to cater to the often perverse requirements of marine and locomotive engineers." One can only imagine how many puddlers had a hand in mixing batches of wrought iron feedstock for the *Titanic*, how much experience each of them had, and how variable their results were.

While only established foundries were able to answer the large demands of shipbuilders, Harland & Wolff often made use of small, relatively unknown iron foundries, always ordering "Best" quality stock that had been tested in accordance with the requirements. As of 1901, however, iron bars were no longer tested by the Board of Trade surveyors, unless requested to do so. Using wrought iron rivets made in a number of foundries may have helped to speed up manufacturing, but it also would have sidestepped the prolonged testing period and additional charges required for steel rivets. Albeit a solution to mass production problems, this was not a model for consistency in quality.

Every *Titanic* wrought iron rivet that we examined revealed a reorientation of slag particles due to the installation process, when the rivet shank was hammered to produce an inner head. Engineers of the time repeatedly discussed the difficulties in knowing if an iron rivet was installed properly, especially when it was hand driven. On Day 30, in the final arguments of the 1912 Mersey Inquiry, the commissioner questioned Mr. Edwards regarding any regulations that controlled the hammering process.

> THE COMMISSIONER: Is there to be a Rule and Regulation
>   which says how many blows each rivet is to receive?
> MR. EDWARDS: No, my Lord.
> THE COMMISSIONER: He is to exercise his discretion,
>   then? . . . Are there any Rules or Regulations which
>   regulate the hammering in of the rivets?
> MR. EDWARDS: No, my Lord.
> THE COMMISSIONER: Then who is to judge whether that
>   work has been properly done? I am told that hammer-
>   ing is a most important part of riveting.
> MR. EDWARDS: There are certain tests—tests when they
>   are forged—as to the character of the rivets; there are
>   certain tests as to the kind of rivet holes; there are cer-
>   tain tests as to the flanges of rivets.
> THE COMMISSIONER: Are there any Rules or Regulations
>   as to the hammering of them in?
> MR. EDWARDS: No, my Lord.

When steel rivets would become brittle when heated too hot during installation, they would thus be recognized as bad and then replaced, but iron rivets could still be riveted without any indications of a problem, resulting in poor joints that were sometimes undetectable to shipbuilders. By the mid-1800s, builders knew that hand riveting required near perfect quality to produce a clean, tight joint, and so machine riveting quickly came into vogue as a faster, more accurate method. As a nineteenth-century shipbuilding text explains, the trickiness in monitoring the temperature and time events when using steel rivets necessitated quick and efficient hammering, making machine riveting ideal.

As mentioned earlier, in the end Harland & Wolff specified that the wrought iron rivets were to be hand-riveted, while the steel ones hydraulically riveted. This made the sturdiest part of the ship even sturdier by using the hydraulically driven, stronger steel rivets to doubly, trebly, or quadruply join the plates of the three-fifths length. On the other hand, paying riveters to bash wrought iron was cheaper, it was physically easier, and human beings could squeeze into the confined spaces at the bow and stern where a hydraulic riveter could not. In McCarty's dissertation, computer modeling showed that hand hammering of wrought iron produced stresses that were the closest to reaching failure within the head. The result was a ship that contained rivets with potential weaknesses that were highly stressed after hand hammering and cooling throughout the joints of the outer-fifths' length. Worse still, even then they might still pass the "tap" test.

In the case of the wrought iron rivets, we know very little about the men who were hand riveting them. We know that there was a massive influx of new unskilled employees at Harland & Wolff during the early 1900s, helping to fulfill part of their plan to train local unskilled countrymen during the ramp-up in processing. The company's meeting minutes mention potential incentives devised to encourage faster production and continued concern over a shortage of riveters at the yard. After the return of the *Olympic* to the gantry after the loss of her propeller, Harland & Wolff was under extreme pressure to complete construction of the world's two largest ships *simultaneously*. Considering the increased level of production, specifically during the years 1909–1911, quality-control procedures for wrought iron rivets, if they existed, may have been relaxed.

Now couple this information mentioned before with the fact that seventeen out of the eighteen *Titanic* wrought iron rivets were missing at least one head, and the photographic evidence shows empty rivet holes, as seen in plate 10, after the RMS *Olympic*'s collision with the HMS *Hawke*, first pointed out by Foecke in his 1998 NIST report. Sonar evidence from the 1996 expedition showed damaged seams within the outer-fifths' length of the bow. Eyewitness testimony suggests that most of the damage was within the outer-fifths length and highlights the direct observation of empty rivet holes corresponding to Barrett's opened seam. Harland & Wolff supposedly pulled out all the stops to build a technological masterpiece, following every regulation, and in most cases surpassing them. But the "unsinkable" ship sank in the North Atlantic and sustained only a limited amount of damage—a series of six slits across the hull in areas where it was held together by hand-riveted, wrought iron rivets. All this suggests a common thread.

McCarty's studies on another Harland & Wolff ship, the SS *Arabic*, built in 1903, confirm a similar microstructure. The *Arabic* rivets contained nearly 16 percent slag in some regions and showed the same large, coarsely distributed stringers as those seen on the *Titanic* rivets. The reorientation of slag at the junction of the head and shaft is clearly visible. On August 19, 1915, the *Arabic*, en route to New York, was torpedoed and sank off the coast of Ireland. The *Titanic* rivets studied, no matter how small a percentage of the 3 million on the ship, do not represent an anomaly of the era.

The Final Step in the Investigation

Computer models, if you are not careful, can suffer from GIGO—garbage in, garbage out. Just because the model results fit the theory, does not necessarily mean that it is proven. Actually, to test the weak rivet theory, a riveted joint, manufactured under conditions similar to those that existed during *Titanic*'s construction, had to be tested. Unfortunately, getting a real sample from the wreck site is out of the question, both for logistical and preservation reasons. After ten years of investigation, we were able to do the next best thing—test a reproduction of the riveted joint, made possible by the filming of a National Geographic Channel *Seconds from Disaster* series episode entitled "Sinking of the *Titanic*."

The producers of the show put us in contact with Chris Topp, a blacksmith in Yorkshire, England, who is an expert in the reproduction of iron artifacts, and has displayed his skills on projects such as a replica five-hundred-year-old cannon from the *Mary Rose*. Through a series of conversations and specifications, we provided Topp with all the details necessary to create a double-riveted *Titanic* hull joint, namely, the spacing of the rivets, the geometry of the heads, the thick-

ness of the steel plates, and a request simply to use riveting best practices, as he understood them, for early-twentieth-century wrought
iron. Topp, who had Edwardian era wrought iron already available in
his shop, produced the riveted joint exactly to our specification, using
a double row of 1-inch-diameter rivets holding together two 1½-inch-
thick steel plates. Within a few weeks, the samples were in the laboratory and ready for testing (see plate 13, bottom). The samples were
loaded in a manner shown in plate 14 (top). The bottom was supported on steel blocks, representing a pair of structural ribs inside the
hull. The load came down from above, pressing on one side of the
rivet with a large steel mass driven by screws, representing the impact
load from the iceberg (see two lower photos of plate 14). The steel
plates began to bend and load the rivets in tension. Eventually the rivets failed, and produced very surprising results.

The total stretching of the rivet shaft was less than 2 percent, and
most of it seemed to have been taken up by the tearing of the head.
The geometry of the actual failure was of the greatest interest. For all
tests, the heads popped off the rivet shafts and left a fracture profile
that was remarkably similar to those from the *Titanic*.

During the stretching of the joint, another detail, which had not
previously been considered, became apparent. As the joint was pushed
inward, the bending of the plates actually did not put the rivets into
pure tension, but rather into a combination of tension and bending.
This brings into play another factor, discussed in chapter 10, namely,
the presence of stress concentrations. The corner where the head and
shaft meet is quite sharp, and the bending imposed on the rivet greatly
increased the stress at that point. This stress concentration was not a
detail that was included in the computer model, but is an important
factor that would have made it even *more* likely for the heads to pop
off the rivets under this unusual type of loading.

Experiments on the steel hull plating that were more appropriate
to the rate of the actual iceberg collision have put the brittle steel theory firmly to rest. The photographic evidence, the eyewitness testimony, the subsurface sonar results, and the expedition observations all
point in the direction of the rivets. Using extensive metallography, mi-

croscopy, mechanical testing, and computer modeling has revealed a metallurgical weak link, exacerbated by poor manufacturing, high variability in feedstock, and a shipbuilder's race to finish. Our investigation has shown that the quality of the wrought iron rivets installed in the bow is the most quantifiable factor in the iceberg damage to, and the loss of, the *Titanic*. Regardless of all the unsinkable features on *Titanic*, the ship had her own structural Achilles' heel. Just like every other riveted ship in history, the *Titanic* was only as strong as its weakest riveted seam.

It is time to synthesize the findings with the solid facts surrounding the night in question.

CHAPTER 12

THE COLLISION
SCENARIO

*It will never be known, now that the ship has sunk,
whether the immense impact involved any shearing
of rivets of the inner as well as the outer bottom,
and consequently the admission of water to many
compartments. Or did the ship in the first place
glide along the berg, or ultimately sheer off from
the berg?*

—*Engineering*, April 19, 1912

This chapter tries to answer the very questions posed by those 1912 engineers, grappling to understand the mechanics of what actually occurred that night. We have chronicled the technological advances that made the *Titanic* possible and have presented the history of events during her construction. We now have a solid understanding of the basic facts on the night of April 14, 1912, the eyewitness experiences, the location of flooding, as well as an insider's understanding of how the materials performed, how the ship was built, who had a hand in it, and how it was checked for performance and quality. As much as possible, what is known has been distilled from what is surmised or theorized. Along the way, evidence has been presented to refute many of the alternative theories floating around, at least those that are slightly plausible. Using analysis of key eyewitness testimony, the results of past forensic studies, and combining these with forensic studies on the hull steel and rivets, this chapter explains the most likely collision scenario that occurred that night. This is where the forensic science ends, and we venture into suppositions about what may have been probable, or even possible.

PROBABILITIES AND POSSIBILITIES

Conclusion #1: The brittle steel theory is wrong.

As shown through analysis of steel recovered from various locations on the wreck of the *Titanic*, as well as through photographic evidence of the damage to the *Olympic* due to her collision with the *Hawke*, the brittle steel theory is categorically wrong. The hull sample that was tested in Canada after its recovery in 1991 was already fractured on three sides and thus might have come from a particularly low-toughness hull plate. In any case, the mechanical test that was applied to analyze the toughness of the steel, the Charpy impact test, is a nonstandardized method used in the industry roughly to measure the toughness of steels—the test being too severe to replicate accurately the conditions of the collision. The photographic evidence of the damage to the *Olympic* that was cited to support the brittle steel claim was misconstrued, and an analysis of other photos from the collection clearly show high-speed ductile tearing of the hull plates. Foecke's mechanical tests of other hull steel recovered from the wreck, which were much more controlled, standardized, and performed under appropriate conditions, show adequate fracture toughness in the steel at ice water temperatures, fairly close to steels used to build bulk carrier ships today. The brittle steel theory does not stand up to close scrutiny and is wrong.

Conclusion #2: The wrought iron feedstock supplied to Harland & Wolff for the construction of the *Titanic* was not the highest quality available and would not have qualified as rivet-quality material.

Government records and surviving Harland & Wolff books verify that the company utilized numerous manufacturers to supply them with thousands of tons of material at any one time. The early twentieth century brought the age of the ocean liner to its fruition, meaning that Harland & Wolff were not the only ones who were scrambling to acquire the necessary feedstock. Both steel and iron manufacturers and shipbuilders dealt with the ramp-up in production however possible—bigger furnaces, widespread ore deposits, more employees, and numerous suppliers as necessary. Yet from hull plates to boilerplates and rivets to girders, every piece began as part of the charge in a forge's furnace, and in particular, for wrought iron that meant a size-limited, time-consuming process requiring hard manual labor by many different people. Since the manufacture of wrought iron was an apprentice-learned handmade process, it was simply impossible to scale up production if there was a shortage, without having quality suffer. The first question that a forensic investigator will ask when studying a disaster is, "What changed recently?" In this case, it was the ramp-up in production and the onslaught of workers and suppliers to fill the shipyard's needs. The forensic evidence supports the supposition that a significant amount of the wrought iron provided was fabricated incorrectly, whether worked too little or at the wrong temperature or both.

Conclusion #3: Installation of wrought iron rivets from variable, and often inferior, feedstock would result in a distribution of different seam strengths along the hull.

This conglomeration of wrought iron feedstock, produced from multiple sources and manufacturers, was formed into rivets and installed in batches by the hands of different riveting teams, different heater boys, and different rivet bashers. The result was most definitely an increased level of variability in quality and workmanship among the rivets on the ship. The presence of substandard rivets within a seam would naturally result in an array of riveted seams along the hull of questionable quality: variability in rivet strengths produces variability in riveted *seam* strengths. Any compromise in the strength of a riveted joint resulted in a region of *Titanic*'s hull that was more sensitive to external loads. Even in modern-day failure analysis of riveted structures, the main failure mechanisms usually depend on the strength of the riveted seams. Based on the metallurgical data, when the *Titanic* set sail, it is highly likely that some of her rivets were already near their material's ultimate tensile strength, creating riveted joints with insufficient strength to withstand any additional load.

Conclusion #4: The installed substandard rivets could not have been detected unless they were loose after they cooled, since the quality control and certification procedures used at the time of construction were insufficient to the task.

If the variability in feedstock and installation methods produced rivets that varied in their microstructure and chemistry, then their mechanical strength would have varied as well. During the formation of a rivet head over the outside of a plate, the strain in the rivet material increases up to 20 percent where the head material comes in contact with the metal plate. This is especially high at the corner junction between the head and the shaft. For those rivets that contained too much slag in large stringers, their microstructural irregularities would only have increased this highly stressed region, making the rivets extremely fragile to any additional stress. If any of these rivets had been poorly riveted (hammered off center or heated too hot, for example), it would only add to this weakness. Any combination of these factors would have resulted in the presence of weakened rivets throughout the ship. As is already apparent from the limited quality control used in early-twentieth-century shipbuilding, these rivets would have most likely gone unnoticed. With those rivets made of wrought iron, the inspection methods used in 1911 would have made it next to impossible to detect a rivet embrittled through installation at too high a temperature or one weakened by the presence of too much slag,

Conclusion #5: The nature of the impact between the hull and the ice (bumping, scraping over a significant distance) was very unusual and happened to stress the rivets in a manner that exposed their weakness.

Ice-ship collisions are extremely complex, and despite thousands of collisions in the last century, scientists still have difficulty in predicting the stress of an iceberg encounter, especially at higher speeds. In the case of *Titanic's* encounter, several things are undisputable. First, the collision lasted for a number of seconds, based on witness descriptions. Passengers and crew recalled the feeling as "a long grinding sound," "a noise like a cable running out," "a trembling of the ship"— all clearly indicative of a slightly prolonged, rather than instantaneous, impact. It wasn't a split-second bang that threw passengers across the floor, but an eerie rumbling that tossed them in their beds or caught them off balance on the decks. Second, this drawn-out, bumping collision of ice with the hull produced a nonuniform load along the ship's side.

During the collision, decreased pressure between the iceberg and the ship caused them to be sucked toward one another again and again, fluctuating between the momentum of each impact that threw them apart and the forces that pulled them together. Since the two bodies were roughly a factor of ten different in mass, the force of the ship running alongside the iceberg would have caused the iceberg to move as well. Both ship and iceberg were displaced by the impact, and this bouncing effect would result. *Titanic's* collision with the iceberg was not the catastrophic collision imitated by the Charpy impact test from the brittle steel theory, but a series of nonuniform, poking, prodding blows that served to disperse the force of the impact along the riveted seams of the ship—in effect, the weakest links. Physically speaking, the longer the time over which the force is distributed, the more spread out the impact will be. This translates to the likelihood of rivets failing and seams opening, rather than steel fracturing mid-plate, as would be the case in a high-intensity, head-on collision, where the impulse, and therefore the force of the crash, is confined to a much shorter time.

Conclusion #6: *Titanic* experienced significant damage to her starboard bow due to the collision with the iceberg. This collision loaded the riveted seams in a manner contrary to their design, thus opening them to the sea. She may have also damaged her bottom, but the evidence is inconclusive.

There are two possible theories as to the geometry of the collision: the first is sideswiping the starboard bow, supported by eyewitness accounts and the results of two scientific expeditions to the wreck site, or the second, grounding the front portion of her bow on an underwater spur, a newer theory backed by critical variations in the 1912 eyewitness testimony. In either scenario, the iceberg loaded, or effectively "tested," the riveted seams directly at intermittent points along the starboard side or continuously along the bottom under the ship's weight. Either way, the *Titanic* suffered mechanical loading of the riveted joints in the outer-fifths length of the starboard bow where the wrought iron riveted seams were located.

As mentioned, riveted seams are designed to be loaded uniformly over the surface. In this way, the rivets are loaded in shear, and the joint is usually stronger than the plates they hold together. However, if the joint is loaded nonuniformly, as with a sharp impact, something quite different and unintended happens. As the iceberg pushed one plate of a joint inward, the other plate remained stationary, or deflected in the opposite direction, prying at the rivet heads that held the joints together. The result was a complex combination of high tensile stresses and bending. These tensile stresses developed in the rivets following each subsequent load applied to *Titanic*'s hull. This type of contact between the iceberg and the hull would stretch the weaker rivets beyond their limits (which wasn't very far, as we saw).

The only force keeping the plates together was the integrity of the rivet heads. Unfortunately, because loading a joint nonuniformly actually puts leverage on the rivet heads (see plate 15, top), the regions around the joint were the most highly stressed places in the impact area. As each rivet failed, the load it was carrying was transferred to the neighboring rivets. These rivets, which may or may not have been of suitable quality, were certainly not designed to see an instantaneous jump in load that could be as high as 20 percent. Whether poorly made or downright perfect, the neighboring rivets were then forced to share the additional stress but were unable to withstand it for long. As they failed, a domino effect ensued, distributing the increased loads to other rivets until the damaged seams began to open up.

The grounding theory of David G. Brown suggests that the most significant damage occurred to the double bottom of the ship when *Titanic's* bow ran aground on the ice. As the bow hinged on the ice, it was flexed upward, causing significant strains along the starboard side seams, resulting in rivet failure. As will be discussed later, Brown's assertion that only a bottoming of the ship on an underwater ice feature can explain the sinking does not hold up to rigorous analysis. The bottom of the ship may indeed have suffered damage during the collision, but there is simply insufficient eyewitness or physical evidence to support a claim that damage to the double bottom was the fatal wound to the ship. The analysis relies too heavily on a selective reading of the inquiry testimony and hand-waving, unsubstantiated mechanical engineering arguments.

Conclusion #7: Riveted joints are not a fail-safe design when loaded in the manner that occurred during the collision with the iceberg. Once failure started in a seam, it spread along the joint.

In theory, riveted joints are "balanced" designs in which all different, possible types of failure occur simultaneously under loading that is high enough to tear them apart. Riveted joints are designed to be stronger than the plates they join. Yet, as a practical matter, this very rarely happens. In the *Titanic's* case, the unusual loading by the iceberg collision caused the failure to be a combination of the weakest rivets failing in tension just under the rivet head, and then the remaining rivets failing one by one until the seams "unzipped."

Although it sounds like a scenario unique to the *Titanic*, this mechanism is all too common in riveted structures. In a finite-element analysis of the explosion that sank the USS *Maine* in 1898, highly localized stresses developed around the rivet heads and steel plating until the riveted seams unzipped without any appreciable stretching, and the rivet heads failed and pulled through the plate material—a result that was supported by photographic evidence from the USS *Maine*'s wreck site. In 1945, the USS *Enterprise*, an aircraft carrier that served during World War II, suffered popped rivets and opened seams after the impact of the engine of a Japanese suicide plane blew a 2- by 3-foot hole in her shell plating. In 1970, the USS *Wiltsie*, a World War II destroyer, was damaged while in port when high winds battered her against the destroyer *John W. Thomason* and resulted in the opening of riveted seams. And, of course, it is hardly surprising to hear suggestions that the Harland & Wolff ship *Arabic* may have sunk as a result of the failure of its riveted seams or that wreck surveillance indicates possible failure of riveted seams on the port side of *Titanic*'s sister ship *Britannic*.

During the British Inquiry, Mr. Roche, representing the Marine Engineers' Association, hinted at riveted seam failure as the source of flooding on the ship when he questioned Fireman Barrett about the water coming into Boiler Room No. 6. Unfortunately, Barrett could not offer any information on the subject.

> MR. ROCHE: But did it look as if it were a hole, and as if a
> hole had been made by something outside puncturing
> the bunker, or did it look as if a rivet had been started
> by the shock?
> BARRETT: That would be a question for an engineer.

A number of witnesses recalled water trickling through the ship's side, not enough to be considered continuous, but a steady pour onto the deck floors. This is consistent with the notion of seams that steadily bulged open as rivets failed, rather than a gaping hole produced by plate fracture, but it doesn't explain how so much water filled the ship so quickly. Whether the damage to the ship's starboard side was the only source for flooding is debatable.

Conclusion #8: At least some of the rivets would have failed no matter their quality or strength.

Rivets fail when loaded beyond their design capabilities, and some argue that even the best rivets would not have survived the impact. It is entirely likely that some rivets of normal quality would have failed during the impact of the *Titanic* with the iceberg, particularly at the very initial point of contact, where the loads on the ship and the stresses on the rivets would have been highest. Although there is no information regarding the shape of the portion of the iceberg that made the initial contact with the *Titanic*, it is reasonable to assume that any sharper protrusions would have broken off or dulled as the collision progressed. This implies that the initial impact would have been the most severe and probably would have broken at least some of the rivets in the hull.

Conclusion #9: If, on average, the wrought iron rivet feedstock had been of higher quality, not as many seams would have opened to the sea, not as many compartments would have flooded, and the *Titanic* would have stayed afloat long enough for rescue ships to save more lives.

We now come to the most significant conclusion, and the one that has been logically supported throughout the analysis. The impact of the iceberg and the hull of the *Titanic* was a long, scraping, glancing blow that loaded the steel plates discontinuously from the point of first contact until the two masses parted ways. The collision would have been most severe initially, gradually growing lighter until it ended. Therefore, the riveted seams that held the hull plates together would have been loaded to different amounts depending on their location along the side. As the iceberg loaded the hull, it mechanically "tested" an unknown number of seams below the waterline, unknown because we have no idea of the shape or size of that part of the iceberg that came in contact with the ship. In addition, some of the seams outside those first six compartments would have been stressed by the iceberg during the collision. Under this load, the seams fabricated with subpar quality rivets would break, and the higher-quality rivet seams would hold. Since the beginning of the impact was harder, it would be more likely that a poor-quality seam would reach its failure load and break. But as the iceberg moved along the ship, the impact became weaker and weaker, and it became less and less likely that the seams would break under the reduced loading. At some point, the load of the iceberg was low enough so that none of the seams, regardless of quality, would have broken.

The manner in which the ship and the iceberg collided is fixed—it happened. The quality of the riveted seams is the variable in this analysis. As built, the ship experienced parted seams totaling about 12 square feet, distributed over the front six compartments. The number of compartments open to the sea would determine how fast the ship sank, which in this case caused the ship to sink in just under three hours. To reduce the rate of flooding would require a lower number of broken seams. If, on average, the rivets that made up the seams had been of higher quality, the seams that they formed would have been stronger. Stronger seams, on average, would have limited the length of damage along the ship's side, reducing the flooding and potentially eliminating the flooding of compartments further amidships. If, on average again, the rivet quality had been better, it is likely that the ship would not have suffered as much damage; the last seams that broke under the ever-lightening load might have held. Under this scenario, the ship would have taken more time to flood and sink. Since the nearest rescue ship, the *Carpathia*, was only two hours away, keeping the ship afloat an additional two to three hours would have allowed those forced to stay behind on the sinking ship to have been shuttled to the *Carpathia*, and many more passengers might have survived.

This analysis does not mean that the quality of the rivets was a determining factor as to whether the ship would have sunk. Any quality rivets would probably have failed under the load of the initial impact and opened a number of compartments to the sea, potentially dooming the ship to sink eventually, depending on the effectiveness of whatever heroic actions were taken by the crew or rescuers to save her. The analysis instead supposes that a better quality of the feedstock that went into the rivets would have changed the length of time of the sinking. If it sank just a little slower, the word "Titanic" would not have had its meaning permanently changed in the English language.

PART IV

THE REST OF THE STORY

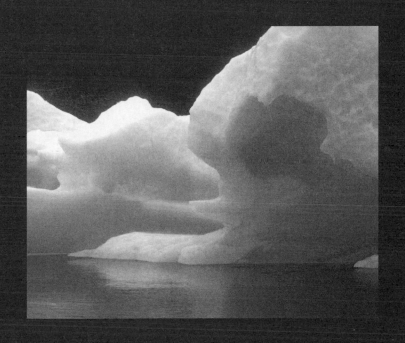

CHAPTER 13

OTHER TIDBITS YOU MAY HAVE HEARD ABOUT

For close to a century, stories of *Titanic*'s sinking, the biographies of passengers, details of life on the ship, and more, have infiltrated our common knowledge. This chapter provides a brief look at some of those other theories, stories, or urban legends that you may have heard about but never really questioned or maybe were just afraid to ask.

THE COAL BUNKER FIRE

THE COMMISSIONER: Did the fact that there was fire in that bunker in any way conduce to the collision as far as you know? Had it anything to do with it?

FIREMAN FREDERICK BARRETT: I could not say that.

THE COMMISSIONER: Do you think it had? Do you think that the fire had anything to do with this disaster?

FIREMAN FREDERICK BARRETT: That would be hard to say, my Lord.

THE COMMISSIONER: Very well; perhaps I am asking you a riddle.

—Excerpt from Day 4, British Inquiry

With the details we now know about *Titanic*'s steel, there is one more curious aspect of the puzzle to examine—the coalbunker fire in Boiler Room No. 5. Many have questioned the presence of a smoldering coal fire during the ship's journey as a potential player in the *Titanic*'s sinking. Their interest centers around the following: whether a coalbunker fire in the vicinity of the flooding caused damage to a bulkhead, weakening its ability to keep back the water, ultimately resulting in the flooding of the critical sixth compartment. What can science tell us? With mechanical and metallurgical analysis, it's possible to examine how prolonged heating by a coal fire would affect the properties of the steel. Did the coal fire have any verifiable effect on the sinking?

By the time that Fireman Barrett testified before the Board of Trade, it was already revealed that a fire had occurred in the forward coalbunker of Boiler Room No. 5 along the starboard side. He also recalled that while he was assisting the engineers below after the collision, a great wall of water rushed through the passageway between the boilers, sending him scurrying above decks for good. Had the bulkhead between Boiler Rooms No. 6 and No. 5 given way? On any normal steamship journey this would not have made much difference—when there was a fire, it was put out and the coal removed from the bunker. However, in this case, the ship in question sank, and to make matters worse, Barrett had witnessed water spewing in through an opening that spanned the bulkhead between Boiler Rooms No. 6 and No. 5—the same bulkhead that acted as a wall to the coal bunker.

Three witnesses testified that they recalled the fire in the coal bunker, which began in Belfast. Two of those witnesses testified that the bulkhead was damaged as a result.

> Fireman Charles Hendrickson: You could see where it had been red hot; all the paint and everything was off. It was dented a bit.
>
> Fireman Frederick Barrett: The bottom of the watertight compartment was dinged aft and the other part was dinged forward.

The bulkhead would have been "dinged" because the heating of the steel plate would have caused it to expand. Since it was held tightly around its edges by rivets and angle iron attaching it to the hull and decks, this expansion could not happen in the plane of the plate, and it underwent a membrane instability. This is just a highly technical term for what is usually known as oil canning, where a sheet of metal has slack in it and can pop in and out like the lid of a can. The ding relieved the stress in the plate at a high temperature when it couldn't break loose from the edges. When it cooled, it would attempt to shrink back to its original size, but now would be dented. As a result, it would pull slightly on the rivets that held it to the hull and decks, but nowhere near enough to compromise the strength of the connections.

Despite their testimony, the commissioner saw little gain in pursuing any line of questioning regarding the fire. In his opinion, spontaneous combustion of coal was "by no means an unusual thing." Trimmer Thomas Dillon remembered the fire and their efforts to clear out the coal, but had little evidence to suggest that it was anything out of the ordinary. It is quite possible that there was nothing special about the fire in the coal bunker. However, the testimony of Fireman Hendrickson and Barrett was very consistent in its description of the damage to the bulkhead. From their words we can surmise the following:

A fire began smoldering in the forward coal bunker of Boiler Room No. 5 at some point around the ship's departure from Belfast. According to the two firemen, it took until Saturday to put it out, mostly because it required the removal of all the coal inside the bunker. In fact, the fire was not actually put out until the coal was removed. According to Barrett's testimony, water was used to try to extinguish the fire. It is possible that the bulkhead itself was heated to red hot, but no one actually claims to have seen it in that condition. Hendrickson alluded to the fact that it may have been red hot, while Barrett clearly insisted that there was a fire, not just heat. The bulkhead, which forms the side of the bunker, was damaged as a result—the paint had peeled off and it was warped.

The question is, did the coal fire weaken the bulkhead's atomic structure substantially, hastening its failure during the collision? To answer this, we'll use the clues from the 1912 testimony and a bit of metallurgical data in order to simulate the actual fire and determine what, if any, mechanical effect the fire had on the bulkhead.

Spontaneous Combustion and the Properties of Coal

Spontaneous combustion was, and still is, one of the most serious causes of coal fires, particularly with stored coal. Self-ignition usually begins in areas deep within the reserve of coal when it absorbs oxygen from the air. At about 150° to 300°F, the coal starts to give off small, but measurable, amounts of gas—aerosols, hydrogen, carbon monoxide, and carbon dioxide—which are precursors of combustion. As a result of the burning, heat is generated and the coal temperature begins to rise. Depending on the amount of combustible matter in the coal, once the temperature reaches about 750° to 850°F, the early stages of combustion, and eventually burning, begin.

High temperatures will hasten the reaction of coal absorbing oxygen, so it is no surprise that bunkers built next to boilers would catch on fire. In 1898 a U.S. Navy report warned that if "the bunker coal next to the bulkhead [is] kept at 120°F, any coal with a tendency to absorb oxygen will run a great chance of igniting within a few days." Coal fires on ships were, as the Board of Trade Commissioner stated, a very usual thing. Shipping lines were instructed to keep coal dry, to reduce its chance of oxidation, especially if the coal contained a lot of sulfur. This applied even to fighting the fire, when removal of coal was preferable to using water, since the moisture could cause a steam explosion. This is still the case today, in which water is only used to fight the fire as an absolute last measure.

The Facts

From the testimony, we are certain of the following:

1. There was a fire in the forward coal bunker of Boiler Room No. 5.
2. The fire was hot enough to cause damage, that is, mechanical deformation, in the bulkhead steel.
3. The fire began smoldering on Wednesday, April 2, and was put out on Saturday, April 11, by removal of coal and the use of water.
4. As a result, when the collision occurred on Saturday evening, the empty bunker allowed Barrett to see the damage to the side shell of the ship.

From our metallurgical analysis it is apparent that:

- The bulkheads were formed of mild steel with 0.2 percent carbon, 0.5–1.0 percent manganese, and a small amount of impurities, namely, sulfur and phosphorus. This is similar to modern 1018 steel, which has been studied extensively in the scientific literature.
- The bulkhead steel has a yield strength of 30,000 psi, has a UTS of 58,000 psi, and is tough at room temperature, as has been measured.

The Suppositions

Supposedly, the bulkhead steel became red hot, although it is not actually clear if Hendrickson saw this or not. He explained during his testimony that he wiped off the region and rubbed black oil on the warped area, which implies that it probably was not exceptionally hot. Red-hot steel would correspond to approximately 900°F. We know that thermodynamically, coal will burn at a constant temperature with a fixed oxygen supply. Assuming that there was no draft in the bunker, this correlates to about 750°F.

The problem here, though, is that if the steel was hot enough to glow red hot, the bunker would have lost a lot of coal, significant fumes would have been produced, and the draft would have increased. It is highly unlikely, considering the coal strike of 1912 and the resultant shortage, that the engineers would have allowed the fire to get so out of control. However, for the sake of a conservative argument, we will assume that the fire was hot enough to heat the steel to a glowing red-hot temperature—900°F.

The Metallurgical Picture

In addition to thinking about how the bulkhead mechanically deformed, it is important to consider what may have happened to the microstructure to weaken the steel after cooling. When this type of steel is heated to a red-hot temperature, the grains within it grow very, very slowly over time. As a result, the steel becomes softer and tougher. If the bulkhead steel simply increased in temperature and then gradually cooled over the period of nine days, there is no scientific reason to believe that its structure was weakened. In fact, very little would have changed at all.

However, if the bulkhead heated up to red hot and then it was hit with cold seawater, either during the collision or even by a stream of water from a hose, it would quench at some rate. If it cooled fast enough, a phase could form in the structure, known as martensite. Martensitic steel is extremely brittle and will fracture catastrophically under stress. But quenching from even our maximum estimate of 900°F would produce very little martensite. Therefore, under the circumstances, even if any martensite was formed, it is highly unlikely that it would have affected the low-temperature strength properties of the bulkhead. Bottom line: the coal fire probably had no effect on the sinking whatsoever.

BOTTOMING OF THE *TITANIC*

A theory advanced by Brown in his book *The Last Log of the Titanic*, as well as a research paper by Brown and Parks Stephenson on the website EncyclopediaTitanica.org, asserts that the *Titanic* was in fact damaged by the impact of the bottom of the hull with an underwater ice shelf on the iceberg. They claim that the damage to the starboard side of the ship was, in fact, produced secondarily—an effect of the bottom impact—and was not the key factor in the sinking. While the scenario we have proposed does not preclude damage to the bottom of the hull and thus does not make the theories exclusive to one another, we should examine the evidence that Brown and Stephenson advance to support their "grounding theory."

Brown and Stephenson refer to the "fact" that a sideswipe would whip people around, throwing them from their feet, using as additional evidence their own experience of running into a dock with a much smaller ship. The *Titanic* and the iceberg are not immovable objects like a dock secured to land. Their masses are within a factor of 10 to 20 of each other. They are supported in a liquid and are far from fixed in one position. During the collision the side of the ship would crush part of the iceberg and, as a result, would deflect inward like a spring, considerably cushioning the blow. If you think of the knobby, rough side of the *Titanic* as a big file moving past the ice at 22 miles per hour, one can imagine quite a bit of grinding away of the ice.

Brown and Stephenson's discussions make use of several things that forensic scientists take pains to avoid during investigations. For example, they compare the damage on the *Titanic* with the damage to the liner *Queen Elizabeth II* when she struck an underwater rock outcropping and damaged her hull. Similarly, others have advanced the notion that since the *Olympic*, made of the same materials and from the same plans as the *Titanic*, had experienced a number of collisions during her twenty-eight-year career and did not sink, scenarios such as the "weak rivet theory" could not have happened. Both of these are termed *forensics by analogy*, and from an actual scientific and forensic perspective of an incident, are nearly worthless. *Titanic* underwent a unique collision event and was damaged because of that specific event. What happened to other ships that experienced other accidents is not relevant to the investigation.

In his book, Brown relies heavily on the testimony of one or two survivors and discounts for various reasons the testimony of many others as a means to reinforce his hypothesis. He also relies on his interpretation of the early-twentieth-century meaning of certain words used in testimony, such as "struck," which in Brown's view can only mean the bottoming of the ship and not a sideswipe, to bolster his argument. Again, this is an example of not allowing the data to lead you to the answer, and trying, consciously or unconsciously, to fit the evidence to the preconception. Finally, the book cites scientific evidence from dubious sources concluding that iceberg ice is nearly as hard as steel and could have cut the steel of the hull bottom. As discussed earlier, top researchers in the field of the mechanics of ice utterly dismiss this conclusion.

In the end, Brown has withdrawn his theory via postings on the Internet, after video taken on an expedition in 2005 "discovered" (actually rediscovered—they were seen in 1996, 1998, and 2001, as well) two sections of the hull's double bottom lying upside down on the seafloor, and no evidence was found of ice damage to that portion of the bottom of the ship.

THE BREAKUP

Survivor testimonies have propagated a number of conflicting scenarios about the breakup of the ship and her eventual plunge toward the seafloor. Expedition evidence has helped to shed some light on the details about *Titanic*'s final moments above water.

A computer analysis of the breakup completed in 1996 shows that as the flooding progressed past Boiler Room No. 4, bending stresses within the second expansion joint exceeded the yield stress of the ship's material. The interior walls of the ship were beginning to cave, with the superstructure on the verge of fracture. Baker Joughin was in the pantry on A deck (positioned between the third stack and the aft expansion joint) when he "heard a kind of a crash as if something had buckled, as if part of the ship had buckled." Joughin raced to the top where a crowd of passengers was surging toward the Poop Deck in the hopes of holding on until the last moment. Joughin fought the crush of people and wriggled his way to the well deck just as the ship took a great lurch forward, dumping everyone around him into the water.

The structural failures in the ship were numerous, setting off a sequence of events that signaled the end, all remembered for the sound they made. The lights dimmed to a dull red and then flickered, providing just enough of an outline for survivors to watch the doomed ship take her final plunge.

Many survivors were convinced that the stern of the ship protruded out of the water until it was standing nearly vertical. This idea stems from images that were burned into witnesses' brains, images of the propellers and the colossal rudder ripped straight out of the sea into the night air, floating above them for what seemed like an eternity. Some memories recalled that the stern had risen to an almost perpendicular position, but depending on how close survivors were to the ship, their view would be obscured by an illusion, making the height of the stern tower above them. The inconsistencies among witnesses were very apparent during the inquiries.

> MR. PITMAN: She gradually disappeared until the forecastle head was submerged to the bridge. Then she turned right on end and went down perpendicularly.

> MAJ. PEUCHEN: While the lights were burning, I saw her bow pointing down and the stern up; not in a perpendicular position, but considerable.
> SENATOR SMITH: About what angle?
> MAJ. PEUCHEN: I should think an angle of not as much as 45 degrees.

Who is correct? The 1996 expedition to the wreck site revealed the answer. Underwater observation clearly showed that the boilers were still in their foundations—an impossibility if the ship had sunk vertically as some witnesses claimed, considering that the boilers were held in their cradles by gravity. At most the angle of trim was 35°, still enough to raise the propellers from the water and place approximately 250 feet of hull in the air. As the hull girder approached failure, the bow sank lower into the ocean, the sides of the ship began to fracture, and the decks opened wider.

The final moments of *Titanic*'s plunge were mired in controversy until recently—did she or did she not break apart? The 1985 discovery of the *Titanic* on the seafloor revealed that the ship had broken apart during her sinking. The bow and stern were eventually photographed and mapped and revealed that they were separated by 1,970 feet, facing in opposite directions. Finally, there was proof to support survivors' claims of what appeared to be the bow snapping off in the water, just aft of the third funnel.

> SENATOR FLETCHER: What do you mean by saying she snapped in two?
>
> MR. BULEY: She parted in two.
>
> SENATOR FLETCHER: How do you know that?
>
> MR. BULEY: Because we could see the after part afloat, and there was no forepart to it.
>
> > —Seaman Edward Buley on Day 7,
> > American Inquiry

> MR. MOORE: I saw the forward part of her go down, and it appeared to me as if she broke in half, and then the after part went.
>
> > —Seaman George Moore on Day 7,
> > American Inquiry

> MR. EVANS: She parted between the third and fourth funnels.
>
> > —Seaman Frank Evans on Day 8,
> > American Inquiry

As a representative of Harland & Wolff, the naval architect Edward Wilding felt compelled to assure the public of the considerable strength of his employer's ships, despite the unyielding claims of those present during the tragedy.

> MR. ROWLATT: We have heard something in the evidence about an apparent fracture of the whole ship as she foundered, which is rather why I was going a little minutely into this part of it. Do you believe that happened?
> MR. WILDING: Not in the least. I have tried to make an approximate calculation, and I feel quite sure it did not happen.

The testimony of "reputable" witnesses such as Wilding and other high-ranking crew members, notably Second Officer Lightoller, disputed claim after claim given by ordinary passengers that the structure "parted in two." It did not matter that witness after witness described the same scene. It did not matter that Major Peuchen saw the barber pole from C Deck floating amidst the debris, tangible evidence that the ship had broken apart. It was easy to dismiss the testimonies, partly because the lights had gone out before the ship made its final descent. In the opinion of Edwardian-period judicial proceedings, what could an average person actually see in the dark at 2:20 a.m. from several hundred feet or more?

The stern settled back to the water's surface, still connected by the inner bottom to the submerged bow. Again, it rose upward and began sinking in the water, accompanied by a loud roaring noise that seemed to pull it into the sea. First Class passenger R. Norris Williams watched the stern disappear, "[She] slid into the ocean facing England—no suction, no noise, two or three big waves—stillness." As poetic as it may seem, the physical destruction was not over. Many described hearing sounds, explosions, and thunderous rumbles very clearly due to the implosions and explosions of the stern, which had no time to equalize in pressure before its crash course to the seabed. The

structure of the stern was completely demolished, as evidenced by the
Poop Deck, the only hope for so many passengers to cling to, which
was discovered years later on the ocean floor completely bent backward on top of itself.

In the end, the exact details of the breakup may be unknowable.
Recent efforts have been made by groups of engineers to model the in-
tricate details of the structure of the ship and the massive stresses she
withstood as the stern rose into the air. Unfortunately, there are sharp
corners at hatch openings, floor connections, and many, many other
places on the ship where a crack could initiate in the steel. As the ship
flexed and groaned, any one, or several, of these stress "hot spots"
could have fractured and started the final break. They would have
moved through the structure at about half the speed of sound in steel
(about 5,000 miles per hour) until they linked up into the final failure.
The analysis continues, but the final details may remain a mystery.

CHAPTER 14

AS THE METAL RUSTS

What Is Happening to the
Wreck of the *Titanic* Now?

A s the *Titanic* wreck is visited at least every other year by an expedition, subtle changes in its condition are being observed and, to varying extents, documented. At times, stories in the media have trumpeted the catastrophic degradation of the wreck and have wondered whether visitors are contributing to the problem. Groups with vested interests in the question have used these speculations to press for rapid salvage of artifacts before they are lost forever. Again, here is another aspect of the *Titanic* story that would benefit from an impartial, rational scientific examination. What is happening to the wreck? Is there anything we can do to preserve it? Are visitors destroying it? Is there actually anything unexpected happening here?

A ship that sinks does not stay in her original condition for very long. Seawater is a very nasty environment for most materials and, particularly, the iron of ship hulls. Along with heated discussions regarding who has rights to visit the wreck site and possibly salvage artifacts, a great deal of interest is focused on the future of the wreck of the *Titanic*. The group posed these typical questions: What is happening to her? How long will she last? Is there anything that can be done to preserve her or possibly even salvage her? Are the visits inflicting damage or accelerated deterioration on the wreck site? To some extent, these are all valid questions, and with a review of the facts and the application of scientific principles, there may actually be some answers.

The main causes degrading the wreck today are corrosion and gravity and, to a much lesser extent, human influences. The steel and iron portions of the ship will rust, and the wood will be degraded or consumed by microorganisms. Much of the internal structure of the bulkheads, walls, and floor were probably damaged under the stress of the breakup and the 30-plus miles per hour impact with the ocean floor. As these parts degrade, they will no longer be able to support the weight they were designed to hold or even to support their own weight. Riveted or bolted connections might give way, causing further collapse to occur. Of course, careless or unlucky visitors using sub-mersibles or ROVs can collide with the wreck and cause further damage, as was seen in the case of the Russian *Mir* submersible during James Cameron's first dive to the *Titanic* in September 1995, when it collided with the wreck and tore off *Mir*'s propeller shroud. The strength of any given piece of the wreck is determined by how it has been and continues to be affected by corrosion. What is corrosion? How does it work? How we can affect its rate, and what precisely is happening on the wreck site?

AS THE METAL RUSTS: WHAT IS CORROSION?

In technical terms, corrosion is a chemical process in which metals, in this case iron, react with the environment and turn into other com-pounds. With iron in water, the iron can turn into any of several differ-ent iron oxides, most often known as rust. Copper and copper-based alloys, like brass and bronze, react with oxygen and sulfur dioxide in the atmosphere and form the familiar green patina seen on statues. Silver-ware reacts with sulfur dioxide to form tarnish, which is a compound of silver and sulfur. In all these cases, there is a chemical driving force for metals to react and form other compounds, which is why almost all met-als are found in the form of ores, typically as oxides and sulfides. One notable exception to this is gold, which remains unreactive under normal conditions. To change these oxides and sulfides back to metals, you need to introduce energy, such as in processes like iron smelting. So left alone in most environments, iron will eventually rust away. Rust is what iron wants to be.

Of course, just because metals may be energetically "happier" if

---

Polishing Silver

If you have ever manually or chemically polished silver, you may have smelled that very special odor of rotten eggs. This smell is hydrogen sulfide and is formed when the silver-sulfur bonds are broken and the silver surface becomes clean of tarnish.

---

left to corrode into other compounds does not tell us how fast this change will occur. For example, a piece of silver left to tarnish in most environments will take hundreds of years to disappear completely, because the process is very slow. Witness the recovery of silver and gold artifacts from Spanish galleons in the Caribbean. The gold is pristine, and although the silver is encrusted with marine life and tarnish, once cleaned it is nearly intact. This was also seen for silver and gold artifacts recovered from the *Titanic*. Even stainless steel, which most people think of as a material that is "corrosion proof," does in fact corrode. The chromium and nickel in the stainless steel react with oxygen and form a very thin, transparent, very hard layer of oxide that protects the iron below. The oxide layer forms very quickly on the bare surface, but its rate of growth slows to nearly zero after only a few minutes, shutting down the corrosion process all by itself. In this case engineers take advantage of one form of corrosion to prevent another. Brass and bronze are commonly used for fittings and propellers on oceangoing vessels because they resist marine corrosion very well.

Some materials corrode very quickly, depending on the environment. Aluminum takes an enormous amount of energy to produce from ores (which is why they build aluminum smelters right next to electric power generation stations) and, therefore, rusts back to ore via corrosion relatively quickly. In seawater, the skin of aircraft will last only a couple of months before being eaten away if it is not protected with a highly specialized coating. Navy aircraft are under constant attack by sea spray, and according to the Naval Research Lab, aluminum corrosion is a huge maintenance issue on Navy planes. Other metals can corrode extremely fast. Examples are metals such as magnesium, which in a chipped form is used as a fire starter, and sodium and potassium, which are so unstable in their metallic form that they actually burn when exposed to water or air and must be stored covered in oil. Since these metals are converting to other compounds when they burn (in this case, hydroxides), this process can be thought of as another form of corrosion, although an extreme case.

Among common metals, iron alloys sit in the "middle range" of corrosion rates. Most people understand corrosion of iron alloys as rusting car body panels and outdoor furniture. From a practical standpoint, if you keep them clean, dry, and painted, they will not rust. Scientifically, what you are doing is removing electrolytes and highly reactive chemicals, such as road salts and dirt, which can enable current to flow during corrosion. If removing these compounds will cause corrosion to halt, then having them in overabundance will cause a great deal of corrosion to occur.

When unpainted iron is immersed in saltwater (which is the case at the *Titanic* wreck site), it creates one of the most corrosive environments for iron and steel. One particularly special form of iron, considered fairly corrosion resistant, is wrought iron. This is obvious when examining the wrought iron pieces recovered from the wreck of the *Titanic*. As described in chapter 3, wrought iron is pure iron mixed with slag fibers to give it strength. Since slag is a glass, and does not corrode, the iron grains in the wrought iron are eaten away while the fibers remain. During this process, more and more slag fibers are exposed until a very rough surface (that looks like wood) is produced, that is covered by slag (see fig. 12b, p. 146).

This protects the underlying iron from further corrosion and is the reason that wrought iron was commonly used for exterior architectural pieces, such as fences, gates, furniture, and fire escapes, in the nineteenth and early twentieth centuries.

Of course, the speed at which a shipwreck will rust away, even in this highly active environment, depends on many other factors, some that can be controlled and many more that cannot. The makeup of the water that surrounds the wreck is probably the most important factor. Saltwater corrodes iron faster than fresh water, because it is a better conductor of electricity and has more chemically active species dissolved in it. As iron turns into an oxide, the presence of a high concentration of oxygen in the water produces a higher rate of corrosion. Keep in mind that the oxygen does not need to be in the water itself, as some of the highest corrosion rates on ships actually occur in the "splash zone," where the metal is alternately exposed to water and air. If the exposed surface is bare, obviously it will be eaten away faster than if it was painted, coated, or even covered with a layer of mud or sand.

THE ENVIRONMENT OF AN OCEAN WRECK SITE

The wreck of the *Titanic* is located on the ocean floor, 12,600 feet down, in the North Atlantic Ocean. At these depths, the hydrostatic pressure (pushing equally from all sides) is about 6,000 pounds psi. (A good analogy to visualize this high pressure is to imagine two cars parked on your thumbnail.) The water temperature at the wreck site is approximately 34°F, and there is obviously no light. The current can vary from zero to several knots, and frequently changes direction. A common misconception is that because it is so far from the surface there is no dissolved oxygen in the water to eat away at the wreck. While the oxygen content is lower (about 40 percent of that at the surface), there is still oxygen present, which is easily evidenced by the images of fish and crabs seen swimming into the view of the cameras during numerous expeditions to the wreck site. The wreck is buried to a depth of 5 to 50 feet in the mud bottom, depending on the location. This mud is a waterlogged mixture of silt, sand, and biomaterial that has floated down over the centuries. In addition, as the wreck has corroded, it has added fallen rust and rusticles to the depth of the mud piled next to it. Compared to the highly aggressive and ever-changing marine environments experienced by offshore oil rigs, for example, the region around the *Titanic* is fairly stable and consistent. This stability is what gives us a chance of predicting her remaining lifetime.

Protecting the Wreck: Is It Feasible?

The enormous difficulty and huge expense of reaching the location of the wreck ($300,000 per expedition day) makes finding a practical preservation plan nearly impossible. An obvious way to slow down or prevent corrosion is to change the environment completely—take the wreck out of the ocean. Suffice it to say that this solution is completely impractical for any number of reasons.

So if the *Titanic* cannot be removed from the environment, can the environment be removed from the *Titanic*? One might imagine wrapping the wreck site in plastic—a nice idea, yet a solution that would not only be challenging but completely ineffective at removing the water from *Titanic*'s surface. The original paint on the ship protected the steel for a time, but the water has seeped under and through it, and rust that formed between the paint and the steel has caused the coating to flake off. Reapplication of another protective coating is a slightly more plausible solution, but it would be an environmental disaster that, similar to the original paint job, would only be temporary.

During the study of steel and iron artifacts recovered from the *Titanic* wreck site, scientists discovered another very effective way of protecting the ship material from corrosion. It is possible to reduce exposure of the metal by simply burying it in the sand or muck of the seafloor. Large bulkhead sections that were riveted to angle iron were recovered, and the encrusted mud was left on them as they dried. During cleaning in the laboratory the steel of the bulkhead plate, angle iron, and heads of the wrought iron rivets showed considerably less corrosion damage and thinning than the sections that were exposed directly to seawater. It is not clear whether this muck was mud from the ocean bottom or rusticle material, as seen at other locations of the wreck. Regardless, this layer acted as a barrier to the inflow of fresh seawater and, as a result, slowed the corrosion process. Given these observations, another potential solution to protect the *Titanic* might just be to bury it. While the wreck would probably last longer, researchers would not be able to see it to verify this. And, of course, given the depth, it would be very hard to accomplish. Perhaps the wreck can be saved with a more modern solution.

Protecting the Wreck Using Slightly Higher Tech

Theoretically, the wreck of the *Titanic* could be protected using some of the same methods currently used to protect ocean vessels, oil rigs, and underground pipelines. First, this requires understanding a process called anodic corrosion. Basically, this is what happens inside a battery. Two different materials are connected to one another in the presence of an electrical conductor (the electrolyte). One metal corrodes and passes electrons to the other metal. This makes a current that can be used to power devices. A simple example of anodic corrosion is to bite on a penny, assuming you have at least a couple of silver-mercury amalgam fillings in your teeth. The "metallic" taste you sense with your tongue is actually a tiny current that flows as the penny corrodes and passes electrons to your filling. The important factor in this process is that to produce a flow of current, the two metals in contact must have very different corrosion potentials. Put plainly, one of them must want to rust a lot more than the other one does.

Now, the phenomenon of anodic corrosion can be helpful or hurtful, depending on how things are set up. Take the Statue of Liberty as an example. She was assembled with copper sheets riveted to wrought iron inner members. In the presence of a conductor (in this case, salt spray and humidity from the New York harbor), the electrons flowed from the wrought iron to the copper, and the iron rusted, necessitating the refurbishment that she underwent in the 1980s. When they rebuilt her, they tried to match the skin, rivet, and frame parts chemically as much as possible, and when this was not possible, they used Teflon and other nonconducting materials in the joints to break the circuits and prevent anodic corrosion.

How can anodic corrosion be helpful? Suppose there is a steel

Myth: Anodic Corrosion Sank *Titanic*

It has been proposed that corrosion may have had a role to play in the sinking of the *Titanic*. Robert Baboian suggests that anodic corrosion of the rivets may have occurred, beginning shortly after her launch, explaining that a battery of sorts existed between two different materials on the ship—the wrought iron rivets and the steel plates. He speculated that stray currents from dc electrical equipment may have somehow created the problem. However, there are several fundamental weaknesses in this theory. First, if this were a serious enough problem to endanger the ship after little more than a year at sea, why was it not a more prevalent issue among other ships produced with rivets and hull plates made of different materials? Second, for anodic corrosion to occur at a rate that would cause a problem on the *Titanic*, the difference in chemical potential between the two metals would have to be huge. Wrought iron and steel are chemically nearly identical, and the anodic corrosion current would be tiny, almost zero. Finally, Baboian hasn't examined the wreck other than looking at magazines and television programs, and from this cursory view he attempted to observe enhanced corrosion that happened in the first year of the ship's life and to separate that from the eighty or so years of corrosion on top of it. At the time of his publication, Baboian happened to work for Intel in the corrosion program and was dealing with corrosion problems endemic to microelectronics. In microelectronic devices, metals such as copper and gold come into contact with aluminum. The chemical driving force for corrosion in this situation is huge, and corrosion failures of circuits in computers can actually be a big problem. But it just doesn't happen in steel ships riveted with iron rivets. A quick check of an elementary corrosion textbook would have revealed that.

structure that needs protecting, like a shipwreck. By attaching a piece of metal that has a much lower corrosion potential, it will corrode in place of the ship, thus protecting the steel. This method, using a sacrificial anode, is widely utilized to protect ships and buried pipelines. To slow corrosion down using this method, the whole structure must be electrically connected to the anode metal. A commonly used metal for this is zinc. The same effect can be accomplished, if the structure is accessible enough, by attaching a power lead directly to it and applying a voltage that is roughly the same as a battery. In fact, this is exactly what happens when recharging a rechargeable battery—the corrosion process is driven backward to its starting point so that it can happen again and make more power. Applying a voltage makes it unnecessary to either replace the anode or deal with the production of corrosion products from the anode. This is another method of corrosion protection in a broad category known as anodic protection.

Protecting the wreck of the *Titanic* with a power source is impractical for several reasons: The wreck has seen a great deal of corrosion already. Aside from the damage that occurred during the breakup and impact with the seafloor, many pieces of the wreck have fallen away, and many more have probably become disconnected from one another due to the buildup of rust layers between the metal pieces. This would require either connecting the wreck portions together with cables or individually connecting sacrificial anodes or power cables to every piece to protect them. Also, the logistics of dropping huge anodes to the site and hooking them up or somehow providing power to the site would be daunting.

Currently, Foecke is helping to protect the wreck site of the USS *Arizona*, in which these same methods are being contemplated. Unfortunately, the USS *Arizona* is disconnected into dozens of different parts, requiring consideration for the practical and aesthetic factors in draping cables over the wreck or securing big silverish hunks of zinc alongside her. Despite the fact that this wreck is accessible, located within only forty feet of water inside a harbor, the project is moving ahead very slowly. Given the enormous logistical, technical, and even political issues involved, it is extremely unlikely that some active protection scheme will be applied to the wreck of the *Titanic*. She will probably be left to rust away.

What About the Wood?

Expeditions to the wreck have observed that sections of the wood decking remain intact, when the mud and ooze are wiped away. Although it looks to be unharmed, admittedly it is impossible to know whether it is solid or has been eaten away internally. Most of the wood that survives is teak, which is naturally high in rubber (imparting a waterproofing effect) and toxic oils (providing an antibiotic effect) and is commonly used in situations where the wood will be exposed to extreme weathering and marine environments. A similar phenomenon of natural protection from the environment includes the leather luggage recovered from the *Titanic*, which was found to contain the remains of paper documents. The paper was in the form of waterlogged pulpy masses, but by carefully freeze-drying the pulp, it could be reconstituted to its original form. It turns out that the tannic acid used to preserve (or tan) the leather likely kept the pulp-eating microorganisms at bay. These two examples highlight the importance of considering not only what something is made of but its entire environment when determining its ability to resist corrosion.

As the Ooze Forms:
Biologically Assisted Corrosion and Rusticles

Biology and the wreck of the RMS *Titanic* as a topic has probably generated the largest amount of erroneous speculation and ill-informed common knowledge of any other topic related to the wreck. This section will provide guidance to decipher the general misconceptions that are out there, as well as the latest and greatest theories, injecting a fair amount of science into the discussion to reveal the real facts.

Biology has a role to play in corrosion, of this there is little doubt. By changing the environment at the spot that the corrosion is occurring, the presence of biological organisms becomes one of the huge factors that determines how fast a piece of metal will rust. Locations where organisms are attached to the *Titanic* show a different rate of rusting than the cleaner surfaces. These biological organisms on shipwrecks can be as large as shellfish or as small as bacteria. On the *Titanic*, these biological colonies are made of bacteria and fungi and can increase the corrosion rate, forming a small region where the steel becomes thinner than other regions on the ship. They do this through a change in the pH or the amount of oxygen available at that spot. At other locations, biological debris that has fallen off the ship covers large areas of the steel near the mud line, actually protecting it from attack by limiting how the water and dissolved oxygen can circulate past the steel.

However, the studies about biological organisms on the *Titanic* suffer from the old saying that "a little PBS is a dangerous thing." The many television science programs produced on the *Titanic* have glossed over the details, falling victim to easy-to-digest sound bites like "bacteria are eating the ship." Statements such as this one offer an explanation to the public that seems very simple. But as you will see, the situation is not simple.

Rusticles

One of the more persistent stories, retold ad nauseam on the Internet, is the "fact" that the *Titanic* is being consumed by bacteria. According to this theory, bacteria are extracting iron from the hull and somehow living off the extracted material. The initial observations of such bacteria, coined "rusticles," came from the first expeditions to the wreck, when the crew remarked that the structures hanging from the hull resembled icicles of rust. In years since, and during subsequent expeditions, Dr. Roy Cullimore of the University of Regina has studied the composition, makeup, and structure of these materials. According to Cullimore, the rusticles are extremely porous, solid masses composed of colonies of bacteria and fungi intertwined with solids that drift down from the surface of the ocean (floc, or flakes), as well as sand and corrosion products from the hull of the ship. Fine so far.

It is Cullimore's contention that the bacteria are using a compound of iron for respiration, just as humans use oxygen, for the conversion of food into energy. Similar life-forms have been identified around deep-sea geothermal vents, where bacteria use various elements and compounds, primarily sulfur, in the same way. Cullimore's description of these bacteria has been misconstrued by many people into an oversimplification of what are very complex life systems. The rusticles' activity is boiled down to "sulfur or iron-eating" bacteria, as if the bacteria are approaching the source of these elements and taking a nano-bite out of it. This explanation is occasionally combined with other mistaken impressions concerning the ship, such as the high sulfur content in the steel, which has been proposed as a cause of brittleness. In this incarnation of the theory, the bacteria are consuming the ship at an alarming rate because they are sulfur-eating bacteria, and the steel is riddled with the stuff. There is even the occasional reference to the corroded steel as "swiss cheese" because all the sulfur particles are being eaten away, leaving holes throughout.

Where Cullimore takes a leap with no net is in his attempt to connect the actual corrosion to the bacteria themselves. For example, he describes in general terms the ways that the bacteria or other organisms could "extract" iron from the ship in order to be used for food. However, he never describes *how* this happens. He offers no biological mechanism to explain this, but rather relies on plain-old corrosion. Furthermore, he has stated that corrosion simply cannot occur in the absense of bacteria, that all lab tests have some form of bacteria present, and that they are in fact causing all the corrosion to happen. According to his notions, without biology, corrosion does not exist.

Corrosion is, in fact, a chemical process, and to be more precise, an electrochemical process. Iron atoms are removed from the surface when an electron transfers to an oxygen atom in the surrounding water, and the charged iron and oxygen atoms rapidly combine to make iron oxide, or rust. The presence of bacteria only changes the local environment, whether by giving off acids or other chemicals as waste products or by forming a layer on the metal that restricts movement of water, oxygen, or other chemicals to the surface. All these processes will change the corrosion rate. It is kind of a chicken-or-the-egg argument. We assert that the rust is coming off the ship, the bacteria are taking advantage of the windfall, and, in some cases, the bacteria are increasing or decreasing the rate of corrosion locally by changing the environment. Cullimore would assert that the bacteria are attacking the ship itself by some process that no one has managed to describe. Every other corrosion expert that has consulted on the *Titanic* or on other shipwreck preservation projects agrees that this interpretation of biological consumption of the wreck makes no sense.

Take the case of rusticles that form on bent steel. Corrosion of deformed steel has been studied for decades. The act of bending both increases the energy of the steel and creates many defects in the crystals that make up the steel plate. These defects make perfect sites for corrosion to start because they form tiny pits on the surface of the steel. Thus, corrosion happens considerably faster on bent steel than on a piece of the same steel that has not been bent. Taking this a step further, since the bacteria and fungi seem to make use of the rust to live and multiply, rusticles form more easily and get larger faster at locations where the steel is bent because there is more rust being formed that they can use for their purposes. This is what is seen on the wreck of the *Titanic*. Asked about this at a scientific meeting several years ago, Cullimore asserted that the rusticles are bigger and form faster on bent steel because the bacteria know it is a better place to feed and go there by choice. Again, a chicken-or-the-egg situation, and unfortunately for Dr. Cullimore, science shows that he is picking the wrong one.

DOCUMENTATION OF THE WRECK

Most of the visits to the wreck site since its discovery in 1985 have included at least some photography, which can be used to document the rate of degradation. Availability of this information is, unfortunately, limited in some cases as it belongs to various television production companies or to one of the sponsors of the expeditions. However, once the television programs are broadcast or the books are published, the photos become publicly available and provide a way to map how the wreck is falling apart over time.

A program begun by NOAA under the leadership of Lt. Jr. Gr.

Jeremy Weirich of the NOAA Corps keeps an eye on the condition of the wreck as part of the U.S. commitment to the international treaty signed to preserve the wreck site from exploitation. He has assembled an excellent team of researchers who are experienced in wreck conservation and surveys and include those responsible for the wrecks of the USS *Monitor*, the CSS *Hunley* (Confederate sub that was the first to sink a ship during a war in 1863), and the USS *Arizona* in Pearl Harbor. Team members hail from NOAA, NIST, and the National Park Service, as well as nonprofit organizations and universities. Each brings his or her own unique set of skills to the task, looking at the wreck site from the point of view of an archeologist, mechanical engineer, metallurgist, or biologist. NOAA mounted an expedition in 2004, in cooperation with the National Geographic Channel, to launch this monitoring effort.

Currently, detailed observations of the collapse of specific rooms and features of the ship are being documented, and more informal observations from other expeditions have been presented in books, in broadcast programs, and on the Internet. Unsupported speculation regarding the "who," "when," and "how" concerning collapsed features continues to reign. This discussion will not attempt to detail the range of subtle to very large changes the wreck has undergone since 1985—that would be enough to fill another entire book. Each collapse or structural change depends on many factors: the local corrosion rates, the amount of damage the area has in the first place, or the possibility that something else has fallen onto the structure you are interested in, among other things.

Some observations during the most recent expeditions have relied on the amount of rusticles to indicate an increase in the rate that the wreck is rusting away. Yet, rusticles form and fall off the wreck all the time. Their size is not controlled by the rate that the steel is rusting, but rather the change in current strength and direction, which acts to knock the rusticles off continually. Seeing a temporary increase in larger rusticles on areas of the wreck during that particular dive does not necessarily mean that the ship is falling apart faster. The answer may just be perfect timing. The bottom line is that forecasting how long any one thing will stay together on the wreck of the *Titanic* is likely an exercise in futility. With tens of thousands of photos and thousands of hours of video, our efforts to understand this process are definitely a work in progress.

STABILITY OF THE WRECK: HOW IS SHE HOLDING TOGETHER?

Recent trips to the wreck site have documented that both parts of the ship have undergone large changes, and that portions of decks and the superstructure have collapsed between the discovery in 1985 and today. There is concern that the wreck is falling apart, and the more alarmist contributors to this discussion topic have pinned the collapse observations to the effects of the visits of submersibles over the years. From an engineering point of view, nothing surprising is happening on the wreck of the *Titanic*. From a mechanical point of view, the present degradation of the structure can be roughly described as a "midlife crisis."

Recall one of the characteristics of corroding steel: deformed (bent) steel corrodes faster than undeformed steel. As seen in numerous photographs of the wreck site, much of the steel of the hull, decks, and bulkheads of the *Titanic* was massively deformed during the breakup and sinking. Also, when the ship broke in half and came to rest on the seafloor, sections near the break site were left partially unsupported, with decks and beams cantilevered out free, putting enormous stresses at their points of connection to the wreck. These connections rust faster, releasing the stress and precipitating collapse of these pieces. If there happen to be notches or cracks at these highly stressed points, another process called stress corrosion cracking can occur. Studied extensively in steels, stress corrosion cracking is when the rate of corrosion at the very tip of a stressed crack is hundreds of times faster than elsewhere, driving the crack to grow in length. Once the crack gets to a certain length under its load, it suddenly snaps forward, causing a local area of the ship to collapse.

When the *Titanic* first sank, the condition of the steel of the ship could be considered very good, excluding the damage inflicted by the iceberg and the destruction on impact with the sea floor. The ship sat at the bottom of the ocean rusting for decades before she was discovered, easily supporting her own weight and holding herself together in her approximate original state. Over the years, the steel members thinned at different rates, producing isolated regions that were no longer weight bearing, and, as a result, *Titanic* began to collapse. As upper regions fell onto the sections below, the problems compounded and accelerated, with changes happening at a fast and furious rate. By chance, her discovery in 1985 seems to have roughly corresponded to the time in the life of the wreck when the changes were beginning to accelerate. As things continue to rust into thinner and thinner dimensions, eventually all the decks will fall in, and finally the hull plates will fold in (or out). Once most of the potential energy of the standing sections has been spent and the ship is a chaotic pile of rusting steel and debris, the rate of change of the site will slow down dramatically.

With a calculation of the approximate surface area of the ship that is iron or iron alloy, including the inside of the hull and the underside of the decks, it is possible to make a back-of-the-envelope estimate of how fast the wreck is disappearing. The textbook value for the amount of steel that corrodes away in marine environments is one ten thousandth of an inch per day, or about a hair thickness (100 micrometers) every four days. If you multiply this by the estimated surface area and multiply that number by the density of iron, you get the following result: an estimate of one half to one ton of iron being turned into rust every day. This seems like a lot, but recall there are tens of thousands of tons of steel down there. Eventually, in a century or two, *Titanic* will return to her lowest-energy, natural state—an iron ore deposit. It is not glamorous, and some regard it as highly tragic, but that is not how a scientist and engineer see it.

It's all just chemistry and gravity.

NOTES

In chapters 6 to 12, the Brit. Inq. numbers (e.g., Brit. Inq. 1851–52) refer to question numbers, and the Am. Inq. numbers (e.g., Am. Inq. 37) refer to page numbers because questions were not identified.

Chapter 1: The Yard
Information about the managing directors of Harland & Wolff and the general situation at the shipyard: (PRONI Document D/2805/MIN/1-2 1907–1914), (PRONI Document D/2805/MISC/1 1883–1919); Labor conditions in Belfast and other shipyards: (Rebbeck 1950; Bardon 1982; Lynch 2001); "read like a roster . . ." (Connolly 1915).

Chapter 2: Building the Great Leviathan: A Guide to *Titanic*'s Details
"There is . . . the larger and more important national view . . ." (James 1903; "the essence of modernity" (McCaughan 1998); "The White Star Liners . . .": (Rebbeck 1950; hull materials: (Kirkaldy 1862); "We have been solemnly told . . ." (*The Shipping World Magazine*, vol. XLVI, issue 993, June 12, 1912); "But, however excellent the staff of builders . . ." (*Marine Insurance Correspondent*, May 17, 1912); "In view of the reports . . ." (July 8, 1912); "[The door] is held in the open . . ." (*The Shipbuilder* 1995); "On [the ship's] way across . . ." (Hamilton 1899).

Chapter 3: What the *Titanic* Was Made Of: The Science of Iron
"Scientific investigation and civil . . ." (White 1913); "The task of the smith . . ." (Smith and Gnudi 1990); The puddling process—a method . . . : (Aston and Story 1936), (Calvert and Johnson 1857), (Harris 1988, 39–40), (Wiley 1882), (Wengenroth 1994). *The Glory Days of Wrought Iron*: (Gale 1969), (Aston and Story 1936), (PRONI Document

D/2805/MISC/1 1883–1919), (Morgan 1999). *Scientific Enlightenment:* Kirkaldy studies (Kirkaldy 1862).

So What About Steel? ("The White Star Line," *The Engineer,* vol. 109, June 24, 1910, Supplement).

Turn of the Century Developments: What Did Titanic Use? (PRONI Document D/2805/MISC/1 1883–1919), (British PRO Document MT15/78 1906), (Moss and Hume 1986, 46), (British PRO Document MT15/212 1912; McCluskie 1998).

Chapter 4: The Riveting Process

Riveting "is a difficult trade to learn . . .": *Transactions of the Institute of Naval Architects,* 1899; Great Eastern boxed text: (Murphy 1959), (Reed 1869).

Rivet Material: Iron vs. Steel and the Red-Hot Rule: (Jeans 1880, 739); "It would appear to be . . ." (*Lloyd's Report of Steel for Shipbuilding.* London: Lloyd's Printing House, 1877); "In hand-riveting it will be observed . . ." (Fairbairn 1856, xiv), (Jeans 1880).

Adding Machinery to the Assembly Line: (*Engineering,* March 16, 1900); "The [riveting] machine produces . . ." (Fairbairn 1856, xv); "Hydraulic riveting is nearly always . . ." (John July 10, 1914), (*Engineering,* June 12, 1908), (*Engineering,* December 10, 1880), (*Transactions of the Institution of Naval Architects,* 1899, 121; Pollard and Robertson 1979).

The Standards of the Industry: "iron forgings and bars . . ." (British PRO Document MT9/710 M15667 1902), (British PRO Document MT15/78 1906).

What About the Rivets? (British PRO Document MT15/78 1906).

Best Practices: The Secrets of Good Riveting: "After working about . . ." (Wilson 1873); "Every loose rivet . . ." (Thorpe January 27, 1905), (Thearle 1891), (Walton 1904), (Hammond 1986).

The Inspection Process: "As strong as . . ." (Bullock 1999), (PRONI Document D2805/WB/15/7 1920–1924); "[The rivet counters] had few friends . . ." (Hammond 1986); "The tightness of . . ." (Walton 1904), Fellowes Wilson 1926; Cameron 1998), (Thearle 1891); "The differences in the results . . ." (Reed 1869).

Chapter 5: Harland & Wolff's Protocols

Employment at Harland & Wolff: (McCaughan 1989), (PRONI Document D/2805/MIN/1–2 1907–1914), (Lynch 2001), (Rebbeck 1950); "Country men fresh . . ." (Hammond 1986), (Moss and Hume 1986); "idling workers on No. 401" (PRONI Document D/2805/MIN/1–2 1907–1914); "The workmanship is of . . ." (British PRO Document MT15/212 1912); "In the event of work . . ." (PRONI Document D2910/1–2, 1888).

The Riveting Plan: The Clyde Riveters Piece-work Price List published in 1926 indicated that workers would be paid an additional 5 percent on listed pay rates when steel rivets were used (British PRO Document LAB 83/913 1926).

By Hand or by Machine: A Measure of Consistency: (Engineering 1911); "The Shell to be hydraulically riveted..." (British PRO Document MT 9/920A/1, 1912).

Titanic's Materials: Tying Harland & Wolff's Specifications to Standards of the Day: (British PRO Document MT9/710 M2213 1902; British PRO Document MT9/710 M15667 1902); (Rebbeck 1950; Moss and Hume 1986), (PRONI Document D/2805/MISC/1 1883–1919).

Wrought Iron or Steel: Harland & Wolff's Rationale: "for all hand riveting..." (British PRO Document MT15/212 22818 1912), (British PRO Document MT15/212 1912); "The tendency to use..." (Thearle 1891).

Why Was Titanic Different? (PRONI Document D2805/WB/15/7 1920–1924); "knocked down and finished..." (Reed 1869), (British PRO Document LAB 83/913 1926), (British PRO Document MT9/710 M15667 1902).

Chapter 6: April 14, 1912—What Are the Facts?
"By the time..." (Biel 1996).

Boxed text on survivor testimony: (Brandon and Davies 1973), (Loftus and Ketcham 1991), (Widley, 1993 #194), (Arts & Entertainment 1994).

Latitude 41° 46' N, Longitude 50° 14' W: As the sun dipped... (Brit. Inq. 1851–52, 3981, 5506), (Brit. Inq. 13615–17), (Am. Inq. 37, Brit Inq. 13635–36), (Brit. Inq. 15547–53); "a stack of personal messages..." (Brit. Inq. 16490–91); five ice warnings: (Am. Inq. 50, 139, 907, 1061, 1115; Brit. Inq. 8943, 15689, 16099, 16122, 16176); "In lat. 42°N..." (Brit. Inq. 16221), (Butler 1998); very dense field ice: (Am. Inq. 715); "Say, old man..." (Am. Inq. 735); dropping temperatures: (Brit. Inq. 13578); fresh water supply: (Brit. Inq. 13593–95); "West-bound steamers..." (Brit. Inq. 13462), (Brit. Inq. 13621); Lightoller's shift: (Brit. Inq. 1349), (Brit. Inq. 13531–35, 13547, 13538–52), (Am. Inq. 438); "If it becomes..."(Brit. Inq. 13635); "absolutely flat" (Brit. Inq. 13575); "to keep a sharp..." (Brit. Inq. 11334–39, 13657); At 10:00 p.m.... (Am. Inq. 439, Br. Inq. 14270–77), (Brit. Inq. 14353–54); "small ice..." (Am. Inq. 361).

Question: What was the ship's speed? "You have no..." (Brit. Inq. 25046); 75 revolutions: (Br. Inq. 2213–14); low on coal: (Am. Inq. 273); Quartermaster Robert Hichens (Brit. Inq. 965–96); suprise finish: (Brit. Inq. 2217–18, 2232–33) (Brown 2001).

Question: What was the size, shape, speed and location of the iceberg? "looking all over" (Am. Inq. 322); "haze right ahead" (Brit. Inq. 2401–2); "black mass" (Am. Inq. 318); "two tables put together" (Am. Inq. 320); estimation of iceberg height: (Am. Inq. 320, Brit. Inq. 2439), (Am. Inq. 230–31), (Am. Inq. 539), (Am. Inq. 343), (Am. Inq. 974), (Stoermer and Rudkin 2003); iceberg "was too close" (Br. Inq. 15355); "the grinding noise . . ." (Am. Inq. 450); just before the foremast" (Br. Inq. 17471–72, 2452); chunks of ice on A deck (Am. Inq. 537, 643, Br. Inq. 2800–2, 4525–29); "running mostly . . ." (Br. Inq. 14962–67), (Br. Inq. 2452–54); "the bilge . . ." (Am. Inq. 969); hard aport maneuver (Brown 2001), (Am. Inq. 527).

Question: How severe was the collision? (Brit. Inq. 986–87, 1856–60; Am. Inq. 1141); "Shut all dampers!" (Brit. Inq. 1864); "a slight shock" (Brit. Inq. 3713–20); "It seemed as though . . ." (Am. Inq. 603); "There was just . . ." (Brit. Inq. 3995), (Brit. Inq. 1417); "There was a sound . . ." (Am. Inq. 275); "narrow shave" (Am. Inq. 321), "like she touched . . ." (Am. Inq. 520); "I felt as though . . ." (Am. Inq. 333); "just a grating . . ." (Am. Inq. 643), (Brit. Inq. 1867); "Water came pouring . . ." (Brit. Inq. 1868), (Brit. Inq. 4201–7); "I cannot believe . . ." (Brit. Inq. 20423), (Bedford 1996).

Question: How, when, and at what speed did the ship flood? "I saw the water . . ." (Br. Inq. 4866), (Brit. Inq. 1905–6, 1917–21), (Am. Inq. 1141); "just abaft . . ." (Brit. Inq. 4849); Minutes later . . . (Brit. Inq. 4859–64, 4870–71, 4912–23), (Brit. Inq. 4903), (Brit. Inq. 1931–32); "pierced" (Am. Inq. 425); "the mailroom . . ." (Brit. Inq. 15362–67, 15371–74, 15581), (Am. Inq. 232), (Brit. Inq. 2452–54); "the mailroom was afloat" (Brit. Inq. 14946–48, 14950, 14957–60); From these examples . . . (Brit. Inq. 10910–17, 13277–81, Am. Inq. 1042); "Come at once . . ." (Brit. Inq. 17103), (Brit. Inq. 3816–3827); "Come on quickly . . ." (Brit. Inq. 17141), (Brit. Inq. 2038–45, 2304–7, 4264–67, 4282–4317).

Chapter 7: Materials Investigation: The Goal
of the Recent Expeditions

The Search for forensic evidence . . . (Ballard 1985; Ballard 1987; Michel 1987; Michel 1994); 1991: (Brigham and LaFreniere 1992); 1996: (Garzke et al. 1997); 1998: (Garzke, Matthias, and Wood 2002), (Weihs, personal communication with Hooper McCarty, September 1998; Wood 1998); boxed text on Disrespect and Stupidity: (Broad 2003).

Chapter 8: Distilling the Facts: What Are the Possible Scenarios?

Fact #1: "just before . . ." (Br. Inq. 2452), (Br. Inq. 14964–66), (Br. Inq. 1868–75), (Br. Inq. 1043), (Am. Inq. 343, 537, 643; Br. Inq. 52, 2800–02, 4525–29).

Fact #2: "The sound . . ." (Am. Inq. p. 520); "It seemed . . ." (Am. Inq. p. 587); "I was awakened . . ." (Am. Inq. 634), "No shock . . ." (Am. Inq. p. 643); "I did not feel . . ." (Am. Inq. 832); "It gave just . . ." (Am. Inq. p. 275); "Just like thunder . . ." (Br. Inq. 662); "There was just . . ." (Br. Inq. 10338); "What awakened . . ." (Br. Inq. 11347); "There was a slight . . ." (Br. Inq 13734); "This contact . . ." (Br. Inq. 20267–68); Wilding testimony box: (Br. Inq. 20269–84).

Fact #3: "Water came . . ." (Brit. Inq. 1868), (Br. Inq. 1907–21); "the hole was . . ." (Br. Inq. 1965).

Fact #4: (Br. Inq. 2821–22), (Br. Inq. 4856–66, 4870); mailroom testimony: (Br. Inq. 3384, 10909–14, 13275–78, 15375–79, Am. Inq. Day 13); Collision in boiler rooms: (Br. Inq. 1868–74, 1899, 1905, 1917–21, 1926, 1937, 2105); Barrett testimony: (Br. Inq. 2252–55); "damp" (Br. Inq. 3819–24).

Fact #5: "My estimate for the size . . ." (Br. Inq. 20422), (Bedford 1996); "The collision with . . ." (British Board of Trade 1912); *BCM Trawler* collision: (Ryan, February 2003).

Chapter 9: The 300-Foot Gash

While it may get as cold . . . (Gagnon and Gammon 1997); An iceberg's strength . . . (Gagnon and Gammon 1997); "I cannot believe . . ." (Brit. Inq. 20347); "It can only . . ." (Br. Inq. 20423); Support for the "aggregate of holes" (Garzke 1997).

Chapter 10: Hull Steel = Brittle Steel?

DREA tests: (Brigham and LaFreniere 1992), (KarisAllen, 1995); Chemical analyses of 1991 hull steel: (Brigham and LaFreniere 1992); "15–20 tonnes . . ." (Moss and Hume 1986); Chemical analyses of 1996 steel: (Reemsnyder 1997; Felkins 1998); AISI 1018 steel: (United States Steel Corporation 1971); 100 percent brittle manner: (Matthews, DREA, personal communication to T. Foecke, October 1996); (A. J. DeArdo and Hamburg 1974, 309); sulfur content in steels: 0.04 percent (1906); 0.055 percent (Wilson, Mather, and Harris 1931); 0.05 percent (American Iron and Steel Institute 1946); Liberty Ship failures: (United States Navy 1946); Charpy V-notch test: (Charpy 1912); ordinance steel testing: (Tipper

1962); stress concentrations: (M. Williams 1953); cracks at rivet holes: *Encyclopaedia Britannica*, 11th ed., S.V. "Process of Shipbuilding." (Reed 1869); plate variability: (Brigham and LaFreniere 1992; Felkins 1998), (Tipper 1962), (Eaton and Haas 1986).

Can We Re-create the Collision with the Iceberg? Observations of hull: (Livingstone, private communication to W. Garzke, 1996; Weihs, personal communication with Hooper McCarty, September 1998); Computer simulations: (Garzke 1997); Charpy impact test: (Federal Railroad Administration 1994); Fireman Barrett's torn seam: (Brit. Inq. 1856–93); empty rivet holes: (Garzke, Foecke, Matthias et al. 2002); (Matthews, DREA, personal communication to T. Foecke, October 1996).

Chapter 11: Does the Answer Lie with the Rivets?

How the Ship Was Built: (British PRO Document MT 9/920A/1, 1912 #181) (British PRO Document MT15/212 22818 1912), (British PRO Document MT15/212 1912).

Historical Evidence: (Foecke 1998).

Clues from the Collision: "water came ..." (Brit. Inq. 1868, 1875), (Garzke, Foecke, Matthias et al. 2002, Garzke 1997).

Revelation: The data in this section came from Foecke's initial studies on the first two rivets retrieved from the 1996 expedition, and formed the initial hypothesis of the weak rivet theory. Stresses in rivets: (John 1914; Hogg 1903); In Victorian times ... refinement of wrought iron: (Calvert and Johnson 1857); strength of wrought iron: (Clark 1858; Fairbairn 1869; Kirkaldy 1862).

Probing for Clues: The remainder of this chapter relies on work completed by McCarty during her Ph.D. diss. at Johns Hopkins University and provides the additional metallographic data, mechanical testing, and computer modeling to support the weak rivet theory further.

The Search for Slag: Thousands of digital images of the *Titanic* rivets were taken with the help of numerous undergraduate students and high school summer interns, including Julia Deneen, Melody Augustin, Jason Hughes, and Robb Wissman. Data on slag taken from (Hooper 2003), nineteenth to twentieth century observations of wrought iron strength: (Brull 1868; Urbin 1868; Carnegie Steel Corporation 1917; Clarke and Storr 1983); "further attention ..." (Rosenhain September 24, 1909).

Mechanical Testing: mechanical test data on *Titanic* materials taken from (Hooper 2003).

Taking the Computer to Task: The computer modeling work was completed with the help of Dr. Lori Graham at Johns Hopkins University and Dr. Li Ma at NIST.

The Rivet Geometry: (*Encyclopedia of Shipbuilding* 1911; British PRO Document MT15/212 22818 1912; *The Shipbuilder* 1995).

Cooling Down a Red-Hot Rivet: (Maxtone-Graham 1985; Burton 1994); temperature scale: (Greenwood 1907).

Building the Case: (Smith 1960), (Calvert and Johnson 1857; *The Technical Educator: An Encyclopedia of Technical Education*, 1905; Morgan 1999), (Hooper 2003), (Brull 1868; Urbin 1868; Carnegie Steel Corporation 1917; Clarke and Storr 1983), (PRONI Document D/2805/MISC/1 1883–1919), (Wiley 1882; Wengenroth 1994); "There is no question . . ." (Hand 1925), (British PRO Document MT15/212 1912), (British PRO Document MT9/710 M15667 1902), (Jeans 1880), (Fairbairn 1856; Walton 1904), (Reed 1869), (PRONI Document D/2805/MIN/1–2 1907–14; Rebbeck 1950), (Hammond 1986; McCaughan 1989), (Garzke et al. 1997); eyewitness testimony on damage: (British Board of Trade 1912; United States Senate 1912), (Garzke, Matthias, and Wood 2002).

The Final Step in the Investigation: The experiment described in this section was completed with the support of the National Geographic Channel for their *Seconds from Disaster* series.

Chapter 12: The Collision Scenario

This chapter compiles information that has been presented throughout the text, therefore the following references serve just to clarify specific supporting information for our conclusions.

Conclusions #3 & #4: Modern-day failure analysis and rivet strain analysis (Langrand et al. 2002).

Conclusion #6: David G. Brown's grounding theory: (Brown 2003; Brown 2001).

Conclusion #7: (Cunningham 1967), (Butler 1998), (Louden-Brown 1999; Mills 2005), (Brit. Inq. 2250).

Chapter 13: Other Tidbits You May Have Heard About

The Coal Bunker Fire: 1912 Merscy Inquiry Testimony (Brit. Inq. 2038–45, 2061, 2088–91, 2299–2308, 2338–42, 3936–43, 5232–52, 19634).

Spontaneous Combustion and the Thermodynamics of Coal: (Stevens 1869), (U.S. Department of Energy 1993).

The Breakup: (Garzke et al. 1997), (Brit. Inq. 6040–48, 6052–53), (Am. Inq.

280, 329, 563, 591, 733), (Brit. Inq. 20258); Quote from First Class passenger R. Norris Williams from John Eaton's private research.

Chapter 14: As the Metal Rusts: What Is Happening to the Wreck of the *Titanic* Now?

(Parisi 1998), (Wels 1997); Boxed text on the Myth: Anodic Corrosion Sank *Titanic* (Baboian 2001).

BIBLIOGRAPHY

Abell, Westcott. *The Shipwright's Trade*. Cambridge: Cambridge Univ. Press, 1948.

Agricola, G. *De Re Metallica*. Translated by Hoover, H.C. and L.H. Hoover. New York: Dover Publications, 1950.

American Iron and Steel Institute. "Section 2: Semifinished Carbon Steel Products." In *Steel Products Manual*. Pittsburgh, 1946.

Arnold, A. J. *Iron Shipbuilding on the Thames*. England: Ashgate Publishing Ltd., 2000.

Arts & Entertainment. "Titanic: Death of Dream." 55 min. United States, 1994.

Aston, James, and Edward B. Story. *Wrought Iron: Its Manufacture, Character-istics and Applications*. 1st ed. Pittsburgh, PA: A. M. Byers Co., 1936.

Baboian, R. "Anodic Corrosion." *Discover Magazine*, 22, no. 8 (August 2001).

Ballard, R. D. *The Discovery of the Titanic*. Toronto: Warner/Madison Press, 1987.

———. "A Long Last Look at Titanic." *National Geographic* 1986, 698–727.

———, and J. L. Michel. "How We Found Titanic." *National Geographic* 1985, 696–719.

Ballard, Robert D. *Exploring the Titanic*. New York: Scholastic, 1988.

Banbury, Philip. *Man and the Sea*. London: Adlard Coles Limited, 1975.

Bardon, Jonathan. *Belfast: An Illustrated History*. Belfast: Blackstaff Press, 1982.

Bealer, Alex. *The Art of Blacksmithing*. Edison, New Jersey: Castle Books, 1995.

Bedford, C., and J. G. Hackett. "The Sinking of the Titanic, Investigated by Modern Techniques." Paper presented at The Northern Ireland Branch of the Institute of Marine Engineers and the Royal Institution of Naval Architects 1996.

Beesley, Lawrence. *The Loss of the Titanic.*

Bessemer, Henry, F.R.S. *An Autobiography.* London: Engineering, 1905.

Biel, Steven. *Down with the Old Canoe: A Cultural History of the Titanic Disaster.* New York: W. W. Norton & Co., 1996.

Brandon, R., and C. Davies. *Wrongful Imprisonment.* London: Allen & Unwin, 1973.

Breese, Martin, ed. *The Titanic Story: The Ocean's Greatest Disaster, 1912.* 2nd ed. London: Breese Books Ltd, 1998.

Brigham, R. J., and Y. A. LaFreniere. "Titanic Specimens." CANMET Metals Technology Laboratories, 1992.

British Board of Trade. "Report on the Loss of the S.S. 'Titanic'." 1912.

British PRO Document BT110/426/2. "Board of Trade." In *Form No. 19 Transcript of Register.* London, 1912.

British PRO Document MT9/148 M731 1885. "Board of Trade Documents." In *Mr. Wimshurst's report regarding the use of steel on ships.* London, 1878.

British PRO Document MT9/258 M12470. "Board of Trade Inspections." In *Testing of rivets in steel boilers.* London, 1884.

British PRO Document MT9/710 M2213. "Board of Trade Inspections." In *Steel testing for Harland & Wolff's boilers.* London, 1902.

British PRO Document MT9/710 M15667. "Board of Trade Inspections." In *Inspection of rivets complained of made from rivet bars inspected at Sunderland for Young and Co.* London, 1902.

British PRO Document MT15/78. "Board of Trade." In *British Standard Specification for Structural Steel for Shipbuilding.* London, 1906.

British PRO Document MT15/212 22818. "Titanic Surveys and Inspections." In *Form L.L. 9: Comparison of Scantlings of Unclassed Iron and Steel Ships with the Rules of Lloyd's Register for 1885,* 1912.

British PRO Document MT15/212. "Titanic Surveys and Inspections." In *Board of Trade Form L 24: Surveys 24 Surveyor's Report of Steel Tests.* London, 1911.

British PRO Document MT9/920/A/1. "Titanic Surveys and Inspections" In *Board of Trade and Ministry of Transport and successors: Marine, Harbours and Wrecks* (M, H and W Series) Files, 1854–1969, 1912.

Brogger, A. *The Viking Ships.* Translated by Katherine John. 2nd ed. London: C. Hurst & Co., 1971.

Brown, David G. *The Last Log of the Titanic.* New York: International Marine/McGraw Hill, 2001.

——, and P. Stephenson, *White Paper on the Grounding of Titanic.* Presented for consideration by the Marine Forensic Panel (SD-7) chartered by The Society of Naval Architects and Marine Engineers Arlington, Virginia, May 31, 2001, updated 2003.

Brull, A. *A Comparison of the Resisting Properties of Iron and Steel*. Philadelphia: H. G. Baird, 1868.

Bullock, S. *Thomas Andrews: Shipbuilder* (1912). Belfast: Blackstaff, 1999.

Burton, A. *The Rise and Fall of British Shipbuilding*. London: Constable, 1994.

Butler, D. A. *"Unsinkable": The Full Story*. Mechanicsburg, PA: Stackpole Books, 1998.

Calvert, F. G., and R. Johnson, "On the Chemical Changes Which Pig Iron Undergoes During Its Conversion into Wrought Iron." *Philosophical Magazine* 14 (1857), 165.

Cameron, S. *Titanic: Belfast's Own*. Dublin: Wolfhound Press, 1998.

Carnegie Steel Corporation, *Pocket Companion for Engineers, Architects, and Builders Containing Useful Information and Tables Appertaining to the Use of Steel*. Pittsburgh: Carnegie Steel Company, 1917.

Charpy, M. *Association Internationale pour l'essai des materiaux*. VI Congrès, rv, New York, 1912.

Clark, E. "An Inquiry into the Strength of beams and girders of all descriptions from the most simple and elementary forms, up to the complex arrangements which obtain in Girder Bridges of wrought and cast iron. *The Artizan* (1858), 6–43.

Clarke, J. F., and F. Storr. "The Introduction of the Use of Mild Steel into the Shipbuilding and Marine Engineering Industries." Occasional Papers in the History of Science and Technology. Newcastle upon Tyne Polytechnic, UK 1: (1983).

Coburn, J. L., F. W. DeBord, J. B. Montgomery, A. M. Nawwar, and K. E. Dane. *A Rational Basis for the Selection of Ice Strengthening Criteria for Ships*, *Vol. 1*, SSC-309 (1981).

Corlett, E. *The Iron Ship: The Story of Brunel's SS Great Britain*. London: Conway, Maritime Press, 1990.

Cunningham, D. C. *Marine Riveting on the Great Lakes*. ed. Washington, DC: U.S. Government Printing Office, 1967.

David Colville & Sons. *List of Manufacturers. Brands, Qualities for Steel Plates, Sections, Joists, Rails, Steel and Iron Bars*. Motherwell, Scotland, 1919.

DeArdo, A. J., Jr., and E. G. Hamburg. In *Sulfide Inclusions in Steel*. Metals Park, OH: American Society for Metals, 1974.

"Detailed Construction Plan for the Rimutaka, Ship No. 634." Glasgow, 1894.

Dickinson, H. W. *A Short History of the Steam Engine*. London: F. Cass, 1963.

Eaton, J. P., and C. A. Haas, *Titanic: Triumph and Tragedy*. New York: Norton, 1986.

Encyclopaedia Britannica, 11th ed., S.V. "Process of Shipbuilding."

Fairbairn, W. *Iron: Its History, Properties, and Processes of Manufacture*. Edinburgh, Scotland: Adams and Charles Black, 1869.

———. *Treatise on Iron Shipbuilding, Its History and Progress*. London: Longmans, Green, 1865.

———. *Useful Information for Engineers*. London: Longmans, 1856.

Federal Railroad Administration. "Charpy Energy of Head Plate Absorption," 1994, FRA 14139e

Felkins, K., H. P. Leighly, A. Jankovic. "The Royal Mail Ship *Titanic*: Did a Metallurgical Failure Cause a Night to Remember?" *JOM* 1 (1998): 12–8.

Fellowes Wilson, V. S. *The Largest Ships in the World*. London: Crosby, Lockwood & Son, 1926.

Foecke, T. *Metallurgy of the RMS Titanic*. Gaithersburg, MD: National Institute of Standards and Technology, 1998.

Fox, F. A. "The Brittle Fracture of Structural Steel," *Science News* 36: (Year) 76–77.

Gagnon, R. E., and P. H. Gammon. "Flexural Strength," *Journal of Glaciology* 41 (1995): 103–11.

———. "Thermal profiles," *Journal of Glaciology* 43 (1997): 569–82.

———. "Triaxial Experiments on Iceberg and Glacier Ice," *Journal of Glaciology* 41 (1995): 528–40.

Gale, W. K. V. *The British Iron and Steel Industry, A Technical History*. Newton Abbot (Devon) UK: David & Charles, 1967.

———. *Iron and Steel*. London: Harlow, Longmans, 1969.

Gannon, R. "What Really Sank the *Titanic*?" *Popular Science* 246, no. 2 (1995): 49–55.

Gardiner, R., and D. Van der Vat, *The Riddle of the Titanic*. London: Weidenfeld and Nicolson, 1995.

Garrison, E. *A History of Engineering and Technology: Artful Methods*. Boca Raton, Fl: CRC Press, 1999.

Garzke, W., T. Foecke, P. Matthias, and D. Wood, *A Marine Forensics Analysis of the RMS Titanic*. Paper presented to the Chesapeake Section of the Society of Naval Architects and Marine Engineers, Norfolk, VA, June 10, 2002.

Garzke, W. H., Jr., D. K. Brown, P. K. Matthias, R. Cullimore, D. Wood, D. Livingstone, H. P. Leighly, Jr., T. Foecke, and A. Sandiford, "*Titanic*:

Anatomy of a Disaster" *Proceedings of the 1997 Annual Meeting of the Society of Naval Architects and Marine Engineers*, "SNAME." Jersey City, NJ, 1997, 1–47.

Greenwood, W. H. *Iron: Its Sources, Properties, and Manufacture*. Rev. ed. Philadelphia: David McKay, 1907.

Guilmartin, J. F., Jr. *Galleons and Galleys*. London: Sterling, 2002.

Hamilton, F. A. "Marvellous and Wireless, Immense Importance of Marconi's Telegraph System," *The Halifax Daily Echo*, 1899.

Hammond, D. *The Steel Chest, Nail in the Boot and the Barking Dog: The Belfast Shipyard*. Northern Ireland: Flying Fox Films, 1986.

Hand, T. H. "Progress in British Rolling-Mill Practice," *Journal of the Iron and Steel Institute* 109 (1925): 52.

"Hand and Machine Labour," *Engineering* (March 16, 1900).

"Harland & Wolff Contracts No. 7 Iron and Steel Departments, Belfast, 1883–1919," *Journal of the Mechanics and Physics of Solids*, PRONI Document D/2805/MISC/1.

"Harland & Wolff Private Collection of Piecework Wages," PRONI Document D2805/WB/15/7, Belfast, 1920–24.

"Harland & Wolff Rules," PRONI Document D2910/1–2, 1888.

Harris, J. R. *The British Iron Industry 1700–1850*. London: MacMillan Publishers 1988.

Hill, J. R., ed. *The Oxford Illustrated History of the Royal Navy*. New York: Oxford University Press, 1995.

Hogg, A. "Some Points in the Construction of Large Steel Steamers and the Riveting of Lapped Butts," in *Transactions of the North-East Coast Institution of Engineers and Shipbuilders*. London: Andrew Reid, 1903.

Hooper, J. J. "Analysis of the Rivets from the RMS *Titanic* Using Experimental and Theoretical Techniques." Ph.D. diss., The Johns Hopkins University, 2003.

Hooper McCarty, J. J. Analysis and Metallography of SS *Arabic* rivets (2005).

Hough, R. *A History of Fighting Ships*. London: Octopus Books, 1975.

Howe, H. M. *Iron, Steel, and Other Alloys*. New York: McGraw-Hill, 1906.

Hurley, E. N. *The Bridge to France*. Philadelphia: J. B. Lippincott, 1927.

"Hydraulic Keel Riveter," *Engineering*, 30 (December 10, 1880): 535, 41.

James, M. C. "On Passenger Accommodation in Steam Ships," in *Transactions of the North-East Coast Institution of Engineers and Shipbuilders*. London: Andrew Reid, 1903.

Jeans, J. S. *Steel: Its History, Manufacture, Properties, and Uses*. London: E & F. N. Spon, 1880.

Jenkins, M. F. "The Technology of the Ironclads," *Naval Gazette* 2 and 3 (1998).

"John Brown's Atlas Works." *The Times* 1861.

John, T. G. "Shipbuilding Practice of the Present and Future." *Engineering* 98 (July 10, 1914): 68–71.

Jones, L. *Shipbuilding in Britain*. Cardiff: University of Wales, 1957.

KarisAllen, K, and J. Matthews. "*Titanic* Steel: A Shattering Tale," *Popular Mechanics*, February 1995.

Kirkaldy, D. *An Experimental Inquiry into the Comparative Tensile Strength and Other Properties of Various Kinds of Wrought Iron and Steel*. Glasgow, Scotland: 1862.

Kozasu, I., and J. Tanaka. *Sulfide Inclusions in Steel*. Metals Park, OH: ASM Press, 1974.

Langrand, B., L. Patronelli, E. Deletombe, E. Markiewicz, and P. Drazetic. "Full Scale Experimental Characterisation for Riveted Joint Design," *Aerospace Science and Technology* 6 (2002): 333–42.

Livingstone, D. private communication to W. Garzke, 1996.

Lloyd's Report on Steel for Shipbuilding. London: Lloyd's Printing House, 1877.

Lloyd's Rules and Regulations for the Construction and Classification of Steel Vessels. Lloyd's Printing House, 1910, 1911, and 1912.

Loftus, E., and K. Ketcham. *Witness for the Defense: The Accused, the Eyewitness, and the Expert Who Puts Memory on Trial*. New York: St. Martin's, 1991.

Lord, W. *A Night to Remember*. New York: Holt, 1955.

The Loss of the Titanic, 1912. Edited by The Stationary Office, "Uncovered Editions." London: Biddles Limited, England, 1999.

Louden-Brown, P. "Steel Ships and Iron Rivets," *The Titanic Commutator* 23 (1999): 4–13.

Lynch, J. P. *An Unlikely Success Story, The Belfast Shipbuilding Industry, 1880–1935*. Belfast: Ulster Historical Foundation, 2001.

MacAyeal, D. R., L. Padman, M. R. Drinkwater, M. Fahnestock, T. T. Gotis, A. L. Gray, B. Kerman, M. Lazzara, E. Rignot, T. Scambos, and C. Stearns. "Effects of Rigid Body Collisions and Tide-Forced Drift on Large Tabular Icebergs of the Antarctic." 2002.

Marine Insurance Correspondent. "The Construction of the *Titanic*: Absence of Classification," *The Times*, London, May 17, 1912.

Maxtone-Graham, J. *Liners to the Sun*. New York: Macmillan, 1985.

McCaughan, M. *Steel Ships and Iron Men: Shipbuilding in Belfast*. Belfast, Friar's Bush Press, 1989.

———. "*Titanic*: Out of the Depths and into the Culture" in *Symbols in Northern Ireland*. Ed. by A. Buckley. Belfast: Institute of Irish Studies, Queen's University of Belfast, 1998.

McMillin, B., S. Lehrer, and the staff of the Mariner's Museum. *Titanic: Fortune and Fate*. New York: Simon & Shuster, 1998.

"Messers. Harland & Wolff's Works at Belfast," Engineering, 85 (June 12, 1908): 791–3.

Michel, J. L., and R.D. Ballard. "The RMS *Titanic* 1985 Discovery Expedition." Proceedings at *Oceans '94: Oceans Engineering for Today's Technology and Tomorrow's Preservation*, New York, NY, 1994, 132–37.

Michel, J. L., J. M. Raillard, and B. Jegot. "La Decouverte Du RMS *Titanic*: Role et Importance de la Navigation," *Navigation* 35 (1987): 457–69.

Mills, S. *HMHS Britannic Expedition Summary 1976–1999* (2005). http://britannic.marconigraph.com/muw_expeditions.html.

"Minute Book of Managing Directors, Harland & Wolff." PRONI Document D/2805/MIN/1–2, Belfast, 1907–14.

Moore, T. *Handbook of Practical Smithing and Forging*. London: E. & F. N. Spon, 1919.

Morgan, J. "The Strength of Victorian Wrought Iron," *Proceedings of the Institution of Civil Engineers-Structures and Buildings* (1999): 295–300.

Moss, M. S., and J. R. Hume, *Beardmore: The History of Scottish Industrial Giant*. London: Heinemann, 1979.

———. *Shipbuilders to the World: 125 Years of Harland and Wolff, 1861–1986*. Belfast: Blackstaff, 1986.

———. *Workshop of the British Empire: Engineering and Shipbuilding in the West of Scotland*. London: Heinemann, 1977.

Murphy, J. S. *How They Were Built: Ships*. London: Oxford University Press, 1959.

Napier, J. *The Life of Robert Napier*. Edinburgh, Scotland: William Blackwood, 1904.

National Maritime Museum. *Aspects of the History of Wooden Shipbuilding*. London: Greenwich Publishers, 1970.

———. *From Viking Ship to Victory*. London: Her Majesty's Stationery Office, 1977.

Olympic and Titanic: Ocean Liners of the Past: Based on a Facsimile Reprint of the Original Souvenir Number of "The Shipbuilder" (1911). Mattituck, NY: Ameron, 1995.

Parisi, P. "Lunch on the Deck of the Titanic," *Wired News* no. 6.02 (February 1998).

Parkinson, J. R. *The Economics of Shipbuilding in the United Kingdom.* Cambridge: Cambridge University Press, 1960.

Peebles, H. B. *Warshipbuilding on the Clyde*: Naval Orders and the Prosperity of the Clyde Shipbuilding. Edinburgh, Scotland: J. Donald, 1987.

Pellegrino, C. *Ghosts of the Titanic.* New York: William Morrow, 2000.

Pollard, S., and P. Robertson. *The British Shipbuilding Industry: 1870–1914.* Cambridge, MA: Harvard University Press, 1979.

The Practical Magazine. "The Birkenhead Iron Works." 1874.

Rebbeck, D. "The History of Iron Shipbuilding in the Queen's Island up to July, 1874." Ph.D. diss., Queen's University, 1950.

Reed, E. J. *Shipbuilding in Iron and Steel.* London: J. Murray, 1869.

Reemsnyder, H. *Report to the Marine Forensics Panel (SD-7) of the Society of Naval Architects and Marine Engineers,* 1997.

Rinebolt, J. A., and W. J. Harris. *Transactions of the American Society of Metals* 43 (1951): 1,175.

———. *Transactions of the American Society of Metals* 44 (1952): 225.

Ritchie, R. O., J. F. Knott, and J. R. Rice. *Journal of the Mechanics and Physics of Solids* 21 (1973): 395.

Roberts, I. *Craft, Class, and Control: The Sociology of a Shipbuilding Community.* Edinburgh, Scotland: Edinburgh University Press for the University of Durham, 1993.

Rosenhain, W. "The International Association for the Testing of Materials: Slag Enclosures in Steel," *Engineering* 88 (September 24, 1909): 409–11.

Ryan, M. "Iceberg Wrangler." *Smithsonian Magazine,* February 2003. www.smithsonianmagazine.com.

Schubert, H. R. *History of the British Iron and Steel Industry, from c. 450 B.C. to A.D 1775.* London: Routledge & K. Paul, 1957.

The Shelburne Museum. *Blacksmith's and Farmer's Tools at Shelburne Museum.* Burlington, VT: George Little Press, 1966.

The Shipping World, June 12, 1912.

Smith, C. S. *A History of Metallography: The Development of Ideas on the Structure of Metals Before 1890.* Chicago, IL: University of Chicago Press, 1960.

———, and M. T. Gnudi, eds. *The Pirotechnia of Vannoccio Biringuccio: The Classic Sixteenth-Century Treatise on Metals and Metallurgy.* New York: Dover, 1990.

Stephenson, R. *Remarks and Calculations on the Best Form for Railway Bars and on the Defects Which Exist in the Present Methods of Supporting the Same* (1834). British Transport Commission Archives RAIL 384/107, 1–26.

Stevens, R. W. *On the Stowage of Ships and Their Cargoes: With Information Regarding Freights, Charter-Parties, &c. &c.* London: Longmans, 1869.

Stoermer, L. S. A., and P. Rudkin, "Tabular Icebergs: Ice Season 2002 and the past," *Mariner's Weather Log* 47 (2003).

"Sulfur Content Standards in Structural Steels." In *American Testing Society*. Chicago, 1906.

Thearle, S. J. P. *The Modern Practice of Shipbuilding in Iron and Steel*. London: W. Collins 1891.

The Technical Educator: An Encyclopedia of Technical Education. Vol. III. London: Cassell and Company, Ltd., 1905.

Thorpe, W. H. "The Anatomy of Bridgework," *Engineering* 79, no. 4 (January 27, 1905): 103.

Tipper, C. F. *The Brittle Fracture Story*. Cambridge: Cambridge University Press, 1962.

"Titanic and Lloyd's Register," *The Times*, July 8, 1912.

Transactions of the Institute of Naval Architects (1899).

Tylecote, R. F. *A History of Metallurgy*. London: Maney, 1992.

United States Navy. Brittle Fracture of Welded Ship Structures: Final Report of a Board of Investigation. Washington, DC: Government Printing Office, 1946.

United States Senate, *Report 806: Inquiry into the Causes Leading to the Wreck of the White Star Liner "Titanic."* Ed. by Washington, DC: Government Printing Office 1912.

United States Steel Corporation. *The Making, Shaping, and Treating of Steel*. 9th ed. Pittsburgh: Herbrick & Held, 1971.

U.S. Department of Energy. The Fire Below: Spontaneous Combustion in Coal. Environment Health and Safety Bulletin EH–93–4. Washington, DC, 1993.

Urbin, E. D. *A Practical Guide for Puddling Iron and Steel*. Philadelphia: H. G. Baird, 1868.

Wall, R. *Ocean Liners*. London: New Burlington, 1977.

Walton, T. *Steel Ships: Their Construction and Maintenance* (London: Charles Griffin, 1904).

Wels, S. *Titanic: Legacy of the World's Greatest Ocean Liner*. New York: Time-Life Books. 1997.

Wengenroth, U. *Enterprise and Technology. The German and British Steel Industries 1865–1895*. Cambridge: Cambridge University Press, 1994.

White, A. *The Titanic Tragedy: God Speaking to the Nations*. Bound Brook, NJ: The Pentecostal Union, 1913.

White, C. *Victoria's Navy: End of the Sailing Navy 1830–1870*. England: Kenneth Mason, 1987.

"The White Star Line," *The Engineer* 109 (June 24, 1910): Supplement.

"The White Star Line *Olympic*," *Engineering* 90 (October 21, 1910): 564–72.

"The White Star Liner 'Titanic,' " *Engineering* 91 (1911): 678–81.

Wiley, E. "Iron" 26 (1882): 411.

Williams, M. "Failures in Welded Ships: An Investigation of the Causes of Structural Failures," *NBS Technical News Bulletin* 37 (1953).

Williams, M. L. *Symposium on Metallic Materials at Low Temperatures*. ASTM STP, 1953, 11.

———, and G. A. Ellinger. *American Welding Journal* 32 (1953): 498.

Wilson, T. D. *An Outline of Shipbuilding, Theoretical and Practical*. New York: J. Wiley, 1873.

Wilson, W. M., J. Mather, and C. O. Harris. *Ill. Experimental Station* Bulletin No. 239 (1931), 3.

"Wise after the Event," *Pall Mall Gazette*, May 22, 1912.

Wood, D. M. *Titanic* Expedition '98: Scientific Findings by the Science Team (September 3, 1998).

GLOSSARY

Aft: Toward the stern, or back, of the ship.

Amidships: The middle part of a ship (between the front and back).

Anisotropic: When a material's properties vary with direction.

Bessemer process: A method of mass producing steel from molten pig iron that involves blowing hot air through the molten iron to burn out impurities. The Bessemer process was very fast but was limited in the types of steel it could make.

Bilge: The compartment at the bottom of the hull of a ship or boat where water collects so that it may be pumped out of the vessel at a later time.

Brittle: A solid material that can be easily fractured.

Bulkhead: An interior wall within the ship.

Butt joint: A riveting technique in which two plates are joined by simply putting their ends together and usually securing with a third plate across the back. This creates a smooth surface on the front of the joint.

Cast iron: A type of iron that contains up to 4–5 percent carbon and 1–2 percent silicon, giving it a lower melting point that allows it to be easily poured into molds for casting. Cast iron is typically very strong in compression but also very brittle.

Center keel girder: The component of the ship that provides most of the resistance to bending along its length. It lies along the midline, at the bottom of the hull, and is usually made up of several massive iron beams.

Charge: A batch of pig iron that is heated for conversion to wrought iron or to steel.

Charpy impact test: The Charpy impact test is a high strain-rate test that determines the amount of energy absorbed by a material during fracture. This absorbed energy is a measure of a given material's toughness and acts as a tool to study brittle-ductile transition. During the test, a small rectangular bar with a V-shaped notch on the side is broken by a heavy pendulum hammer, which swings from a fixed height and breaks (or bends) the sample when it reaches the bottom. After the specimen is broken, the amount of energy absorbed can be calculated from the height that the pendulum swings up to after the impact—the lower the swing, the more energy the sample absorbs from the hammer and the tougher the material.

Corrosion: Corrosion is a chemical process in which metals react with the environment and turn into other compounds. Iron's corrosion product due to exposure to oxygen is iron oxide, or rust.

Ductility: A physical property that describes the amount of permanent stretching before a material begins to break. The opposite of ductility is brittleness.

Ferrite: Also known as alpha iron—this is the phase of iron found in cast iron and steel that is very pure. Its grains have a very specific structure under the microscope, and it gives iron alloys their magnetic properties.

Finite Element Analysis: A computer simulation technique used in engineering based on a method that separates a structure into many small, discrete elements in order to study how the structure as a whole will respond to various forces applied to it.

Forecastle: Originally a built-up structure comprising several decks in the forward part of a ship. In more modern times, the forecastle (pronounced and often written "fo'c'sle") is the crew's quarters in the forward part of a ship.

Fore/Forward: Toward the bow, or front, of the ship.

Frame: A transverse rib that forms part of the skeleton of a ship's hull.

Gantry: A large overhead framework that supports cranes over the shipyard.

Helm: The steering column of the ship. Understanding the helm orders in 1912 requires some knowledge of the construction of early sailing vessels. Basically, the orders were given with respect to the tiller, or the lever inside the ship that moves the rudder. If the tiller is pushed to the right (starboard), then the rudder moves left (port), moving the ship to the left. "Hard astarboard" would direct the quartermaster to turn the wheel to the right, sending the tiller to the right, the rudder pivoting to the left, and the bow to the left. About twenty years after *Titanic* sank, the helm controls were revamped so that the orders and the wheel movements paralleled the movement of the rudder.

Hot short: A very brittle condition of steel caused when it is heated too hot and cooled quickly and as a result can shatter when hammered.

Impulse: An impulse on a body is equal to its change in momentum. During the collision, passengers on the ship felt the change in momentum as an *impulse*, which resulted in feeling a jerk or shift one way or another.

Ironclad: A warship with a wooden hull sheathed in iron for protection against gunfire.

Isotropic: When a material's properties are similar in all directions.

Joggled surface: The uneven surface that is produced when hull plates are riveted using lap joints.

Keel: A large beam that runs in the middle of the ship, from the bow to the stern, and serves as the spine of the structure, providing the major source of structural strength of the hull.

Lap joint (butt-lap): A riveting technique created by overlapping two plates and riveting through both of them. This type of joint always results in a joggled surface.

Load line (Load-draft line): An imaginary line marking the level at which a ship or boat floats in the water. The more weight added to the ship, the lower this line will sink into the water, indicating the maximum amount of loading for the vessel in various operating conditions.

Longitudinal wrought iron: Refers to the properties of wrought iron along the direction of the slag stringers and, usually, the direction in which the wrought iron has been rolled or extruded.

Malleability: A property that indicates how easily a metal, or other material, can be deformed, especially by hammering or rolling, without cracking.

Microvoids: Microscopic holes that form in a material before it breaks and that indicate the material has stretched before failure.

Momentum: Momentum is the product of the mass and velocity of an object and relates to how hard it is to stop an object from moving. It does not depend on the object's strength or hardness.

Open-hearth method: A method for producing steel using very large furnaces that could reach very high temperatures. This allowed steel to be created in liquid form, since temperatures could rise as high as 1,800°C. The open-hearth process worked slowly, and therefore allowed for constant checks on the chemistry of the steel.

Panting: The in and out vibration of the plates and beams in the bow. The *Titanic* hull was reinforced to resist this motion.

Pearlite: A phase found in cast irons and steel alloys that is composed of alternating layers of ferrite and cementite, an iron carbide. The layered structure of pearlite is easy to spot under the microscope and is the phase that strengthens steel when carbon is added to iron.

Pig iron: Raw iron has a very high carbon content, typically 3.5 percent, which makes it very brittle and not useful directly as a structural material. It is the direct product of smelting and is used to make both steel and cast iron alloys.

Piling: A process of stacking rolled wrought iron product in an alternating pattern. The stack would then be reheated and rolled again to break up remaining long stringers of slag in order to refine the wrought iron.

Pitch: The separation distance between rivets.

Point: The head of a rivet that is formed prior to placing the rivet into the plate.

Port: A nautical term that refers to the left side of a vessel as perceived by a person on board the ship and facing the bow.

Puddling: A process used to make wrought iron that involves constantly stirring a mixture of molten iron and slag, driving out the impurities. It is a slow, difficult, apprentice-learned trade.

Residual stress: Stresses that remain after the loads have been removed. A properly driven rivet contains a considerable amount of residual tensile stress. This develops as the rivet cools and shrinks, clamping the two plates together. Residual stress decreases the amount of additional stress needed to "pop" a rivet during a collision.

Rivet: A fastener, like a two-headed nail, that can hold plates together on ships, skins of airplanes, parts of boilers, bridges, or on any number of other structures. Rivets are designed to hold two large flat plates together against a uniform pressure being applied to the surface.

Rudder: A device hung on the centerline at the stern and used to turn a vessel.

Rusticles: A phrase coined to describe the icicle-shaped microorganisms that have formed on the wreck as a result of the corrosion of the ship's iron.

Shaft (Shank): The length of the rivet between the heads, pre-cut to specific lengths depending on the use.

Shear stress: A stress that runs parallel to a material's surface.

Slag: A by-product of the puddling process. Slags, which are mixtures of iron, silicon, and oxygen, help to refine the iron chemically but can also help to strengthen it, depending on how much is in the final product.

Slipway: An inclined workspace within which the ship is built and eventually launched by sliding into the ocean.

Starboard: A nautical term that refers to the right side of a vessel as perceived by a person on board the ship and facing the bow.

Strakes: Part of the hull of a boat or ship that, in conjuction with the other strakes, keeps the sea out and the vessel afloat. In *Titanic's* case, the strakes were made from steel plates.

Steel: An alloy of iron and carbon with a small amount of other elements; it contains less carbon than cast iron but more carbon than wrought iron. It is easiest to subdivide steels into three categories;

mild steels (less than 0.25 percent carbon), carbon steels (0.25–1.4 percent carbon), and alloy steels (0.2–1 percent carbon plus other elements).

Tensile stress (Tension): A stress applied perpendicular to the surface of the material, like pulling at both ends of a wire, which causes it to lengthen in one direction.

Ultimate Tensile Strength (UTS): The highest tensile stress that a material can withstand before it begins to break.

Uniform pressure: The same pressure is felt in all directions, for instance in water or in air.

Wrought iron: Nearly pure iron having a small percentage of slag. It is tough, malleable, and ductile and is easy for a blacksmith to hammer weld and form into shapes. Wrought iron also has good corrosion resistance, making it useful for outside structural use such as railings or fire escapes. It is the oldest form of iron produced by man.

Yield strength: This is the stress a material can withstand without permanently deforming.

WHO'S WHO
in *What Really Sank the Titanic*

THOMAS ANDREWS

Thomas Joseph Andrews was a managing director and head of the drafting department for Harland & Wolff in Belfast, Ireland. In 1907, Andrews began to oversee the plans for the RMS *Olympic* for the White Star Line, and later, became a designer for the *Titanic*. Andrews and the rest of his design team traveled on *Titanic*'s maiden voyage and took notes on various improvements that might have been needed. Immediately following the collision, Captain Smith had Andrews summoned to help examine the damage. It was Andrews who determined that nothing could be done and that the *Titanic* would sink in less than three hours. Andrews was last seen staring at a painting above the fireplace in the first-class smoking room as the ship went down. Because of his choice to stay with the ship, Andrews is often heralded as a hero.

ERNEST ARCHER

Able Seaman Ernest Archer received monthly wages of £5 for his work with the White Star Line. Mr. Archer was rescued in Lifeboat 16. He testified at both the British and American Inquiries into the disaster. He died on October 17, 1917, of tuberculosis, aged forty-one years.

FREDERICK BARRETT

Leading Fireman Frederick William Barrett was working in Boiler Room No. 6 at the time of the collision and was a key witness to understanding the nature and location of the impact with the iceberg. He felt the collision and then heard a rumbling sound as it tore along the ship's side. The occupants of Lifeboat 13 put Barrett in command. At 4:45 a.m. Barrett brought his boat and its occupants safely to the side of the rescue ship *Carpathia*. Modern forensic studies using subsurface sonar have located what we believe to be the damage described by Barrett during the inquiries.

JOSEPH BOXHALL

Fourth Officer Joseph Groves Boxhall joined the White Star Line on the *Oceanic*, where he met Charles Lightoller. Boxhall testified at both inquiries to hearing the three-bell warning and Officer Murdoch's subsequent orders to Hichens and the engine room. He helped to fire warning rockets before he was put in charge of Lifeboat 2, which was lowered at 1:45 a.m. Boxhall suffered from pleurisy, a painful condition causing inflammation of the lungs' lining but continued to serve with White Star and other International Mercantile Marine ships. He died in 1967 at eighty-three years of age—the last of the *Titanic*'s surviving deck officers to pass away. His remains were cremated, and at his request, his ashes were scattered over the position he had calculated for *Titanic*'s final resting place.

HAROLD BRIDE

Harold Sydney Bride was the Junior Wireless officer on board the *Titanic*. Working with Jack Phillips, Bride helped inform *Titanic*'s Captain Smith about the ships coming to *Titanic*'s assistance. As he and Phillips were preparing to leave the Marconi Room, Bride held off another crew member who was attempting to steal Phillips' life jacket. Bride survived the sinking by clinging to the underside of Lifeboat B, which had turned over as the *Titanic* became submerged. The next morning, after *Titanic* had sunk, Bride was rescued by the *Carpathia*, and despite being injured, he helped the *Carpathia's* wireless operator transmit survivor lists and personal messages from the ship.

EDWARD BULEY

Able Seaman Edward John Buley was sitting in the mess room when he felt a slight jar. Asked to help with the lifeboats, he worked both sides of the ship loading women and children into the boats. He left in Lifeboat 10 and testified to seeing the ship break in two, from about 750 yards away, before her stern finally sank below the water.

FRANCIS CARRUTHERS

Francis Carruthers was the Ship Surveyor who oversaw the construction of the *Titanic* and made the final inspection of her in the ways in Belfast, several months before her departure. Carruthers had sixteen years of experience with the Board of Trade and testified at the British Inquiry that in his Declaration of Survey, he certified that Harland & Wolff had complied with all necessary requirements. During the inquiry he was questioned as to the types of tests that were performed to ensure the strength of the bulkheads and their rivets.

GEORGE CAVELL

Mr. George Henry Cavell had been at sea for eighteen months serving on the *Adriatic*, the *Oceanic*, and the *Olympic*, before joining the *Titanic*. Cavell testified that he was in Boiler Room No. 4 during the collision and stayed down below until the water had risen one foot high. He was rescued in Lifeboat 15.

HAROLD COTTAM

Harold Cottam was the wireless operator on the RMS *Carpathia* when *Titanic*'s wireless operator began sending the distress signals. After receiving the distress signal, Cottam awakened Captain Arthur Henry Rostron, who changed course to try to rescue *Titanic*'s passengers.

THOMAS DILLON

Trimmer Thomas Patrick Dillon served on the *Oceanic*, as well, and received monthly wages of £5 10s. Dillon, along with two others from the engine crew, jumped from the *Titanic* into the water and swam for approximately twenty minutes. Eventually, Lifeboat 4 picked up an apparently drunk Dillon holding a bottle of brandy in his hand.

FREDERICK FLEET

Lookout Frederick Fleet had sailed for over four years on board *Oceanic* before signing on the *Titanic*. Along with Lee in the crow's nest, Fleet testified that he had seen the iceberg pass on the starboard side of the ship and thought they may just have missed encountering a collision. Frustrated with the White Star Line's treatment of its surviving crew, Fleet left the company and sailed with several others until old age, when he took to selling newspapers. After his wife's death, he committed suicide in 1965.

CHARLES HENDRICKSON

Leading Fireman Charles George Hendrickson received monthly wages of £6 10s for his work. He was rescued in Emergency Lifeboat 1. His testimony at the British Inquiry describes the location of the iceberg immediately after the collision and the water coming in through the starboard side.

JOHN HESKETH

Second Engineer John Henry Hesketh joined the White Star Line as an engineer apprentice at 14 years of age and commenced his seagoing career as Sixth Engineer aboard the *Afric*. He served aboard the *Olympic* before moving to the *Titanic* and was the youngest acting person in his post at the company. Hesketh died during the sinking, but his whereabouts during the sinking were told by Barrett at the inquiries to be in the engine rooms.

ROBERT HICHENS

One of six quartermasters on the ship, Robert Hichens was at *Titanic's* helm at the time of the collision, and his testimony was of utmost importance during both inquiries. Hichens manned Lifeboat 6, and his behavior that night came under severe questioning during the inquiry, as many women testified that he refused to return the lifeboat to rescue dying passengers. Years later, his family left him, he resorted to heavy drinking, and was sent to prison for trying to shoot someone. He attempted suicide while in prison, but never succeeded. Upon his release he lasted three more years before dying on the cargo ship *English Trader* in 1940.

BRUCE ISMAY

Joseph Bruce Ismay was the managing director of the White Star Line, and with Lord Pirrie of Harland & Wolff, he conceived of the three *Olympic*-class ships, designed to boost White Star Line's reputation as having the most luxurious liners in the world. Ismay chose to accompany the *Titanic* on its maiden voyage. He has since been criticized for pressuring the captain into attempting a speed record. Following his rescue from Collapsible Lifeboat C by the *Carpathia*, Ismay remained hidden from view and heavily medicated until his arrival in New York. After Ismay had appeared at both the American and British Inquiries, he was ostracized by the public and the press for deserting the ship and letting passengers die. In 1913, he resigned as president of International Mercantile Marine.

REGINALD LEE

Lookout Reginald Lee had transferred from the *Olympic*. As a lookout he received monthly wages of £5. Lee was in the crow's nest with Fleet when the iceberg was sighted. He was rescued in Lifeboat 13. Later he testified at the British Inquiry. Lee died aboard the *Kenilworth Castle* in 1913.

WILLIAM LUCAS

Able Bodied Seaman William Lucas transferred from the *Oceanic* and received a monthly wage of £5. As Collapsible D was lowered, William Lucas yelled up to First-Class passenger Miss Edith Corse Evans, who was standing on deck, "There's another boat going to be put down for you." Unfortunately, there was no other boat, meaning Edith was left behind. She did, however, survive. Lucas was rescued, probably on Collapsible D.

CHARLES LIGHTOLLER

Second Officer Charles Herbert Lightoller began his career with the White Star Line in 1900 as a Fourth Officer on the *Medic*. On the night of April 14, 1912, Lightoller was commanding the bridge watch immediately prior to the one in which the ship's collision occurred. At the end of his watch he retired to bed, relieved by Chief Officer Murdoch. Because Lightoller was the highest-ranking surviving officer, he became a key witness at both the American and British Inquiries. Lightoller insisted that the sea was calmer than he had ever seen it in his life, blaming the disaster on the inability to see breakers against the icebergs' surfaces. Lightoller wrote an autobiography in the thirties entitled *Titanic and Other Ships*. He lived until 1952.

WILLIAM MURDOCH

First Officer William McMaster Murdoch had previously served on the *Arabic*, *Adriatic*, *Oceanic*, *Olympic*, and, finally, *Titanic*. He was on watch at the bridge when the collision occurred, forcing him to make critical decisions about the ship's maneuvers. He worked to load lifeboats and died in the sinking. His body was never found.

ALFRED OLLIVER

Quartermaster Alfred Olliver had been at the ship's wheel until 10 p.m., when he was relieved by Quartermaster Hichens. During the British Inquiry, Olliver testified that he saw the ship break apart and heard loud explosions that he thought were bulkheads giving way. He continued to work for the White Star Line, but never at sea again. He died in 1934.

FRANK OSMAN

Able Seaman Frank Osman served in the British Navy for just over eleven years before joining the White Star Line. After helping load lifeboats, Osman managed to leave the ship in Lifeboat 2. According to his testimony at the American Inquiry, Lifeboat 2 was 60 to 100 yards off when the *Titanic* sank. He recalled that the ship exploded, broke in two, and the stern rose into the air.

ARTHUR PEUCHEN

Major Arthur Peuchen was rescued in Lifeboat 6, manned by Quartermaster Hichens. He kept company with the famous "Molly Brown," who provided much more leadership than Peuchen did in the lifeboat. Some said that Peuchen complained of tiredness and refused to row until goaded by Mrs. Brown. Following his testimony at the American Inquiry, Peuchen fell under severe scrutiny for discrediting Captain Smith and his critique of the officers aboard the *Titanic*. In

1987, a salvage team recovered Peuchen's wallet from the debris field at the wreck site and in it was his calling card, a traveler's check, and some streetcar tickets.

HERBERT PITMAN

Third Officer Herbert John Pitman had served in the Merchant Navy and joined the White Star Line in 1906. Manning Lifeboat 5, he rowed it five miles once the rescue ship *Carpathia* was in sight. Pitman testified at both inquiries and continued to serve with the White Star Line and several others before his retirement. Pitman received a Member of British Empire Order (MBE) for his service during the war. Pitman died in 1961.

CAPTAIN SMITH

Captain Edward J. Smith was the captain of the *Titanic* on its maiden voyage. Smith joined the White Star Shipping Line in March 1880 as the Fourth Officer of the *Celtic*. After a long and decorated career and two minor collisions, both with the *Olympic*, there were rumors that Smith had chosen the *Titanic*'s voyage to be his last before retirement. Although the 1997 film *Titanic* depicts Smith going down with the ship in the bridge wheelhouse, other survivors claimed to have seem him in a life jacket in the water.

THOMAS RANGER

Greaser Thomas Ranger remained a merchant marine for many more years after *Titanic*'s sinking and died in Southampton in 1964 at eighty-one years of age.

EDWARD WILDING

Edward Wilding was a naval architect for Harland & Wolff, was responsible for the design of the *Titanic*, and sailed on her maiden voyage from Belfast to Southampton. At the time it was clear from his testimony that Wilding wanted to protect Harland & Wolff from bad publicity at the British Inquiry, and while he did not believe that the ship could ever break in two, as some eyewitnesses testified, he was the first person to suggest that a very short series of slits in *Titanic*'s side could have been responsible for sinking the ship. It took over eighty years to prove his hypothesis.

ACKNOWLEDGMENTS

This book could not have come to life without the support and efforts of many people. The scientific studies on the rivets were only possible with the expertise and guidance of the wonderful faculty and staff at Johns Hopkins University. Thank you to Professor Timothy Weihs, who offered me the opportunity and provided scientific guidance and critical suggestions throughout my research plan, and to Dr. Lori Graham, who showed me the world of computational models and acted as an advisor and teacher to my dissertation. In addition, Drs. Alexis Lewis, David Van Heerden, Johanna Bernstein, and John Spey provided insightful comments and advice, and the tens of thousands of micrographs would never have been photographed without the time and effort of Julia Deneen, Melody Agustin, Jason Hughes, Robb Wissman, and Mark Koontz.

At the National Institute of Standards and Technology (NIST), I am grateful to the talented scientists who provided their expertise to these studies: Dr. Li Ma, Dr. Steve Banovic, and Maureen Williams. This kind of multidisciplinary work cannot happen without support of organizations and individuals like Dr. and Mrs. Carl Heath, Discovery Communications, National Geographic, and RMS Titanic, Inc.

During my research in the United Kingdom, I was lucky enough to have help from kind individuals at the Ulster Folk and Transport Museum, namely, George Crowe and Michael McCaughan, who took their time to explain the unique qualities of blacksmithing and shipbuilding in Northern Ireland. The staff of the Bodleian Library in Oxford, the Public Records Offices in Kew and in Northern Ireland, Queen's University and Linen Hall Libraries in Belfast, the Lloyd's of London Archive, and the National Maritime Museum, were all extremely patient with my persistent questions. Thank you to Drs. Peter Northover and Chris Salter in Oxford for their invaluable comments on archeometallurgy and to Dr. Steve Roberts for getting my foot in the door. For our careful study of icebergs and ice strength, a very special thanks goes to Brian T. Hill and Robert Gagnon at the Canadian National Research Council and Dr. Erland Schulson at Dartmouth University.

As the writing proceeded, so did our requests for feedback from readers. Thanks to Lisa Foecke, Bernie and Jim Galvin, and Darwin and Jon Cooper for their constructive comments during the editing process. I would like to extend a special thanks to Michaela Hamilton, editor-in-chief of Citadel Press for her positive outlook and motivation during this process.

Finally, I would like to thank my wonderful husband, Dr. Owen McCarty, for sticking with me through all the ups and downs and for watching this manuscript evolve over what must have seemed like an eternity. I can honestly say that I could not have done it without you.

—Jennifer Hooper McCarty

In addition to all the people Jen mentioned, I would like to acknowledge many of my collaborators over the years, including but not limited to Lieutenant Jeremy Weirich of the NOAA Corps; Ed McCutcheon (Cdr–USCG [retired]), a phone call from whom started this whole sleigh ride back in 1996; all my bosses and colleagues at NIST who let me start this work and helped in ways large and small; and Anne Enright-Shepherd, who rode herd on the media when the first NIST report came out the same day that the movie was nominated for twelve Oscars. Also, I extend my gratitude to the thousands of audience members at my presentations and talks, young and old, kids and colleagues, who listened so attentively, asked all those great questions, and helped keep the study on track.

And especially, to my dear wife Lisa and my girls Karen and Kimberly, thank you for all those evenings you endured with Dad sitting in his chair in the bedroom, with the laptop on the little tray table, working on the book. Thanks for sacrificing all that time and giving all your support.

—Tim Foecke

INDEX